PERCEPTION & IDENTITY

IN

INTERCULTURAL
COMMUNICATION

PERCEPTION & IDENTITY

IN

INTERCULTURAL COMMUNICATION

MARSHALL R SINGER

An Abridged and Revised Edition of
Intercultural Communication: A Perceptual Approach

INTERCULTURAL PRESS, INC.

For information, contact:
Intercultural Press, Inc.
P.O. Box 700
Yarmouth, Maine 04096 USA
207-846-5168

Book design and production by Patty J. Topel
Cover design and production by Patty J. Topel

Printed in the United States of America

02   01   00   2   3   4   5

Library of Congress Cataloging-in-Publication Data

Singer, Marshall R
  Perception & identity in intercultural communication/
Marshall R Singer.
      p.   cm.
  "An abridged and revised edition of Intercultural commu-
nication: a percepetual approach."
  Includes bibliographical references.
  ISBN 1-877864-61-7
  1. Intercultural communication. 2. Communication and
culture. 3. Interpersonal relations. I. Singer, Marshall R In-
tercultural communication: a perceptual approach. II. Title.
HM258.S488   1998
303.48'2—dc21   98–14688
                                              CIP

Dedication

The second edition of this book is still dedicated to my Israeli son, Shepard; my Afghan son, Attid; and my philosopher son, Paul, as well as to the other important young people in my life—Margaret, Martin, Jeffrey, Mitchell, and Karen Singer—all of whom have taught me how culturally unique every human can be.

It is also dedicated to the memory of the most superb human being I ever knew—Helen Singer—who was mother, sister, friend, and giving tree to us all.

Table of Contents

Acknowledgments ix
Introduction xi

Chapter 1

The Role of Culture and Perception in Communication:
How I Violated a Cultural Norm 1

Chapter 2

The Role of Culture and Identity: I Am Who I Am.
You Are Who You Are. Can We Talk? 55

Chapter 3

The Communication Process:
It Is Not Possible to Not Communicate 103

Chapter 4

Communication at Different Levels of Analysis:
Organizations, Groups, and Nations
Don't Communicate, People Do 163

Chapter 5
Bibliography 239

Acknowledgments:
Things That Are Polite to Say,
But Which Are True Nevertheless

T his book is a revised and condensed version of an earlier edition called *Intercultural Communication: A Perceptual Approach*, which was published by Prentice-Hall in 1987.

In the first edition I acknowledged those students, faculty, and staff at the University of Pittsburgh who had helped me so much with that edition. Here I would like to acknowledge those who have helped me on this edition. In particular, I want to thank George Renwick for his careful reading and incredibly detailed and useful comments which made revising so much easier. I also want to thank all the folks at Intercultural Press, but in particular Kay and David Hoopes, Toby Frank, Patty Topel, and Judy Carl-Hendrick. Indeed, it was Dave's idea that I should write this book in the first place, and his idea that Intercultural Press should put out the second edition. At Pitt I would like to thank Kendall Stanley and Paul Kengor for their help with the manuscript and Interim Deans Edison Montgomery and Martin Staniland for granting me the sabbatical that allowed me to make the revisions.

Introduction:
Only Humor and Frogs Die

In an essay on humor, the noted writer and humorist E. B. White wrote: "Humor can be dissected, as a frog can, but the thing dies in the process...."[1] Since I love to communicate interculturally, I would hate to hurt a process I love. Fortunately, the communication process is not the same as either frogs or humor. The more we dissect and understand it, the better at it we are likely to become. Hence, this work is undertaken with a sense of love and enjoyment of the process. My hope is that, by understanding the communication process, the reader will not only become better at communicating across cultural barriers but will also enjoy it more.

---

[1] E. B. White, *The Second Tree from the Corner* (New York: Harper and Brothers, 1935), 173.

Many years ago I argued that every identity group has a culture of its own. I also argued then that every individual is a part of perhaps hundreds of different identity groups simultaneously and that one learns, and becomes a part of, all of the cultures with which one identifies. I will make those same arguments in the pages that follow.

Several decades ago many anthropologists argued that if the concept of culture was to have any meaning it had to be applied only to very large groups like total societies or large language or ethnic groupings. As I saw it, the way those anthropologists viewed the problem forced them to describe the large degree of cultural variation that exists *within* every society as being "subcultural." For me, that didn't seem to be a logical or useful way to deal with the problem—particularly when I realized that I was in some ways much closer to some "subcultures" in other societies than I was to many within my own. It seemed to me then—and still does today—much more logical and useful to talk about the culture of each group and then to examine—for each total society—the groups that comprise it. Each society is certainly different from every other society, but that is because no two societies contain all of the same groups and only those groups. I suppose it's a little like looking at two different kinds of cake. A chocolate cake is certainly quite different from, let's say, a fruitcake, yet they are both still cakes and as such have more in common with each other than either does with, let's say, a chocolate candy bar. But that does not distract from the fact that the chocolate in the cake and the chocolate in the candy bar are much more similar to each other than they are to any of the other ingredients of either the cake or candy bar.

Culinary analogies notwithstanding, over the course of the decades anthropologists themselves have now independently come to take a position very similar to the position I took then. Certainly they have not done so because of me, but rather because of the compelling logic of the argument. In any event, in the pages that follow I hope to show the reader how the individual interacts with the groups of which she or he is a part and how both the individual and the groups affect each other.

Now with this work, I am pushing the concept still further. I argue here that because no person is a part of all and only the same groups as anyone else and because each person ranks the attitudes, values, and beliefs of the groups to which he or she belongs differently, which is what culture is all about, *each individual must be considered to be culturally unique.* Notice that I am *not* arguing that every person is a culture unto herself or himself. Culture is, after all, a group-related phenomenon. What I will argue is that each individual in this world is a member of a unique collection of groups. No two humans share only and exactly the same group memberships or exactly the same ranking of the importance to themselves of the group memberships they do share. Thus each person must be culturally unique. If I am correct in this assertion—and I hope to be able to convince the reader in the pages that follow that I am—this means that every interpersonal communication must, to some degree, also be an intercultural communication.

Since the publication of the first edition of this work increasing numbers of scholars and practitioners have recognized that intercultural communication is more than just *trying to communicate with foreigners.* It is a multidisciplinary field which has as much relevance in trying to understand—and overcome—the barriers to effective communication between different people and different groups within the same country as it does to trying to deal with barriers to effective communication within large organizations such as public bureaucracies and large private corporations. That is what so much of the work on "cultural diversity" in the workplace is about.

When people start to recognize that every human being is culturally unique, they will begin to realize that *every* interpersonal communication is, to some degree, also an intercultural communication. Once they recognize that, perhaps then they will start to look at the cultural differences that make each of us unique and will ask consciously what they can do to overcome more effectively those differences in values, attitudes, and beliefs.

Through most of human history people have been afraid of groups which are different and have frequently fought violently to oppose them. This is being written while ethnic groups are fighting in Bosnia, Rwanda, Sri Lanka, the Middle East, and approximately three dozen other places around the world. Whether it's because they have a different religion, ethnic identity, race, or whatever, some of us are quite prepared to kill them, whoever they are. Most of us don't hate any one single group enough to kill them (I hope), but virtually all of us have some groups and/or individuals we just do not like. I am not suggesting that we have to like everyone equally. What I am suggesting is that (a) frequently the reason we don't like *them* is because we simply have not taken the time to get to know any of them well. (Studies have shown that when white Americans get to know well, and like, just one African American, their attitude toward other African Americans generally tends to become more positive. The same has been shown to hold true of heterosexuals' attitudes toward homosexuals, and so on), and (b) frequently it is necessary for us to work with one of *them*, whether we want to or not. We can usually work with them more effectively if we have learned how to become interculturally more sensitive and how to apply that sensitivity to specific situations. Hence we have to *develop* the skills to understand the impact of culture, both on ourselves and on others.

One or two additional points: it is a further contention of this study that we are talking here about processes that are applicable on all levels of analysis—personal, group, and national. That is why in chapter 4 I have attempted to apply the concepts developed in chapters 1 through 3 to each of these levels of analysis.

I do not believe that "better communication" is a panacea. Conflict at every level of analysis has always persisted and probably always will. I am convinced that to the degree that interpersonal, intergroup, or international communication can be facilitated (a) there is likely to be less misperception and fear of other actors and (b) at least the actors can be certain, if they are in conflict, that they both agree on what the conflict actually is about.

Finally, in this edition, most quotations and footnotes have been removed in order to make it more readable. Some footnotes and direct quotes from some of the classics in the field have been retained. The bibliography for this edition has been expanded, and the work of all authors referred to in the text can be found there.

The Role of Culture and Perception in Communication: How I Violated a Cultural Norm

L et me begin my discussion of culture by relating a true story. Just before teaching my first graduate course in intercultural communication many years ago, I decided that I would like to do something to illustrate dramatically to the class how pervasive cultural norms are, how much we take them for granted, and how upset we become when they are violated. I hit upon an idea and asked the person who was then my wife what she thought about it. Her reaction was *extremely* negative. She became terribly upset at just the thought that I might actually do what I proposed. She begged, she pleaded, she implored me not to do it. Indeed, her reaction was so intense it convinced me that I had hit upon exactly the kind of illustration I wanted.

The next day before class, I dressed very carefully. I put on a male athletic supporter, underwear, and swimming trunks and was careful to wear a shirt that had long tails I could tuck into my trousers. (I did not want to be accused of indecent exposure.) Then, just before walking into my class, I unzipped my fly. For twenty minutes I paced in front of the room. I sat on the desk. I paced again. In general I tried to behave, nonverbally, as normally as possible, while at the same time not letting the class forget that my fly was open.

The reaction of the students was marvelous. They were terribly uncomfortable and embarrassed. They squirmed in their seats. They blushed. They would glance at my fly, then quickly look away. Some avoided eye contact. Others locked their eyes onto my face and refused to let their eyes go anywhere else. Though not one of them said a word about it, it was perfectly clear that they were very uncomfortable. For ten or fifteen minutes I continued to talk as though I had noticed nothing unusual. Finally I told the class that I was sensing a high degree of discomfort and that I thought it might be related to the fact that one zipper on my person, which in our culture is normally always closed in public, was open. There was a look of stunned disbelief on their faces. One of them actually blurted out: "You mean you know it's open?" "Of course I do," I answered. "I did it to illustrate how much we take cultural norms for granted and simply don't even think about them until they are violated." I then explained to them what I had worn that morning, and why I had done what I did. The expression of relief on their faces was profound. There were smiles, laughter, sighs, and general good feeling. We continued the discussion on the role of culture in molding accepted and expected norms of behavior for another ten minutes or so, but I intentionally still had not zipped my fly. Finally one of them shouted out, "Close the goddamn fly!" I did, and then we discussed why having my fly open was so distressing even knowing what I was wearing and that I had opened it intentionally.

Before we proceed any further, let us take a closer look at what is involved in cultural conditioning.

Culture: Why Can't People Be More Like Me?

Of all the animals known to exist, the human animal is perhaps the most social. Particularly in our earliest years, but throughout our entire lives as well, people exist—and must exist—in relationships with other human beings. Each of the humans with whom one comes into contact brings to that relationship his or her own view of the universe. More important, perhaps, each of the groups in which one has been raised or in which one has spent a good deal of time will have conditioned the individual to view the world from its perspective.

As is true for animals, we must eat, drink, sleep, find shelter, give and receive affection, and meet the other biological requirements "that flesh is heir to." But what we eat, when we eat, and how we eat are behaviors we have learned from the groups in which we have grown up. Not only the language I speak and the way I think but even *what* I see, hear, taste, touch, and smell are conditioned by the cultures in which I have been raised.

Benjamin Lee Whorf, the noted linguist, has written:

> We are thus introduced to a new principle of relativity, which holds that all observers are not led by the same physical evidence to the same picture of the universe, unless their linguistic backgrounds are similar, or can in some way be calibrated.[1]

---

[1] From *Collected Papers on Metalinguistics*, quoted by Franklin Fearing in "An Examination of the Conceptions of Benjamin Whorf in the Light of Theories on Perception and Cognition," in *Language in Culture*, edited by Harry Hoijer (Chicago: University of Chicago Press, 1954), 48.

I would go a step further and substitute the word *cultural* for the word *linguistic*. Every culture has its own language[2] or code, to be sure, but language is the manifestation—verbal or otherwise—of the perceptions, attitudes, values, beliefs, and disbelief systems that the group holds. Language, once established, further constrains the individual to perceive in certain ways, but language is merely one of the ways in which groups maintain and reinforce similarity of perception.

Genetically, we inherit from our parents those physical characteristics that distinguish us as their offspring. Admittedly there is a good deal of individual variation physically and experientially, but there is also a good deal of similarity. Given two white parents, the overwhelming probability is that the offspring will be white. Given two English-speaking parents, the overwhelming probability is that the offspring will speak English. The difference is that physical identity is—within a given range of probability— fixed, while cultural identity is not. The daughter of two white parents will always remain white no matter what happens to her after birth, but the daughter of two English-speaking parents may never speak English if immediately after birth she is raised by a totally non-English-speaking group. Thus while physical inheritance is relatively immutable, cultural inheritance is ever changing. The fascinating aspect of cultural conditioning, however, is that while there is theoretically an almost infinite number of possibilities, in fact the number of group-learned experiences to which most individuals are exposed is amazingly limited. Thus, for example, while there may be a whole world to explore, if not an entire universe, the overwhelm-

---

[2] Here I am using *language* in the broadest sense. It may include the jargon or symbols used by social scientists or mathematicians, for example, to express the concepts peculiar to their group, or it may include the myriad of nonverbal gestures sometimes referred to as body language.

ing majority of individuals who inhabit this planet never stray more than a few miles from their place of birth. They will, in all probability, speak the language that their parents spoke, practice the religion that their parents practiced, support the political parties that their parents supported, and in broad outline accept most of the cultural perceptions that their parents accepted. In sum, they will perceive the world in a manner strikingly similar to the way their parents perceived the world. That is precisely what makes them a part of the same broad cultural groups to which their parents belonged. Children will deviate from the perceptions of their parents, of course (some only mildly, others more radically). Children simply are not born into the same generation as their parents and, therefore, not into the same environment. Every individual is unique. So too are the experiences that every person has. While most of those experiences will be learned from other groups into which the individual will be socialized in the course of his or her life, some of those experiences will not have been group-related.

What is more, cultures themselves are constantly changing (in part because the environments in which people live are constantly changing), and thus people's perceptions of the world around them are also constantly changing. Further, many people—particularly in Western societies and most commonly in their teens—rebel against the attitudes and values of their parents and adopt different group values for themselves, though by the time they are adults the vast majority seem to have returned to the cultures of their parents. Each of us is a member of a finite number of different identity groups (which will be defined and discussed in the next chapter), but that number is relatively small compared to the incredibly large number that exist in the world. A high percentage of the most important groups to which we belong are the same groups to which our parents belonged.

It is a most basic premise of this work that a pattern of

learned, group-related perceptions—including both verbal and nonverbal language, attitudes, values, belief systems, disbelief systems, and behaviors—that is accepted and expected by an identity group is called a culture. Since, by definition, each identity group has its own pattern of perceptions and behavioral norms and its own language or code (understood most clearly by members of that group), each group may be said to have its own culture. Since these first three chapters are about perception, identity, and communication and how they affect each other, in a very real sense these chapters, collectively, are about culture and how it operates.

Years ago Ruth Benedict said:

> The life history of the individual is first and foremost an accommodation to the patterns and standards traditionally handed down in his community. From the moment of his birth the customs into which he is born shape his experience and behavior. By the time he can talk, he is a little creature of his culture, and by the time he is grown and able to take part in its activities, its habits are his habits, its beliefs his beliefs, its impossibilities his impossibilities. Every child that is born into his group will share them with him....[3]

And while she was referring there to total societal groups, everything she said then still holds true with reference to all identity groups.

The early cultural anthropologists wanted to collect data on how different groups met their biological needs and related to their environments. In order to do that, they felt that they had to find remote, isolated, "primitive"

---

[3] Ruth Benedict, *Patterns of Culture*, 1934; reprint (New York: New American Library, 1959), 18.

groups that had not been "contaminated" by contact with Western societies. Thus they went to the South Pacific, to isolated American Indian reservations, to the Latin American mountains and remote jungles, and to the Asian subcontinent looking for people who were presumed to have been so isolated that they would have been living and doing things the same way for millennia. In the process they created the impression that it was only those "quaint" and "primitive" peoples who had cultures that were clearly differentiated from one another. Later anthropologists corrected that misconception by rightly demonstrating that all peoples have unique histories, belief systems, attitudes, values, traditions, languages, and accepted and expected patterns of behavior, and that these ensembles constitute culture. But even there the notion persisted that one had to look at a total society in order to understand its culture. Thanks most, perhaps, to the work of Benjamin Lee Whorf and Edward Sapir, the tremendously important role of language in shaping patterns of thinking—and thus the relationship between language and culture—was established. But in so doing they also created the impression that only peoples who spoke distinctly different languages—not dialects—had distinctive cultural patterns. Only in very recent times have scholars come to accept the notion that *every group* that shares a similar pattern of perceptions— with all that implies—constitutes a culture. Since every identity group has somewhat different learned cultural ensembles, in greater or lesser degree, then every identity group may be said to have its own culture and, usually, its own language to go with it. While the language each group speaks may be called a dialect by the purist, the fact is that it makes communication easier among those who share that language, more difficult with those who do not; and it helps cement our feelings of "belonging."

Why the importance of making this distinction? Because looking at it this way enables us to apply the tools and techniques of intercultural analysis and communication to all interpersonal, intergroup, and international interactions. It enables us to look at any totality—a small informal group, a large organization, a city, or a tribe or nation[4]—and ask: What are the identity groups present in that unit of analysis? To what degree are there linkages among the groupings? To what degree are the unit identities stronger than the group identities that comprise it? To what degree are the group identities stronger? How can communication between groups be encouraged? These and dozens of similar questions must be answered if the effectiveness of personal, group, or national communication is to be increased. And the effectiveness of those communications will be increased if we constantly keep in mind the cultural differences that must be dealt with.

Harry Hoijer has said:

> ...to the extent that languages differ markedly from each other, so should we expect to find significant and formidable barriers to cross-cultural communication and understanding....
>
> It is, however, easy to exaggerate... the...barriers to intercultural understanding. No culture is wholly isolated, self-contained, and unique. There are important resemblances between all known cultures—resemblances that stem in part from diffusion (itself an evidence of successful intercultural communication) and in part from the fact that all cultures are built around biological, psychological, and social characteristics common to all mankind.... Intercultural communica-

---

[4] In this work the terms *nation*, *state*, and *country* will be used interchangeably, even though some political scientists prefer to reserve the term *nation* for those countries that share one and only one ethnic, tribal, racial, and/or religious identity.

tion, however wide the differences
between cultures may be, is not impossible. It is simply more or less difficult,
depending on the degree of difference
between the cultures concerned.[5]

Perceptions and Human Behavior: Fried Caterpillars

My first conscious awareness of the importance of perceptions to human behavior began with an incident when I
was still a graduate student. At that time esoteric foods
like chocolate-covered ants, fried grasshoppers, smoked
rattlesnake meat, and sweet-and-sour mouse tails were the
culinary fad. Upon moving into a new apartment, I received from a friend (as a housewarming gift) a whole carton of these canned delicacies. Having at that time rather
prosaic food habits, I did not consume the food. Indeed,
it sat untouched for the better part of a year while I alter-
nately toyed with the idea of trying one of those less than
tempting "goodies" myself or throwing the entire carton
in the garbage. One evening while putting out a whole
array of cheeses and other edibles in preparation for a cocktail party, it occurred to me that my opportunity had arrived. Without saying anything to anyone about what I
planned, I opened a can of fried caterpillars into a little
white dish and set them out on the table along with the
other foods. Then I waited to see what would happen.
Halfway through the evening one of the unsuspecting
young ladies I had invited to the party came up to me and
said, "Marshall, those fried shrimp you put out were deli-

---

[5] Harry Hoijer, "The Sapir-Whorf Hypotheses," in *Language in
Culture*, edited by Harry Hoijer (Chicago: University of Chicago Press, 1954), 94. Reprinted in *Intercultural Communication: A Reader*, 7th ed., edited by Larry A. Samovar and Richard E. Porter (Belmont, CA: Wadsworth, 1994).

cious." "Fried shrimp?" I asked as innocently as I could. "I didn't serve any fried shrimp." "Yes you did," she insisted. "They were in a little white plate on the table. In fact, they were so good I ate most of them myself." "Oh," I said, pausing for maximum effect, "those weren't fried shrimp, they were fried caterpillars."

Virtually the moment I said that the smile disappeared from her face, her complexion turned markedly green, and she proceeded to become terribly sick all over my living room floor. I realized—as I was cleaning up the floor— that what I had done was a terrible trick to play on anyone, and I have never done it again. But as I reflected on that incident, it amazed me that a food that could have been thought to be so delicious one moment—when it was *perceived* to be fried shrimp—could be so repugnant the next, when it was *perceived* to be something else. Suppose they really had been fried shrimp, and I had merely been pulling her leg? Would that have changed her physical reaction? I doubt it. In this case, as in most cases involving human behavior, reality was less important than one's perception of reality.

It is not the stimulus itself that produces specific human reactions and/or actions but rather how the stimulus is perceived by the individual that matters most for human behavior. It is perhaps the most basic law of human behavior that people act or react on the basis of the way in which they perceive the external world.

Perceptions: I Know What I Know. I Can't Know What I Don't Know

By *perception*, I mean the process—and it is a process— by which an individual selects, evaluates, and organizes stimuli from the external environment. Perceptions are the windows through which a person experiences the world. They also determine the ways in which we behave toward it. That "world" includes symbols, things, people, groups of people, ideas, events, ideologies, and even faith. In sum, we experience *everything* in the world not "as it is"—because there is no way that we can know the world as it is—but only as the world comes to us through our sensory receptors. From there these stimuli go instantly into the data banks of our brain, where they have to pass through the filters of our censor screens, our decoding mechanisms, and the collectivity of everything we have learned from the day we were born. The information stored in the brain—including the "program" we have learned that teaches us how to learn about new data—in turn affects (if not determines) not only what relatively few bits of data we will attend to (from the literally millions available) but also how we will interpret each bit that we do select. The Dutch scholar Geert Hofstede calls this the "software of the mind."[6]

Perceptions, attitudes, values, and belief systems are not the same thing (although throughout this work I will sometimes refer to *perceptions* as a shorthand way of referring to them), but they all affect each other and constantly interact.

Technically speaking, group-related, learned perceptions (including verbal and nonverbal codes), attitudes, values, and belief and disbelief systems, plus accepted and expected codes of behavior taught by the groups with which we identify, are what constitute culture. Perceptions that are not group-taught (such as individual physical differences in sensory receptors, body chemistry, or individual unique experiences) should not be considered part of cultural perceptions. Neither should physical or environmental factors that affect perceptions. The trouble is that the distinction between these types of perception is often blurred.

---

[6] Geert Hofstede, *Cultures and Organizations: Software of the Mind* (London: McGraw-Hill, 1991).

Hence, virtually every message to which we attend will be *at least indirectly* affected by our cultural conditioning. Further, when we have finished discussing the factors that affect perceptions, the reader will see more clearly, I think, what a profound effect our cultures do have on the way we perceive and what a minor effect (by comparison) other factors have in most cases. Thus if I am somewhat imprecise in the way I sometimes use the terms *culture* and *perceptions* synonymously, I ask the reader to forgive me. It should be understood, however, that whenever I do use them synonymously I am referring to *group-related, learned* perceptions only. I suspect that it will be easier for most readers to forgive some imprecision than it would be for them to forgive having continually to wade through the phrase "the totality of all of the attitudes, values, beliefs...."

Figure 1.1

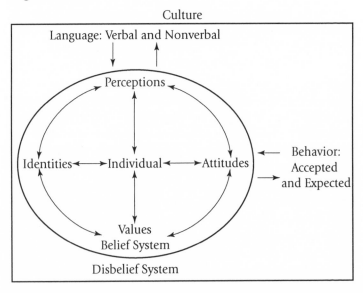

The totality of our group-related, learned perceptions, attitudes, values, and belief and disbelief systems *plus the ranking we make in any specific context* of the groups with which we identify (our identities), plus the behaviors we normally exhibit, are what make us each culturally unique. Some—indeed, many—of those perceptions, attitudes, values, and identities we hold may be totally (more often partially) contradictory. Despite that, we somehow manage to hold them all and to apply different ones to our behavior in different situations. Further, there are times when our own behavior can alter those very perceptions, attitudes, values, identities, and beliefs we hold. Thus what I am suggesting is a circle of causality. Each affects the other and is in turn affected by each. (See figure 1.1.)[7]

At the center is the individual, affected by and affecting all of the components that make up the culture of each of the groups to which she or he belongs. Virtually all of these processes, of course, occur completely below our level of consciousness, and they occur continuously from the moment of our birth. We are hardly ever aware on a conscious level that they are occurring. They are almost totally involuntary processes despite the fact that they are very largely learned. But learned they are, particularly in those early, formative years when our most basic belief systems and corresponding disbelief systems are being formed. And once formed, they change only very slowly— or only when we are confronted by some event that is so dramatic and/or so discordant with an attitude, value, identity, or belief we have held dear that we are forced to reevaluate. Most often we are forced to reevaluate when we interact with people who have different attitudes, values, or belief systems. That is what I meant earlier about getting to know one of *them*. Once we do, they are not nearly so frightening as they were before we got to know them. The trick, of course, is to overcome the enormous problems of learning how to communicate with someone who speaks a totally different cultural language than we do—

---

[7] Although drawn heavily from anthropological and social/psychological literature, this way of viewing culture is my own.

even if the verbal language is the same, or at least intelligible to us. It is the differences in perceptions, attitudes, values, and so on that make communicating so very difficult. But learning how to overcome those differences is what makes us better intercultural communicators.

Factors That Affect Perception: It's Not Just Fingerprints That Are Different for Everyone

There are a great variety of factors that affect perception. There is no question that the learned factors are by far the most important. But before we discuss them, there are some other factors that are not unimportant, and we will discuss those first.

Physical Determinants of Perception

The only way we can know about the world outside our own body is by the impressions of that outside world picked up by our sensory receptors. In another chapter we will discuss the five receptors recognized by Aristotle. Later research, of course, has revealed several things. First, it has shown that it is not really the eye as such that is the sensory receptor but more specifically the nerve endings in the cones and rods of the retina of the eye that pick up those visual sensations and transfer them to the brain for interpretation, organization, and storage.

Second, it was discovered that, in fact, there are many more receptors than the five Aristotle mentioned. Indeed, current research has identified at least thirty-seven differentiated sensory inputs into the human brain, and there are probably many more yet to be discovered.

While most of us have all of these same sensory receptors, we know that no two individuals are identical physically. For example, empirical evidence has proven that the swirls on the tips of every human's fingers are ever-so-slightly different from anyone else's. It must then follow that each person's sense of touch must also be ever-so-slightly different. Yet far more important for the way people view the universe may be the still unanswered questions of physical variations in other sensory receptors. What about the configuration of cones and rods in the retina of the eye, or taste buds on the tongue, or fibers in the ear, or any of the other physical receptors of external stimuli? *If no two individuals have identical physical receptors of stimuli, then it must follow, on the basis of physical evidence alone, that no two individuals can perceive the external world identically.*

Yet physical differences in sensory receptors, while important, may be the least of the factors contributing to differences in perception. Consider for a moment that peculiar combination of physical and psychological factors called personality or temperament that makes each of us unique. Some scholars would argue that temperament is one of the key factors determining how we perceive the external world. While I'm not certain that I would place it in as central a position with regard to perceptions, there is no doubt that it is a contributing factor.

Which of the factors that go into making up temperament are physical and which are learned—and to what degree they are learned—is impossible to say at this point in our knowledge. Nor is it very important to this book that we do so. We know that some children are born with placid personalities, while others are born hyperactive. Certainly that is not learned. What is probably learned, however, are acceptable and unacceptable ways of coping with those physical characteristics. What is learned is that other people react to us in certain ways if we follow one behavior pattern and differently if we follow another.

Before I leave the subject of physical determinants of perception, there are a whole range of other physical differences that make us unique and deserve to be mentioned here because of the ways in which they affect our perceptions. I'm thinking here of the vast array of physical characteristics we inherit at birth. Height, weight, gender, skin color, hair texture, and physical handicaps all have an impact on how we will perceive the world. It is not the physical characteristics themselves that necessarily determine our perceptions, but rather other people's reactions to these physical characteristics that are so important in shaping our view of ourselves and of the world.[8]

In summary, while I do not believe that physical factors are the most important determinant of how individuals perceive the world, what I have attempted to show in this section is that physical differences *alone* make it impossible that any two humans could perceive the world identically. That fact by itself would make it impossible for any two humans to communicate with 100 percent accuracy. As we shall see as we proceed, other factors individually and collectively make the probability of accurate communication even more remote and difficult to achieve.

We will say more about the other, more major learned factors affecting perceptions. Before we get to that, however, we should pause first to consider some of the environmental factors that affect perception.

Environmental Determinants of Perception: It's Just Not Possible to See in Total Darkness

No matter how good, bad, or different people's visual sensory receptors are, in the absence of sufficient light no color can be perceived; in the absence of all light no visual images whatever can be received. Similarly if a sound is made above or below the threshold at which the human ear is capable of sensing it, no sound will be heard. (It is important for us to make the distinction, as we will later in detail, between stimuli that are received on the conscious level and those that are received below the level of consciousness. What I am discussing here are the *factors that*

---

[8] See chapter 3, "Co-Cultures: Living in Two Cultures," in *Intercultural Communication: A Reader*, edited by Larry A. Samovar and Richard E. Porter, 7th ed. (Belmont, CA: Wadsworth, 1994) for a number of articles on what it is like to be female, African American, gay, or disabled in America.

affect the perception of the stimuli, whether at the conscious or subconscious level.)

Physical environment also affects the way we perceive things. There is increasing evidence that people who live in tropical areas of the world may see reds and oranges very differently from the way people living in the Arctic see those colors. People living in a desert environment or a rain forest will certainly have very different perceptions of water. It is not an accident that native peoples who live in far northern climates have many different words for snow. And people who grew up in a big city probably perceive a great many things differently than do people who grew up in the country.

Relationship of stimulus to surroundings. Observe figure 1.2. The figure E is present in F, but it is very difficult to perceive it there consciously because of the surrounding elements in F.

Figure 1.2

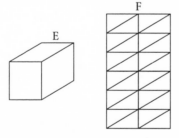

From Willis D. Ellis, *A Source Book of Gestalt Psychology,* Humanities Press, New York, 1967. Reprinted with permission of Routledge & Kegan Paul Ltd. London, 1938.

What has been said thus far also applies to size. Look at figures 1.3 and 1.4. The inner circles in both drawings in figure 1.3 are the same size, as are the lines in figure 1.4. Once again the surrounding elements (circles in figure 1.3, lines in figure 1.4) distort and determine what we see. Subconsciously we may be able to see the similarity

in these figures, but on a conscious level we would swear
that they were different. As I will say repeatedly throughout this work, everything—including perceptions of reality—is relative and contextual.

Figure 1.3

From *Human Behavior: An Inventory of Scientific Findings* by Bernard Berelson and Gary A. Steiner, copyright © 1964 by Harcourt
Brace and & World and renewed 1992 by Ruth Berelson, Linda
Steiner Thomas and Faith Steiner, reproduced by permission of
the publisher.

Figure 1.4

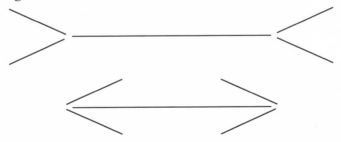

The Muller-Lyer illusion. From "Cross-Cultural Studies" by D.
Price-Williams from *New Horizons in Psychology*, edited by Brian
M. Foss (New York: Penguin Books, 1966), 398.

These figures are presented here merely to demonstrate
that we can't always trust our perceptions—even when they
are culturally neutral. What we see may very well depend
on what surrounds it, or what it is near. But many of the

most important of our perceptions—like our attitudes, values, and beliefs—are not culturally neutral. Rather we have been taught them by the groups that are most important to us. Further, everything that has been shown here about visual perception could be replicated for all of the other senses as well. It is just easier to reproduce pictures than it is to reproduce sounds, tastes, or smells.

What is more, different cultures will not see the same things we do. Go back to figure 1.4. Research has indicated that people in some cultures have no difficulty in seeing that the horizontal lines are of equal length.[9] It is precisely these kinds of differences in perception that are so difficult to deal with. How do I communicate accurately with someone who perceives differently than I do when it would never occur to me that that person could possibly perceive differently?

Learned Determinants of Perception: Death and Destruction or Chicken Soup? It Depends on What You Have Learned

Far more important than either physical or environmental differences in determining an individual's perceptions of the external world are the *learned* factors involved in the reception, organization, and processing of sensory data.

Even identical twins born into and raised by the same family (and thus presumed to have the same physical and learned inheritance) will not have identical perceptions of the world. If one could accurately measure perceptions, there is no doubt that the degree to which twins share similarity of perceptions would be considerably higher than for most other individuals, but those perceptions would be far from identical. Certainly the younger the iden-

---

[9] Cited in D. Price-Williams, "Cross-Cultural Studies," in *New Horizons in Psychology*, edited by Brian M. Foss (New York: Penguin Books, 1966). Reprinted in *Intercultural Communication: A Reader*, 2d ed., edited by Samovar and Porter, 34.

tical twins were at the time the test was given, the more similar their perceptions would likely be, but anyone who lives with twins knows how different they can be, from the earliest age. Looking in from outside, someone who is not a part of the family may not notice the differences. Indeed, the outsider is much more likely to be struck by the similarity of the children than by the differences. But a parent or siblings, from the first weeks, have no difficulty telling them apart physically, and by the end of a few months are amazed at the personality differences. Why this is so is difficult to explain. It's relatively easy to understand that as twins get older their experiences are increasingly dissimilar, but it is startling to see how what appear to be minuscule variations in their exposure to the outside world can produce such profound differences in the very youngest children. Perhaps one caught a cold and the other did not. Perhaps while the twins were resting outdoors a bird flew close to one and startled it but was unnoticed by the other. Perhaps one was scolded or ignored while the other was not. Whatever the specifics, there is no question that while their experiences may indeed be far more similar than for most people, they are never identical. And because those experiences are not identical, the twins will not view the world identically.

If for physical and experiential reasons it is not possible for any two individuals to perceive the universe in exactly the same way, neither is it possible for them to have absolutely no similarities of perception. In a sense there is a continuum of similarity of perception among individuals. One extreme approaches—but never reaches—zero; the other approaches—but never reaches—100 percent. Actually, degree of similarity of perception can probably best be expressed not as a point on a continuum but as a range of points. For example: A Catholic from a wealthy third-generation Boston family and a Catholic from an illiterate and impoverished village in Zaire may share some very small percent of similarity of perception, *as Catholics,* and to that degree they are a part of the broad identity called Catholics. Teachers, considered as a broad group, may also share some small percent of similarity of perception. If we narrow the group to include only college teachers, the range of similarity of perception may increase somewhat. If we further specify that the group consists only of Irish-Catholic, American, middle-class, urban, white, male, heterosexual college teachers of quantum physics, with Ph.D.'s from the Massachusetts Institute of Technology, between the ages of thirty-five and forty, the range of similarity of perception might increase enormously. Notice that while we have decreased the number of people who can be included in our group, we have increased the number of group identities the members share. By so doing, we have greatly increased the likelihood of easy communication among them and thus the likelihood of their sharing still greater similarities of perception in the future. (See premise 4, chapter 2.) It is no wonder that the smaller the group, the greater its cohesion is likely to be.

In order to illustrate how different perceptions of the same stimuli can be, a number of years ago I devised an exercise which I have since run hundreds of times in many different societies. Allow me to describe it here in some detail to illustrate the enormous differences in perceptions of symbols that actually exist.

In this exercise I put four symbols on the board, one at a time, and ask the seminar or class participants to write on a piece of paper all of the meanings that come to their minds when they see the symbols. When they are done writing, I ask everyone in the room to tell me the meanings they attributed to the symbols. (See figure 1.5.)

Figure 1.5

The answers I get vary enormously, depending upon the participants. There is strong indication that they would vary even more if I could do the exercise in remote villages with unschooled individuals in their own languages. As it is, except on three or four occasions when simultaneous translators were present, I have always done the exercise in English, usually with highly educated participants. This has automatically skewed the sample in the direction of *more* similarity of perception because all of the participants shared a certain similarity of perception as speakers of English and usually as highly educated professionals. (Normally the participants are graduate students in public and international affairs or midcareer civil servants.)

The two most common answers I get for the first symbol are "cross"—in the religious sense—and "plus"—in the mathematical sense. Now, since more than half of the participants I get are educated Christians, that is not really a surprising result. Also, since most come from the more developed parts of developing countries, the third most frequent response—"crossroads"—is also not surprising. The surprises, for me at least, usually come because of my own perceptual limitations. I am not really surprised by answers like "the letter T," "quadrants on a map," "the hands of a compass," "check mark" as in *correct*, or "a check mark" as in *incorrect*, the word *yes*, the word *no*, "Red Cross," and "the sign for Switzerland," although they are not answers I would have thought of myself. The first real surprises came for me when I did this exercise at a United Nations school in Costa Rica with a group of senior Central American civil servants from all six Central American republics and a Spanish interpreter. Almost every answer I got for that symbol suggested Latin Catholic romantic symbolism: "death and transfiguration," "life after death," "love," "sacrifice," "eternal life," "suffering," "God's son," "redemption," "crucifixion," "resurrection." These were just some of the meanings that were suggested to that group of people by that symbol. Not having been raised in a Latin

Catholic culture, there was no way I could see those mean-ings in that symbol. From a communication point of view it doesn't matter how I was raised. What is important is that *they* were raised in that culture, and those were the meanings that symbol held for *them*.

The second real surprise for me with that symbol came when I did the exercise at the University of Malaya in Kuala Lumpur, Malaysia, with a group of second-year university students. Virtually every Malaysian of Chinese extraction (about half the students were of Chinese extraction) saw the symbol as the Chinese number ten because—as I dis-covered that day—that, indeed, is the way the Chinese write the number ten. Not having studied Chinese myself, there simply was no way I could possibly have seen the number ten in that symbol. On the other hand, there is almost no way in which a person born of Chinese parents, who has been taught to read and write Chinese as his or her first language, could *not* see the number ten in that symbol.[10]

This is just another example of why communication across cultural barriers is so difficult. If the way in which you perceive a stimulus is completely outside *my* percep-tual ken, how can I possibly begin to communicate with you? The answer, it seems to me, is to constantly remind myself that *everyone* has different perceptions, and I just can-not take anything for granted, which is easier said than done.

At the point where the participants have told me the meanings they saw in the first symbol, I usually ask them which one is correct. Obviously the answer is that all of them are correct—for them. *Symbols have no intrinsic mean-*

---

[10] An interesting variation occurs when I do that exercise in Pitts-burgh. Chinese and Japanese students frequently do *not* see, or indicate they saw, the number 10, although the Japanese write the number 10 the same way. When I ask why, they frequently say that it never occurred to them in the context of a Pittsburgh classroom that an American professor would know Chinese or Japanese.

ing. Meaning resides not in the symbol but in our minds. If you see this + as the number ten or as a symbol of resurrection or as a red cross, who am I to say that you are wrong? What I can say is that it is not the meaning I had in my mind when I devised the exercise. When I first decided to use that symbol, I saw it as one horizontal line and one vertical line crossing more or less at the midpoint. But that is only what was in *my* head at the time. It is no more correct or incorrect than any other meaning that people ascribe to it. Yet if two people are to communicate effectively, each has to know with some degree of accuracy what the symbols they use mean to the other. All language, after all, is symbolic. If I attribute different meanings to your words than you do (and most often I probably do), then there is no way we can communicate accurately. But that is precisely the point being made here. *No two humans can communicate 100 percent accurately because no two humans have learned to perceive identically.*

For the second symbol I have gotten responses that in some ways were even more revealing to me. In one group of participants there was a man from Egypt. When I drew this symbol on the board, he violently threw down his pencil on the desk and in an angry voice said, "I will not draw that symbol! I give my life to oppose it! I will not play games with that symbol!"

"But what if it is only two triangles superimposed upon each other; one pointing down, the other pointing up?" I asked, surprised not at his perception of the symbol as something representing the State of Israel, but by the violence of his reaction.

"No," he said, more angrily than before, "It stands for everything evil in this world! Death! Destruction! Murder! Torture! Violence! Hate! I will not play games with such a symbol!" Whereupon he rolled back one shirt sleeve and asked, "Do you see that scar?" pointing to a long, red scar about three inches above his right wrist. "I got that fighting murderous Zionism in Sinai in 1956." Then putting his wrist on his head he said, "I wear it like my halo of thorns! I will not play games with evil."

Who am I to argue with his perception of that symbol? Obviously for him it really did mean all of those awful things, and nothing that I was going to say could change that perception. I recognized then, for the first time perhaps, at a gut level, why it is so difficult to resolve the Middle East situation.

The more I have thought about that Egyptian's reaction to that symbol and compared it with other reactions I have gotten from different people with different life experiences, the more amazed I am that any communication at all ever takes place. When I have done this exercise with a group of predominantly Jewish, middle-class, American students from New York City I have gotten answers like "Manischewitz wine," "Mogen David products," "Jewish star," "star of David," "peace," "chicken soup," "high holy days," and many other meanings that only an American Jew could associate with that symbol. Being an American Jew myself, none of these meanings really surprised me—not even the chicken soup—though I hadn't thought of them when I designed the exercise. Sharing some degree of similarity of perception with that group, I could certainly understand why they would associate those meanings with that symbol.

The third symbol, I have always drawn carefully the way it appears on page 21. While there is usually some diversity among the answers—depending upon the audience—anywhere from 60 to 100 percent will see it as somehow associated with Hitler, fascism, or Nazi Germany. The fact is that the symbol I put on the board is *not* a Nazi swastika. Hitler's swastika always points to the right, no matter how it is turned, and it is usually turned like this:

But as the saying goes, "Don't confuse me with facts. My mind is made up." It is stylized enough and reminiscent enough of the German swastika to elicit exactly the same depth of emotion—particularly from older Jews who lost relatives during the Nazi period—as a Nazi swastika would. The one I put on the board is really an ancient Aryan (Indian) symbol but that in no way changes the depth of one's perception of and reaction to it as a Nazi swastika.

The fourth symbol is much more ambiguous than the first three and is open to more interpretation. Still, a great many people see it as a "squiggle" or a "signature" or a "corkscrew." More people from developing countries see it as a "river," a "snake," or a "puff of smoke" than do people from developed countries. I once did this exercise at a graduate school of nursing, and more than 60 percent of the participants in that group saw it specifically as an "intrauterine device (IUD)" or simply as a "coil" or a "birth-control device." But if you've never seen an IUD, there just is no way you can know what you don't know.

The last part of that last sentence is at the heart of this exercise and my lengthy discussion of it here. It is so important and so obvious that it is often overlooked. *We know what we perceive; we don't know what we don't perceive. Since there is no way that we can know what we don't perceive, we assume that we perceive "correctly"—even if we don't.* We tend to assume that almost everyone perceives what we perceive and that we perceive everything (or almost everything) that everybody else perceives. Thus we engage people in discussion on a wide range of topics assuming that the people with whom we are attempting to communicate share the same perceptions that we do. The two exceptions to this rule usually are people who look terribly foreign (or don't speak our language) and people who are specialists in fields about which we know nothing.

Beyond those exceptions, however, most of us assume that we know what the other person meant when he or she said something until we discover, by whatever circumstances or accident, that we do not. I automatically assume that someone else perceives what I perceive until proven otherwise. If I didn't do that, even the simplest communication would be exhausting.

The more specific the symbol, the more agreement about its meaning we are likely to find. The more abstract the symbol, the greater the variety of meanings we are likely to find associated with it. A word like *table,* for example, is a symbol. But because it is specific, the range of perceptions associated with it are likely to be fairly limited. One may see a wooden table or a Formica table, a round one or a rectangular one. One might see a mathematical table, a statistical table, a water table, or a table of contents. But the range of choices is fairly limited. On the other hand, the range of choices one might—and does—associate with abstract concepts like "God," "justice," or "democracy" are truly mind-boggling. There probably are as many different meanings associated with those abstract concepts as there are groups in the world.

Attitudes: This Is Beautiful; That Is Ugly

Take any stimulus, whatever that stimulus may be—a person, an event, an idea—it doesn't matter. On the basis of all the previous stimuli that have gone into our brain's data bank and the way we have organized those stimuli, we make judgments about the new stimulus. Those judgments are called attitudes. Something is good or bad, right or wrong, useful or dangerous, beautiful or ugly. Each of the groups into which we have been socialized (and as we shall see shortly, we are socialized into a great many) teaches us *its* attitudes toward those stimuli. Many of the groups with which we identify will teach us conflicting judgments about the same stimuli. In some cases even the same group will, on specific issues, teach conflicting attitudes. Conflicting or not, what is important to note here is that *every* group teaches its members what *its* preferred attitudes are.

Not only does each of the groups into which we have been socialized teach us its judgment toward specific stimuli; even more important, it teaches us an *attitudinal framework* through which we can evaluate *new* stimuli that reach our sensory receptors. These attitudinal frameworks become an integral part of both our censor screens and our decoding mechanism. Many of the groups of which we consider ourselves to be a part may teach conflicting attitudinal frames of reference. Which we will adopt as our own will depend in large part on the way we rank the various group identities we hold. Often these conflicting frameworks cause no difficulty, however, because the context of each is usually different. For example, our religious identity may teach us that life is precious and that all killing—including that of an unborn fetus—is wrong. Yet some of those religious people have gone out—in the name of ending the killing of unborn babies—and bombed family planning clinics and killed doctors who perform abortions.

The variety of judgments about the same stimuli is astounding. In the same city in India one might find men who, as a sign of deference to God, never cut their beard or hair (Sikhs), while a few blocks away at a Buddhist monastery one can find men who shave their head and face completely—as their sign of deference to God. In some places one finds it perfectly acceptable for a man to walk down a city street holding hands with a male friend, while he might be arrested (or at least disparaged) for walking down the same street holding hands with a female. In some places a woman could be killed for sleeping with the brother of her husband. In others she may be married to all the brothers in a family simultaneously. In some places if a man were to sexually molest a prepubescent boy he could be jailed and very possibly killed by other inmates, while in other places it is not considered at all immoral, *provided* the boy is prepubescent. The contrasts and differences are unlimited. Which set of attitudes we adopt and how we rank them will depend heavily on the degree to which we identify with each of the groups to which we belong.

It occasionally happens that we are confronted with a stimulus (it could be a thing, an event, or an idea) to which we simply do not know how to react. At those times we will sometimes check with people from the groups with which we identify and whom we consider knowledgeable to see how they evaluate that stimulus. Their responses then give us our clues as to how we should react.

Sometimes we form an attitude about a stimulus based on the framework that is already in place and then check our judgment of that stimulus with specific others from the groups that matter most to us (people whom we know and trust and whose judgments we respect—meaning that generally their attitudes toward stimuli either conform to our own or are such that we have no difficulty accepting them as our own) just to reinforce our original assessment of the stimulus. But most of the time we don't need to check. Most of the time the attitudinal framework our groups have supplied is sufficient so that we can make judgments about a whole range of issues or events with which we may never before have been confronted.

Values: This Is the Way Things Ought to Be

Obviously, values are closely intertwined with attitudes. We desire certain events or situations above others because we have learned that they are good, right, and/or useful. Which attitudes and values the individual will adopt as his or her own will depend in large part on the ranking he or she makes of the various group identities held at any given time. Yet the complexity of the process is such that those attitudes and values, in turn, will affect our identity which, in turn, will affect how we perceive any new stimulus.

Values refer to our desires, wants, needs, or goals. Those terms are close in meaning, although there are shades of difference. *Needs*, for example, connotes a desire having a physiological base. One needs something in order to survive as opposed to just wanting it.

Every individual, group, or nation holds a number of values simultaneously. Just as with attitudes, some of the values an individual or group holds may be compatible, but some may be in conflict. Or an individual's values may conflict with the values of one or more of the groups to which he or she belongs. In fact, it is almost inevitable that they will. It may not be so much that the values themselves conflict—although that is certainly possible—but rather that the importance we attach to certain values may be different from the importance other individuals or groups attach to those same values. That is, each individual or group ranks the importance of those values (to themselves) differently. Each of the groups of which we are a part teaches us *its* ranking of values. Which ranking we accept, which we change, and which we reject outright is, I believe, a function of the degree to which we identify with each of those groups. That is why I argue that every individual is culturally unique.

Let's suppose that membership in Group I implies acceptance of the hypothetical values listed in figure 1.6. That does not mean that every member of Group I will accept all of these values or will rank them in exactly that order. Indeed they will not. Membership in a group does imply acceptance of some of the basic group values, but it is clear that each member of the group will accept some of the group's values and reject others. Even among those group values that are accepted by everyone, each individual will rank the importance of those group values somewhat differently. Indeed some members of Group I, because of overlapping membership in some other groups, will inevitably hold some values that are completely alien to other members of Group I.

Figure 1.6

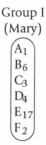

Group I
(Mary)

A_1
B_6
C_3
D_4
E_{17}
F_2

While person 1 of Group I (let's call her Mary) might have ranked the predominant group values as shown, persons 2 and 3 of the same group (let's call them Margaret and Mildred) might have ranked them as shown in figure 1.7. Each individual is still holding all of the same group values but ranking them differently. The combinations possible—even for people holding all and only the same group values—are virtually endless.

Figure 1.7

Group I   Group I
Person 2   Person 3
(Margaret)   (Mildred)

A_1 F_2
B_6 E_{17}
C_3 D_4
D_4 C_3
F_2 B_6
E_{17} A_1

Allow me a personal real-world example to illustrate: One of the groups with which I identify is called "Jewish." For some Jews, being Jewish means praying three times a day, holding the Sabbath sacred, observing all of the traditions associated with Judaism, eating only the foods considered ritually pure, observing all of the holidays, and so on. These Jewish values may be the ones some Jews rank highly, but they are not the ones I do. I rank other Jewish values—which are just as Jewish—like being a good person, the importance of education, the need to be tolerant of other people's values, the importance of family and of good friends to share meals and conversation with, as values that better fit my definition of Judaism. That doesn't make me right and them wrong, or better or worse Jews. It just makes us different kinds of Jews. But it is the different ranking of our Jewish values that makes us different kinds of Jews.

Complicate the picture still further by recognizing that no two humans are members of all and only the same groups. Thus, assuming membership in only twelve different identity groups (which is a vast underestimation of the number of groups of which we are simultaneously members), Mary's value structure might look something like figure 1.8.

Figure 1.8

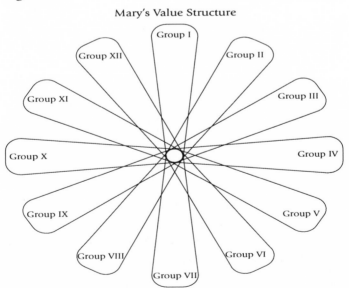

Mary's Value Structure

Mary would be at the confluence of these twelve specific identity groups (remember that each group has a culture of its own) and presumably would rank the values of each of these groups in her own unique way. Another individual belonging to all and only the same groups as Mary—if that were possible—would still be culturally different from Mary because of the probability that the other individual would rank the values of each of those groups somewhat differently from the way Mary ranks them.

Figure 1.9

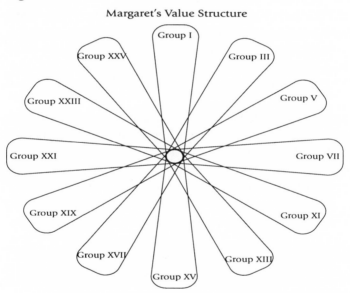

Margaret's Value Structure

Margaret's value structure (also assuming membership in only twelve identity groups), and sharing membership in five of the same cultures as Mary, might look something like figure 1.9.

I don't think the point has to be labored further. Of course every person is culturally unique. That is why every interpersonal communication is also an intercultural communication. Knowing that should allow us to recognize the differences for what they are and strive to find the cultural similarities—which just as certainly are going to be there, since each of us shares some similar group identities merely by virtue of being human—and start by building upon those. The more we explore another individual's value structure, the more we are likely to find that we share. From these explorations we can learn how to learn about those other values we do not share. This is exactly what it takes to communicate effectively across cultural barriers.

Let's return to our discussion of values as such. Whatever we call them—needs, values, goals—the fact is, every individual or group has them. Some individuals and groups may have different values from other individuals and groups or they may have them in different proportions and/or they may rank them differently, but every human has values.

Some have argued that precisely because the human animal is just that—an animal—we must fulfill our most basic animal needs first. They would argue that either we eat, drink, sleep, and find shelter or we die. We either procreate or the species dies. Those are the basic needs to which we must first attend. But as a complex social animal, there are other needs to which we must also attend. Psychologists would argue that we need to feel safe and provide for the safety of those whom we care about; we need to give and receive affection; we need to have a feeling of self-esteem; and ultimately, if there is time and energy left over, and we have the chance to think about it, we have a need for self-actualization.

Abraham H. Maslow describes these as the hierarchy of needs.[11] That is, he argues that we must fulfill our most basic needs *first*, and only when those have been satisfied do we turn our attention to the fulfillment of the "higher order" needs. He goes on to say:

---

[11] Abraham H. Maslow, *Motivation and Personality*, 2nd ed. (New York: Harper and Row, 1970).

> In actual fact, most members of our
> society who are normal are partially
> satisfied in all of their basic needs and
> partially unsatisfied in all their basic
> needs at the same time. A more realistic
> description of the hierarchy would be in
> terms of decreasing percentages of
> satisfaction as we go up the hierarchy of
> prepotency. For instance,…it is as if the
> average citizen is satisfied perhaps 85%
> in his physiological needs, 70% in his
> safety needs, 60% in his love needs, 40%
> in his self-esteem needs and 10% in his
> self-actualization needs.[12]

Regardless of the percentages involved, Maslow would argue that we try to fulfill all of those needs all of the time.

Whether they are actually physiological needs or learned values does not have to overly trouble us here. To the degree that they have a physical imperative associated with them, they may indeed be needs as opposed to desires or wants or goals. Regardless of which they are, however, several things have to be said about them.

For one thing, it is clear that we try to fulfill several or all of them simultaneously. To the degree that those values are compatible that is not a problem. To the degree that one or more of those needs conflict, however, particularly if we rank them as equally important, that could be a problem. We could—and many of us frequently do—find ourselves trying to satisfy two totally conflicting values simultaneously and thus achieve neither. In chapter 2, I will talk more about the importance of prioritizing our needs, goals, and values in order to be able to direct our behavior toward meeting them. But there is no way we can meet all of them simultaneously even if they don't

---

[12] Ibid., 53-54.

directly conflict. Let me give you a concrete example. A number of years ago when I was raising my children as a single parent, I promised my sons that if the Pirates made it into the World Series I would take them to a game. Being a single parent, my identity as a father was naturally very high, and I certainly wanted to be perceived by my sons as being a good one. On the other hand, my identity as a professor is also pretty high, and I certainly wanted my students to think I was a good one. Well, as luck would have it, the Pirates did make it into the World Series and, unfortunately for me, the only game I could take them to was the one being played on the night of my class. Now I had to choose. There was no way I could do both at the same time. Which identity was more important to me? At that point in my life, my identity as father won. I told my class I would be willing to hold a makeup session on a Saturday, but somehow, they weren't impressed. My sons were, however, particularly because we had good seats and the Pirates won.

Second, except in those extreme cases where the deprivation is all-consuming, many—if not most—of these needs or values are perceived only on a subconscious level. Consciously we may deny vehemently—even to ourselves—that we are lonely, yet our actions can indicate loudly to the trained observer that much of our behavior revolves around trying to assuage that loneliness. Most often we are simply unaware consciously of what our needs are or how pressing some of them are at different times. Yet we try communicating with others (who may be no more conscious of *their* value ranking than we are) and oftentimes come away not knowing why we found the exchange so unsatisfying.

Third, fulfilling one need can partially—but only partially—substitute for another. Filling up on water is not really a substitute for food, but it does stave off hunger to some degree. People who eat compulsively don't do so because they are perpetually hungry. They may do so because eating provides instant gratification and substitutes for other needs that are not being gratified. Meeting self-esteem needs may not substitute for love needs, but may be perceived by the individual as a means to an end.

Fourth, and probably most relevant to this discussion, whatever our needs or values or how we rank them, what they are and how they are ranked are learned from the groups with which we identify. We are taught which values we *ought* to hold by each of our groups. What is more, we are also taught in what ways it is acceptable to go about satisfying those desires and in what ways it is not.

But that is just the point. Each group teaches *its* culture, its attitudes, values, perceptions, and so on. That is precisely what makes intercultural communication so difficult. If we fervently value "the greatest good for the greatest number" of our fellow humans, how do we possibly communicate effectively with those who just as fervently value getting all they can for themselves and their families? If we value peace and nonviolence above all else, how do we communicate effectively with someone who believes that one has to take what one wants by whatever means? All of us believe that our values are the best ones to hold. If we didn't, we would hold other values. Because no two groups value exactly the same things or rank their values in the same order, it is inevitable that there will be basic value conflict between individuals from different groups. Yet somehow, if communication among individuals from different groups is ever to be effective, we must not only recognize which values we rank most highly, we must also recognize that "they" are likely to rank perhaps totally different values just as highly. The first step to effective intercultural communication, it seems to me, is to recognize what those value differences are. As I said earlier, we may not like the values "they" hold, but we must recognize that their values are as important to them as ours are to us. I can't stress this fact enough. The second step—and it is perhaps the most difficult one in the intercultural communication process—is to find some way to reach an accommodation between those conflicting values. It is the ability to achieve this accommodation that constitutes the making of an effective intercultural communicator.

On a very practical level just think how important this is to multinational corporations (MNCs) that operate all over the world with workers and managers from a variety of cultures. In his path-breaking book, *Culture's Consequences: International Differences in Work-Related Values,* Geert Hofstede examined the values of employees at IBM (he called it the "HERMES Corp." at the time to disguise it) in forty countries of the world.[13] (He later extended it to sixty countries.) What he found was that there were some major differences in what both managers and employees in different countries thought was "proper behavior" for managers and workers. He summarized those differences in values under four headings: Power Distance (how autocratic or paternalistic the worker and the boss thought the boss ought to be), Uncertainty Avoidance (the extent to which workers and managers feel threatened by uncertain or unknown situations), Individualism vs. Collectivism (whether one preferred to do one's job alone or in groups), and what he called Masculinity vs. Femininity (which referred to men being more assertive, competitive, and tough, and women being more nurturing and concerned with family and relationships and the environment). He later added a fifth dimension, Long-Term vs. Short-Term time horizons. He discovered that people feel very strongly about the correctness of the values they hold on each of these dimensions and are very uncomfortable when put into positions where they feel that those values they hold important are not being respected by those in power. No surprise: We all feel uncomfortable when our

---

[13] Geert Hofstede, *Culture's Consequences: International Differences in Work-Related Values* (Newbury Park, CA: Sage, first published in 1980, 7th printing of abridged edition, 1991).

values are being violated. Yet this must happen thousands of times every day, as workers all over the world are confronted by managers from different cultures who value different outlooks. Though Hofstede does not go into it in detail, it also happens every day in the United States as women, Hispanics, Asian Americans, and African Americans are confronted by an essentially white, European, male-dominated managerial work ethic.

One final point before we leave the discussion of values. The reason I have taken up so much space discussing values is that *so much of human behavior is geared toward satisfying those needs, goals, and/or desires.* Thus we interpret situations and relations with other people and groups in terms of trying to satisfy those needs and values. Having needs and desires, we try to fulfill them. Humans usually attempt to manipulate and/or structure their environment, people, and groups in order to achieve their own needs, goals, and/or values. The fact that most of those efforts are subconscious does not deny the fact that they motivate most of our behavior and are crucial for understanding it.

Belief Systems: I Think, Therefore I Am Right

The totality of all the perceptions, attitudes, values, and identities that we hold—and the way we rank them at any moment in time—is referred to as a "belief system." Holding a particular belief system implies, however, that there are a host of other belief systems that we do not hold. Those are labeled "disbelief systems." If, for example, I believe that people are basically hostile and "out to get me," then I do not believe that people are basically good, friendly, and helpful. If I am a Buddhist believer then I am not a nonbeliever. Nor will I likely be Christian, Muslim, Jewish, Hindu, or any other kind of believer.

Figure 1.10

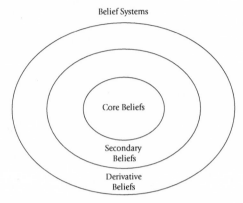

Not all beliefs we hold are equally important to us.[14] See figure 1.10 above. Some beliefs are at the very core of our existence and are central to our thinking and behavior. They frequently have to do with a person's physical and social world. Those are the beliefs that are so basic that the individual cannot conceive that other individuals wouldn't also hold them. And precisely because they are so basic, they are probably the least susceptible to change. This is the range of beliefs, of course, that makes intercultural communication so difficult. We take them so much for granted that they are only rarely, if ever, consciously considered. Thus, it almost never occurs to us that anyone could possibly have different core beliefs. We will come back to these core thought patterns in a moment. First I want to discuss secondary and derivative beliefs.

Secondary beliefs are those that are simply not as basic as core beliefs. A secondary belief might be that I believe the Bible literally or I believe that the best government is the government that governs least. These are not insignifi-

---

[14] For much of this discussion of belief systems, I am indebted to Milton Rokeach, who spent much of his life writing about attitudes, values, and beliefs. See the bibliography for specific references to his works.

cant beliefs, but they are usually conscious, and they simply are not as central to our being as are core beliefs. What's more, over time these could change. Not easily, mind you, but they are easier to change than our core beliefs.

Derivative beliefs stem from our primary or secondary beliefs. For example, because I believe the Bible literally, then in fact I honestly do believe that God created man in His image and created Eve out of one of Adam's ribs, and I don't want some feminist referring to God as She, or some darn fool evolutionist telling my kids that they are descended from monkeys. That's what I mean by derivative beliefs. They can be held very strongly, but they derive from a deeper, even more basically held belief. Thought patterns fall into the category of core beliefs.

One of the most common problems encountered by people from one group trying to deal with someone from a different group is that "they just don't think the way we do." That is quite correct. It shouldn't be surprising. What would be surprising is if they did. Thought patterns are buried so deep in our core belief system that it simply never occurs to us that anyone would think differently—nor is it at all easy to try to understand different thought patterns. Yet we must if we are to communicate effectively interculturally.

In an interesting article on the thought processes of different linguistic groups, Robert B. Kaplan has observed that while English writing and thinking is linear (a statement on which there is virtually unanimous agreement among logicians, linguists, anthropologists, and other scholars), those who speak and write Semitic languages (Arabic and Hebrew) seem to use various kinds of parallels in their thinking, and the writing and thinking of Chinese and Koreans (whom he lumps together as "Orientals" in his study) are marked by indirection.[15] That is, a "turning and turning in a widening gyre." Kaplan has

---

[15] Robert B. Kaplan, "Cultural Thought Patterns in Inter-Cultural Education," in *Language Learning* 16, nos. 1 and 2 (1966).

graphically represented the major groups he studies. (See figure 1.11) One must be careful not to fall into the trap of believing that *all* Chinese and Koreans think by a process of indirection, that *all* English-speaking people think in a linear manner all of the time, and so on, but the fact is that most people probably do, most of the time. And while the specifics of Kaplan's chart are in some dispute, certainly it does not detract from the reality that people from different cultures do think differently.

Similarly, the more different from us they are, the more likely we are to find that some of their core beliefs are actually some of our disbeliefs. How then are we to cope with the differences? The most effective way is by trying to understand rather than to judge. That's very difficult precisely because, as I noted earlier, it is nearly impossible to separate attitudes and values. Yet we must if we are to communicate effectively with someone of a group different from our own. We don't have to like another group's values or way of thinking to communicate effectively with them, but we certainly do have to understand them.

Figure 1.11

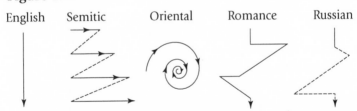

Another interesting aspect of beliefs is how they affect attitudes toward authority. We know that how one views authority determines in large measure how he or she will behave in the world. We have already seen from Geert Hofstede's study how that affects people at work. But there is another part of the problem that is worth mentioning. Milton Rokeach's research has shown that the more a person interprets information coming from the outside world, independent of the authority of the source of that information, the more open to new ideas that person is likely to be. Conversely, the more one relies on authority to determine his or her attitude toward information, the more closed to new ideas that person is likely to be.

What this implies is that an individual or group that is more open-minded in their belief systems will be much more likely to try to understand another individual or group with a different belief system—and thus will be much better able to communicate with "them"—than would an individual or a group with a different belief system. In other words, individuals from cultures that rely heavily on unquestioning acceptance of authority tend to be much less likely to be open to different ideas, attitudes, values, and beliefs than would individuals from more accepting cultures. If that is so, then what it implies is that communication between individuals from different authoritarian-oriented cultures (or between individuals who are themselves more authoritarian than others in their culture) should be much more difficult than communication between open-minded individuals from different accepting cultures.

Reality, Perception, and Misperception: What Is Reality?

Earlier we argued that objective reality may exist but that humans can never know reality: rather, they have perceptions of reality. That is an important enough assertion to warrant further discussion.

Whether in philosophy, politics, religion, or history, one always comes across assertions that there is a knowable reality and that honest people just have to be willing to look at all the facts to know that reality. I must challenge that notion directly. If the people who study the way we learn about the world are correct—and everything I will say in this work assumes that they are—then we learn about the world through our sensory receptors. Further, I believe I have demonstrated here that each individual perceives reality differently. This raises some serious problems. If people's perceptions are valid for them, then how can any accurate communication occur between individuals? Can't individuals be wrong about something? Clearly they can. How then do we get out of the intellectual corner we seem to have painted ourselves into?

First, let me deal with reality. I am not suggesting here that reality does not exist. Indeed, I'm certain it does. There are mountains and people and wars and ideas. Rather, I have been arguing that reality may be less important, both in determining and understanding human behavior, than are perceptions of reality. Since I cannot know reality directly but only through my sensory receptors, I tend to treat my perceptions of reality *as though they were reality.* That is, through a long series of trial-and-error tests, I behave toward objects, people, events, and ideas as though they are what I perceive them to be.

As I write those words I pause to contemplate how to illustrate what I mean. I look up at my bookcase and see row after row of books. Books exist. They are reality. I can hold and touch them. Wouldn't anyone—no matter from where—perceive them to be books? Not necessarily. In the first place, not all books are shaped like these or are made of the same materials. When I show friends a book from ancient Sri Lanka that I have in my collection, written on dried banana leaves, each about two inches wide by fourteen inches long and held together by string running through two holes in each leaf and two painted wooden end pieces, they have absolutely no idea what it is. Second, many people in nonliterate societies have never seen a book and would have no idea what one was even if they were shown one. Have you ever seen a very young child playing with a book? Babies have no idea what a book is or what to do with it until they have been taught by their parents how to deal with it.

Third, ask a physicist what a book is. He might tell you it is a book, but he might also tell you that each page is merely a collection of certain kinds of molecules held together by a force field, while a chemist might tell you that the individual pages are actually wood pulp with a certain rag content treated in certain ways, then rolled into long sheets, dried, and later printed on with certain dyes having such and such chemical content. Some people in the book-printing business, on the other hand, might see the binding, the quality of the paper, and the typeface. Some people collect books merely because they "look nice" as a decoration for a room.

Books are real enough, but each person who comes into contact with them will view them differently. The ideas contained in the books are also real—but they are much more abstract than the physical book itself and thus open to much greater variety of interpretation than the book is. The more abstract the reality, the greater the variety of interpretation one should expect.

What about people? Surely they exist, but what kind of person is anyone? Every term I show my classes a very old film starring Richard Conti called *The Eye of the Beholder*. It is not as good as the Japanese film *Rashomon*, but it is shorter and makes the same point. In this film Conti plays a character named Michael Gerrard. The film asks the question, What kind of person is Gerrard? It then goes on to show several different people's perceptions of him. A waiter in a lounge sees him as a "ladies' man," a taxicab driver sees him as a "hood," his mother sees him as a "good boy" who works too hard, the landlord of the artist's studio he rents sees him as "a lunatic," and the cleaning woman in the building sees him as a "murderer." The movie replays what happened in a twenty-four-hour period from each of those different perspectives and then shows the audience how Michael Gerrard views himself and the events of that period from his perspective. What is very clear is that each person in the film—including

Gerrard—attended to different bits of information in forming an opinion of what he was like and what happened
that day. But questions of "fact" change in each retelling.
From Gerrard's perspective, he told the cab driver to "Please
be quiet. I'm trying to concentrate." From the cabby's telling of it, he said, "Shut up, Mac. I'm busy." Which is reality? I'm not certain that we could know unless there was a
tape recorder to play it back as it happened. But even then
we might not know. The words could have said "Be quiet,"
but the tone could have said "Shut up." Or the words could
indeed have said "Shut up." We don't always say what we
intend to say.

Since others know us less well than we know ourselves
it is inevitable that their perceptions of us (or our perceptions of them) will be very different from our perceptions
of ourselves. Whereas abstract concepts are open to more
interpretation than are concrete concepts, so, too, complex creatures like people are probably open to much more
interpretation than are simple creatures like fish or dogs.

Somewhere out there, there is reality. Trying to know
what that reality is, however, is not simple. In every age everyone has his or her own perceptions of what that reality
is. In medieval times people behaved toward the world as
though it were flat. It wasn't, but never mind that. They
thought it was and therefore tended not to travel too far for
fear of falling off. Now people know it is round and therefore treat it differently. They know that they can get east by
traveling west and they do. They also know that they can
get to the moon by aiming not at where it is when they start
the trip but at where it will be when they get there.

If we all have different perceptions of reality, how can
we differentiate what is more nearly true from what is less
true? After all, there are such things as hallucinations, and
we do recognize when someone has "lost touch with reality" and believes (and behaves) as though he were Jesus
Christ or Napoleon. One could argue that he merely had
a different perception of reality. I know that there are some

mental health theorists who might very well take that point of view. Others would argue that it is only the insane who see reality and that all the rest of us who think we do and call ourselves sane are in fact deceived. Yet intuitively we know that those kinds of answers simply will not do. Neither, it seems to me, can we resort to a vote to determine what reality is. Copernicus and Galileo would both have been overwhelmingly outvoted. So too would Hellenists and Christians in early Rome and heathens and heretics during the Inquisition in medieval Europe.

It seems to me that the scientific solution of observing and noting what our perceptions of reality are, of formulating a hypothesis that helps us to explain what it is we think we observe, and then of monitoring data to test that hypothesis may be the most useful approach. No hypothesis ever holds true indefinitely. Rather, prevailing views of reality are retained so long as they are useful in helping to explain phenomena. As soon as we start finding data that don't fit that view, we begin to try to formulate a different hypothesis that might better help explain what it is we are looking at. The same thing happens in trying to explain things, events, people, and ideas.

Trying to determine what reality is takes a great deal of time and hard work. This is particularly true of situations in which different individuals, groups, or nations have totally different perceptions about the same reality, as they frequently do. But not all situations require that we test our perceptions of them. Indeed, many probably do not. In most day-to-day situations in our life, nothing major is lost by trusting our perceptions of reality to be a fair assessment of what it really is—until we discover that we are wrong. When we do, then often no great harm has been done, nor will any be done, by changing our perceptions and searching for a new hypothesis that will better explain the event or phenomenon we want to know about. This principle says: "Assume our perceptions of reality are correct until proven otherwise." In other cases it is terribly important to come as close to reality as possible before making a decision about whether our perceptions are correct, as in a murder trial or an international event that could lead to war. I would argue that in those cases it is wisest to assume that our perceptions of reality are probably *incorrect*—or at least different from the perception of reality held by others—and hence to keep working to determine what reality is until we are convinced "beyond a reasonable doubt" that we know.

The other device we should be careful to try to preserve is a constant level of analysis. Are we looking at a total system or merely at a subset of a system? Because "he" tends to carry a knife, does that mean that everyone in one of the subsets to which he belongs is also likely to carry a knife? And which subset is it that best helps to categorize and describe his behavior? Is it the subset based on skin color, age, height, socioeconomic class, level of education, intelligence, gender, sexual preference, religious preference, political preference, the food he eats, the movies he likes, his upbringing, some kind of "criminal personality" he has, or his genes? Or is it some other subset that we have not yet formulated?

Of course a book is a book at one level of analysis. But it is just as certainly a collectivity of molecules at another. Indeed it is precisely because of the existence of different levels of analysis that we must come to the conclusion that there is not just one reality but many different realities out there, all of them perhaps equally valid. It may well be the existence of these different realities on different levels of analysis, added to our differences of perception about reality—regardless of level—that makes for so much confusion.

If it is not possible for us to know reality directly, if we can know it only through our perceptions of it, and if each person's perceptions are inevitably different—and probably just as valid for him or her as mine are for me—then what are misperceptions?

If both you and I believe that the other is preparing to attack, and neither of us is preparing to do so, that is a misperception. Further, if, because I believe that you are about to attack, I pick up a gun to defend myself, you are likely to believe that your perceptions of me were correct and to point to my taking up a gun as proof of my intention to attack you. Unfortunately this is precisely how most wars start. My reaching for a gun may indeed have been completely defensive, but can you take a chance in a situation like that? There is, after all, the chance—no matter how remote—that I do intend to attack. Doesn't one have to do something to protect oneself? Of course. Since you can never know reality for certain, you have no alternative but to prepare for the worst. The only trouble is that as *you* prepare, I take that as further proof that it is you who are preparing to attack me.

The point is that people can be, and often are, wrong in the way they perceive situations, motives, or intentions. Whenever they are, we have to refer to that as a "misperception."

There are a great many things external to myself that I cannot know about for certain. But things about myself, in particular, I can know. When someone attributes actions or motives to me that are incorrect, that is a misperception and ought to be clarified as quickly as possible. Just because you and I perceive each other correctly will in no way assure that I will like you or that we won't have conflicts. But at least if misperceptions are clarified, we will know what it is we are disagreeing about and we may be able to resolve our conflict peacefully. Probably, in the overwhelming majority of conflict situations, neither party really knows precisely what it is that they are fighting over because the misperceptions tend to obscure everything else.

Sam Green in Guatemala

Allow me to relate a true story about differing perceptions of reality to illustrate just how important such differences can be to successful intercultural communication. Some time after World War II ended, a successful American businessman by the name of Sam Green retired to the mountains of Guatemala, near Lake Atitlán. He had made his fortune doing business in Guatemala and had fallen in love with the land and its people. Every evening after sunset when the Indians in the region returned from the fields to their villages, he would ride out to their villages on his horse and sit for hours talking with them. He came to know and trust them very much, and they him. He had learned their language, their culture, and their reality world very well. They would tell him of their needs and their dreams. It seemed to him that many of the things these simple people wanted were the same things that people everywhere wanted: health, safety, food, security. He discovered that one of the problems they had in obtaining these basic things was lack of cash—sometimes very small quantities at that. To the peasants in those small villages, a hundred dollars or a thousand dollars seemed like an inordinate amount of money—and given their reality world, it was. But he also learned that these Indians did have a little surplus cash, maybe only a penny or two per person, per day, but they did have some cash. Accordingly he hit upon the idea of loaning them the money to dig the well they needed, or buy the medicine, or whatever (never a lot of money—usually on the order of magnitude of a few hundred dollars). They, in return, promised to pay him back a penny per day, per family, until the loan was repaid. Because these were a very honest people whose word was their bond, Sam Green was always repaid in full for every loan he made. Indeed, his efforts with the Indians were so successful that he eventually established what came to be known as the Penny Foundation in Guatemala to institutionalize this practice.

One year Mr. Green returned to the United States for an extended period. Very shortly after he returned to Guatemala he was met by a representative of the Guatemalan government who wanted to know why it was that he, a foreigner, could get the Indians to pay back loans he made, but they, the government of Guatemala, could not. It seems that in his absence, one of the drinking wells in a village had gone dry, and the Indians had approached the government asking them if they would supply water. Since the village next to the one in question had a more than ample water supply, the government arranged to pipe the water from the oversupplied village to the dry village. The government thought that the villagers had agreed to pay back the government for this service, but when the government tried to collect, the villagers refused. Mr. Green said that he couldn't explain why that had happened until he spoke to the villagers in question. When he rode out to the village and asked what had happened, he was told that yes, the village well had run dry, but that now the government was trying to make them pay for the water they used—the government had imposed a water tax to recover the loan—and everyone knew that God gave water free. Mr. Green agreed that was so but pointed out to the villagers that while God gave water free, metal pipes were made by man, and they cost money. He asked if the villagers would mind paying the government back for the pipe it had bought and installed to bring the water to the village. Of course, the villagers had no problem at all agreeing to pay for the pipe, and thus the issue was resolved.

I think the story illustrates well my contention that for intercultural communication, perceptions of reality may be more important than trying to establish any intrinsic reality itself.

Propositional Summary for Chapter 1

Culture: Culture is defined as a pattern of learned, group-related perceptions—including both verbal and nonverbal language, attitudes, values, belief systems, disbelief systems, and behaviors—that is accepted and expected by an identity group.

Group culture: Since, by definition, each identity group has its own pattern of perceptions and behavioral norms and its own language or code (understood most clearly by members of that group), each group may be said to have its own culture.

Perceptions: Perceptions are defined as the process by which an individual selects, evaluates, and organizes stimuli from the external environment. Those perceptions that are group-related are the ones that are sometimes used synonymously with the word *culture* in this work.

Misperceptions: The term "misperceptions" is used here to describe those situations when two (or several) individuals or groups are wrong about the way other individuals or groups perceive an object, event, person, or idea.

Attitudes: Attitudes are defined as likes and dislikes. They are our affinities for, and our aversions to, situations, objects, persons, groups, or any other identifiable aspect of our environment, including abstract ideas and social policies.

Value: A value is defined as our belief in the way things or behaviors ought to be. Values refer to our desires, wants, needs, or goals.

Value system: A value system is defined as a configuration of our ranking of the values of the groups into which we have been socialized. Since each individual and group ranks the importance of the values of the group differently, it is inevitable that some of the values an individual holds will be in conflict with the values of one or more of the other groups to which the individual belongs.

Belief system: A belief system represents all of the beliefs, conscious and unconscious, that a person accepts as true of the world she or he lives in at a given time.

Disbelief system: A disbelief system is composed of a series of subsystems rather than merely one and contains all of the disbeliefs, conscious and unconscious, that to one degree or another, a person rejects as false at a given time.

Determinants of perception: Three sets of determinants of perception were analyzed: physical, environmental, and learned. It was argued that no two individuals can perceive identically because no two individuals have exactly the same physical sensory receptors. More important than physical differences among individuals are the learned differences among them. No two humans can have exactly the same life experiences—either group-related or individual—yet these learned differences account for the greatest variation in perception that individuals hold.

Reality: Reality exists, to be certain, but since our knowledge of the external world is learned, and since no two individuals perceive reality identically, it is argued that, for human behavior, perceptions of reality are more important than reality itself.

The Role of Culture and Identity: I Am Who I Am. You Are Who You Are. Can We Talk?

I said earlier I believed that becoming an effective intercultural communicator meant recognizing the impact of culture on everything we do and think and say. This chapter is intended to help the reader understand how what we now think and believe got there, that is, how we developed the perceptions, attitudes, and values we hold. Once we recognize the way culture molds all of us, we will begin, I hope, to see ways to understand our own and their own cultures better. This analysis is based on a model I developed a number of years ago and have been refining ever since. Essentially it is a systematic set of premises and hypotheses designed to help explain human behavior in general and intercultural communication in particular. Although these have been reproduced in many different places many times, I present them here in greatly revised form because I believe they relate so specifically to problems of identity, behavior, and intercultural communication.

Basic Premises

Any study of cultural or identity groups[1] really has to start with an earlier step: perceptual groups.

> *Premise 1. A perceptual group may be*
> *defined as a number of individuals who*
> *perceive some aspect of the external world*
> *more or less similarly, but who do not*
> *communicate this similarity of perception*
> *among themselves.*[2]

We established in the last chapter that not all people respond to the same stimulus identically, but here we should look at the other side of that coin. That is, a number of people who have, or have had, some shared experience—whether it is having a baby, digging coal, or speaking a particular language—have a higher degree of similarity of perception about that experience than they do

---

[1] Because I argue that every identity group has a cultural ensemble somewhat different from every other identity group, I will use the terms *cultural groups* or *cultures* interchangeably with the term *identity groups*.

[2] As I have used the term in this work, perceptual groups are not groups in the traditional sense. In order for a group to exist in the sociological and anthropological sense, some communication among members must exist. By definition, individuals who belong to perceptual groups do not communicate among themselves, hence they may be thought of as a "collectivity." And since culture in the true sense is something that is taught, perceptual groups, as such, cannot have culture. They share something in common, to be sure, but they don't know it. As soon as they do communicate about the fact that they perceive some aspect of human existence similarly, they become an identity group. Identity groups do have cultures.

with people who did not or do not share that experience. Urbanites, country dwellers, mothers, fathers, first children, second children, middle children, secretaries, bookkeepers, accountants, businesspeople, steelworkers, miners, carpenters, peasants, teachers, students, fat people, skinny people, tall people, short people, young people, old people, doctors, lawyers, Indian chiefs, rich men, poor men, beggar men, thieves, sick people, healthy people, religious people, atheists, communists, capitalists, socialists, fascists, black folk, white folk, yellow, red, and tan folk, virgins, nonvirgins, acrobats, and curly-haired, straight-haired, and bald men, all share some degree of similarity of perceptions with others who do the same things they do, who value the things they value, or who are the way they are. But if they don't communicate with each other, they don't know that others think or feel as they do. I will remain an "I" until somehow you and I communicate and discover that together we form a "we."

Let us take the example of the peasant. Peasants the world over have an extraordinarily high degree of similarity of perception.[3] Most tend to be fatalistic, religious, awed by natural phenomena, tradition-bound (whatever that tradition happens to be), with a deep sense of suspicion of outsiders. There are probably a great many additional perceptual and attitudinal traits that peasants have in common with each other, but my intention here is not to list all of their similarities of perception. Rather, I mean to establish the fact that those similarities do exist. Despite the wide range of similarities among them, peasants notoriously do not communicate with other peasants, except perhaps with those from the next village. Part of the reason, of course, is the fact that the worldview of peasants is so limited that they probably do not know that others with

---

[3] For one of the classic works on the subject see Robert Redfield, *Peasant Society and Culture: An Anthropological Approach to Civilization* (Chicago: University of Chicago Press, 1956).

very similar views to their own exist by the millions and tens of millions on other continents. For many peasants the world does not exist any farther than perhaps fifty miles from where they were born, and if it does exist, it does so in only some dimly thought-through, abstract way. In addition, the peasant is almost by definition voiceless. It is true that sons and daughters of peasants increasingly are going off to the big city to get their education, but once they have gotten that education they cease being peasants. Rarely, if ever, do educated children of peasants return to the land of their forebears. But if people do not communicate with one another, they don't know that there are others out there who feel much the same about many aspects of the world as they do. Unless they communicate, they cannot become a group. Given that they do not communicate among themselves, how is it possible for them to share such a high degree of similarity of perception? Indeed, in premise 3 below I will argue that the less communication occurs, the less likely it is that there will be similarities of perception. The answer, it would seem, has to do with the rather universal relationship of the peasant to nature. Everywhere peasants are equally at the mercy of the vicissitudes of nature for sun, rain, food, shelter, and even life and death. My guess is that this universally perceived dependency on nature—or on the gods—produces a rather universal response.

The same could be said of many urban poor people. There is after all a *culture of poverty*. There is a high degree of similarity of world outlook, attitudes, and belief systems poor people seem to share, again perhaps because of the universality of their experience—in this case, extreme poverty. Like the peasant, a poor person from Mexico City probably doesn't know that Calcutta exists, let alone that there are poor people there who share a similar worldview. Yet despite the differences in language, religion, food preference, and the like, if poor people could communicate, they would probably be amazed to discover how similarly they perceive the world.

Just because certain people don't know that there are others out there who think the way they do—about something—doesn't mean that they comprise an unimportant category of people. In fact it may be the most important category. Underlying every identity group is a perceptual group.

> *Premise 2. A number of people who perceive some aspect of the external world more or less similarly and recognize and communicate this similarity of perception form an identity group.*

The key words here are *recognize* and *communicate.* Sometimes I recognize that I share a similarity of perception with someone else merely by looking at that person. Recognition is, after all, a form of communication.

Individuals who share some similarity of perception but do not (or are not able to) communicate about the similarity of perception are not a group. A group—a sense that we are not alone—cannot form until two or more individuals communicate the fact that they share a common identity or view of something. Once they do communicate that similarity, verbally or nonverbally, they have become an identity group.

Knowing who "we" are is a learned process. That is, while it is true that one may just be born into a particular family, or have skin of a particular color, or what have you, that by itself is not what establishes identity. What establishes identity is the learning that occurs in the process of being socialized into the group that tells us that one particular characteristic or another distinguishes "us" from "them." We have to learn that he or she is one of us, but that this other person is not. What's more, subtly, ever so subtly, from the moment of birth we learn how "we" do things. Most often we learn just by the way we are held or spoken to or fed or by listening to adults talk. No one ever sits down and says to us, "OK, now I am going to hold you this way and I want you to remember that because when you grow up and have babies that is the way you will have to hold your children if you want them to grow up to be one of us." No. It's far more subtle than that. Learning who we are and how *we* do things and how *we* see the world occurs in much the same manner as learning our first language. We just hear words over and over again, and gradually—very gradually—we come to identify those words with particular meanings. In the same way we also learn the attitudes, values, and belief systems our parents and other group elders teach us. Children don't begin learning to differentiate skin color or hair texture or size and shape of nose or those other little differences that adults find so very important until well after they are old enough to talk. But learn them they do. Identity-group learning occurs whenever we experience something that others in our identity group have experienced.

Think of a number of people working at the same kind of task or job. It doesn't matter whether the job is raising young children, studying chemistry, or working at a particular kind of occupation. In the course of doing that work, experiences are being shared by all of the people doing the kind of task that is unique to that work. No other collectivity of individuals doing other kinds of tasks will share exactly the same experiences. In the course of becoming specialists in the accomplishment of those tasks, they will all learn to use the same kinds of tools. A shorthand language will be learned, which will be understood by other people doing the same kind of task but not understood by people doing different kinds of tasks. Acronyms will develop rather quickly. A way of thinking about how to accomplish the task will be developed, as will common expectations and acceptable patterns of behavior. The more everyone involved in accomplishing a certain task shares these similarities of perception, the easier it is for those people to communicate—thus the more efficiently the task can be accomplished.

Those examples were all task- or job-oriented, but there

are many, many similarities of perception which develop around other things. Think, for example, of people from the same ethnic background. Again, certain ways of thinking about the world are shared, a taste for certain kinds of foods, a preference for a certain kind of dress. Certain folk heroes are esteemed by one group and are unknown to others. Do you know how long it takes to cook chitterlings?[4] Do you know who Crispus Attucks was? If you are an African American, the probability is that you know. If you are not, the probability is that you do not know. What about Garibaldi? Or Asoka? An Italian would know the former, an Indian from India, the latter.

Similarly, adherents of religious, political, or other ideologies also form identity groups. Catholicism as practiced in Latin America is certainly markedly different from the variety practiced in Dublin or Chicago. Despite those differences, however, two religious Catholics, wherever they are from, can usually communicate *about religious matters* with a much higher degree of similarity of perception and identity than may, say, a Catholic and a Hindu, both from Chicago.

It should be noted that it is not only important whether a specific group views itself as different; it is also important whether the society in which the group lives *accepts* its members as "one of us" or views them as alien. Thus, for example, while the Jews in Nazi Germany may have

---

[4] Chitterlings is a food widely eaten by African Americans, particularly by poorer blacks in the southern part of the United States. The reference here is to something called the chitterlings test, which was developed to demonstrate to middle-class white Americans the enormous cultural bias that is built into so-called intelligence tests. Few if any whites could answer most of the questions on the chitterlings test, yet poor African Americans would rarely miss more than a few. It demonstrated effectively how very much each group takes for granted that "everyone knows," when in fact that "everyone" is most often only "everyone in our group."

viewed themselves—or may have wanted to view themselves—primarily as Germans, their society viewed them, at best, as a particular kind of German (German-Jews) and, at worst, as not German at all. Faced with that circumstance, regardless of personal preference, most German-Jews had no choice but to see themselves as members of a group separate from other Germans.

Let me take a moment here to discuss further this question of the relationship of identity to the way others see us, as opposed to the way we see ourselves. Some groups are highly inclusive, and others are highly exclusive. White America tends to be highly exclusive. If you have even 1/64 African ancestry you are considered by American society as black. Now it makes absolutely no sense from any point of logic that someone who is 63/64 white should be considered black by society. But there is nothing logical about group identity. The prevailing white sentiment is that anyone with a drop of black blood is black, and most whites will treat that person accordingly, regardless of how white his or her physical features may be.[5] If society treats one as though he or she were black, there is no way the individual can come to think of him- or herself as anything but black.

> Premise 3. Other things being equal, the
> higher the degree of similarity of perception
> that exists among a number of individuals,
> the easier communication among them is
> likely to be, and the more communication

---

[5] For a fascinating fictionalized account of what this meant in the society of the southern United States several decades ago—and the sentiment would be only somewhat less today—read Sinclair Lewis, *Kingsblood Royal* (New York: Random House, 1947). Interestingly, in 1997, *for the first time*, the U. S. Census Bureau "considered" including a category called "mixed" race for the year 2000 census with which to classify people of a mixed racial ancestry. The proposal was rejected.

among them is likely to occur. Conversely,
where there is little or no communication
among individuals there tends to be a
decrease in similarity of perception, which in
turn tends to make further communication
more difficult.

This premise postulates a spiraling of communication or noncommunication. Stated simply, it argues that, all things being equal, the easier communication is, the more we tend to communicate. The more we communicate, the more we share our perceptions with others. The more we share our perceptions with others, the easier still communication becomes. And so it spirals, with increased communication tending to lead to greater sharing of perceptions, and with greater sharing of perceptions tending to lead to greater ease of communication, and greater ease of communication tending to lead to further increased communication. The problem with intercultural or intergroup communication is the spiraling in the opposite direction. That is, the very similarity of perceptions and sharing of common values, attitudes, beliefs, and languages that make communication within a group so much easier make communication between different groups that much harder. Less communication tends to lead to *less* sharing of perceptions (or greater dissimilarity of perception), and with less similarity of perception, communication tends to become more difficult. The more difficult communication becomes, the less people tend to communicate. Actually this is more than merely a premise. There is empirical evidence to support it.

One is almost forced to believe that this process is precisely how the proliferation of different cultures came into being. Somewhere back in history, living conditions likely became too crowded for all the people who lived on the mountain, so they probably sent out a colony of their own kind, who started living in the valley. Because environmental conditions in the valley were different from con-

ditions on the mountain, people had to do things somewhat differently there. And because it was probably difficult for people from the valley to get back to the top of the
mountain to visit friends and relatives, they probably did
so very infrequently. As time and generations passed, probably fewer people had the inclination to "go back to the
old country" because there wasn't anyone there any longer
whom the people in the valley knew. So people in the valley would communicate almost exclusively with other
people in the valley, while people on the mountain would
communicate almost exclusively with other people on the
mountain. As the years and decades and centuries passed,
someone from the valley venturing to the mountain would
almost certainly find that "they don't do things on the
mountain the way we do them back home." What is more,
our adventurous traveler would probably find that the
people on the mountain couldn't understand him when
he spoke and that he couldn't understand them. And so it
has gone for centuries as "people from the mountains" on
every continent have ventured into their valleys, setting
up new homes and new cultures, ever increasing the differences among humankind. At least that was the way it
was until the communication and transportation revolutions of the nineteenth, twentieth, and now the twenty-
first centuries, which make it increasingly easy and necessary for valley and mountain people to communicate with
each other.

> Premise 4. As the number and importance of
> identity groups that individuals share rise,
> the more likely those individuals are to have
> a higher degree of group identity. That is, the
> more overlapping of important identity
> groups that an individual shares with other
> individuals, the more important that particu-
> lar group of people is likely to be to him or
> her.

From what has been said thus far, it should be clear that the more groups we share in common with people, the easier communication with them is likely to be. Conversely, the fewer group perceptions or identities we share with people, the more difficult our communications with them are likely to be. The reasons should be obvious. The more group perceptions we share with people, the greater will be the range of subjects on which we can communicate easily. Sharing the same values and perceptions on a wide range of issues will make it less necessary to probe constantly in order to find out which of their beliefs or attitudes or values are simply outside of our perceptual ken. In addition, the more groups we share in common, the more cultural languages we will share, thus making communication (including feedback) that much easier.

Having said that, however, let me be very explicit: It could be much more intercultural for me to try to communicate with, say, a steelworker in a different neighborhood of Pittsburgh than it might be for me to communicate with another college professor of international affairs in, say, Malaysia. Despite differences of race and nationality, my Malaysian counterpart and I would share a very high degree of similarity of perception—as social scientists—because of our education level (some of us would even have studied with the same professors), social class, professional identification, and the like. To be sure, there are some group identities I would share with the steelworker—being Americans, Pittsburghers, Democrats, fathers, men, and so forth—but even there, my attitude toward people who are different, for example, would probably be much closer to my Malaysian counterpart's than it is to the American steelworker's.

Obviously it is not just the number of group identities one shares with another but also the importance of those group perceptions in molding one's most basic attitudes, values, and beliefs that determines just how intercultural any communication will be. Of course, how difficult communication will be will depend in large part on the subject under discussion. Little as I may know about baseball, it would be much less intercultural for me to discuss the standing of the Pittsburgh Pirates with a steelworker than it would be for me to try to discuss that topic with a Malaysian college professor. On the other hand, if Plato is what I want to discuss, I'd better look for someone with a college education to discuss him with.

In most societies the family enjoys the highest degree of group identity and loyalty. One reason this is so is that the members of the family group are also concurrently members of so many other perceptual groups. Thus, with rare exceptions, traditionally, adult members of a family speak the same language, are from the same locality, are of the same ethnic group or tribe, are of the same religious persuasion, have approximately the same educational level, are of the same socioeconomic class, are very likely to be employed in the same occupation grouping, and so on. Some of this is changing in our fast-moving postindustrial society, but it is still widely true.

What is more, particularly in more traditional societies, the family or clan is the group that members are taught to trust most. That perception is reinforced by positive, supportive behavior from other family members, and thus all the messages coming to the individual support the notion that the family is, and should be, the group in which there is the greatest ease of communication and to which one owes his or her highest loyalty. (More will be said about this in premise 7.)

In the more mobile societies of urban industrial areas, this sense of loyalty to family begins to break down. This happens in part because family members share fewer and fewer common perceptions and identities. It is not rare in more urban societies for the children to be better educated than the parents; to marry someone of a different religion, ethnic group, or race; to live in a different city; and to be part of a different class. In some countries it is not especially unusual for the children to prefer speaking English or French as their first language at home, instead of the mother tongue their parents speak. This has been true of immigrants coming to the United States and Britain for decades, and is increasingly true of North Africans going to France today. No wonder that the intensity of family identity breaks down. But what replaces it when it does break down? In large degree it is replaced by those friends with whom we share many group perceptions and identities.

Think for a moment of the five people you would consider your closest friends. Define *close* here as the ease with which you can communicate with them on a wide variety of subjects. Now think of all the group identities you share in common with them. (You may well find that you share some identities with one or two of those people and different identities with others. That's fine.)

If you are like most people, you have probably left out the most important identities—the ones that are so basic one doesn't think of them—like race, economic class, status, educational background, age, political preference (not necessarily party affiliation), and religious predilection (again not necessarily membership in the same religious organizations—although that is possible). There is a reason for this—it is not an accident. Similarities of perception and group identities are often such subtle phenomena that we are simply unaware of them until (a) we come across others with whom we do not share those similarities of outlook, values, worldview, and so on, and/or (b) until someone violates a group norm we so take for granted that we don't even think of it as a group norm. Sharing of group attitudes, values, and beliefs is a very subtle process. Most often that sharing remains below the level of consciousness. There is something about each of us—whoever we are—that tends to make us feel comfortable with one of our own. Of course, this is not true in every case, but it is true in so many more cases than it is not true as to go almost unnoticed.

One further note: We have already established that no two individuals can perceive identically. But suppose they could. Would any communication between them be necessary? I would argue that it would. In the first place, as we shall see in the communication chapter, feedback is an integral part of the communication process. I would not know that the other person's perceptions were identical to my own unless there was a great deal of feedback on a wide range of topics. Communication would be easy, certainly (like the transfer of energy without any friction), but it would have to occur. Second, there is a strong probability that I would communicate *more* with someone whose perceptions were identical to mine precisely because of the ease of communication and because I would be assured that the subjects that interest me most would also be the subjects that interest that other person most.

David Hoopes has argued that "communication is a process by which human dissimilarities are negotiated."[6] I agree with that statement, but I think that communication is also a process by which human similarities are shared. Thus I could carry on an enormously satisfying conversation with that other person who shared 100 percent the same perceptions, while at the same time having my own perceptions, attitudes, values, and beliefs reinforced with no loss of energy. What a satisfying fantasy! What is more, I wouldn't have to feel guilty about talking to myself.

> *Premise 5. Any "we" (identity group) comes into much sharper focus when juxtaposed against any "they" (a different identity group).*

Cultural values and identities are so pervasive and subconscious that we simply take them for granted, only rarely, if ever, being aware of them on a conscious level. The

---

[6] Personal communication.

moment we are juxtaposed against some other group we have no choice but to become conscious of that identity. Nearly every group perceives itself (and members of the group) as being essentially "good." (Some exceptions to this rule will be discussed in a moment.) "We" may recognize individual differences among ourselves and admit that not all of us are perfect, but by and large we consider ourselves trustworthy, loyal, helpful, friendly, courteous, kind, obedient, cheerful, thrifty, brave, clean, and reverent. In addition, we are intelligent, industrious, and generally nice people. Regardless of what we may be engaged in at any particular time, we genuinely believe ourselves to be acting from the best of motives. Of course we want what is best for everyone. It just usually happens that our definition of "what is best" is based on a subconscious definition of self-interest, rather narrowly defined. The industrialist sees the country's best interests as being served by allowing industry to accrue huge profits, which will "naturally" (the industrialist genuinely believes) be reinvested, thus creating jobs for workers and well-being for everyone. The worker, on the other hand, sees the country's best interests as being served by ensuring high wages for the worker, which will, just as "naturally" (the worker just as genuinely believes), mean that the workers will have more to spend on things the industrialist produces, thus creating well-being for everyone. Of course, both perceptions are equally valid (remember our discussion of differing reality worlds?), but each accuses the other of being out to improve "their" position at "our" expense.

Whoever we are, we tend to trust one of "us" more than we trust one of "them." If we know nothing about two individuals save that one of them is a member of one of the primary groups with which we identify and the other is not, we are likely to trust the one who belongs to our group and to be suspicious of the other.

Every group tends to see itself as noble, just, honest, and virtuous—and "them" as the opposite. The ancient

Athenians—like everyone else before and since—divided the world into two classes of people: we and they, Athenians and non-Athenians. Do you know what word the Athenians used to describe someone who was not from Athens? *Barbarians.* Even the word *they* is itself mildly pejorative. The degree of hostility expressed toward other groups increases as the group becomes more specific. Thus while *they, stranger,* and *alien* all have mildly pejorative connotations, words like *spic, mick, honkie, kike, nigger, wop,* and *queer* are both specific and strongly hostile. Recall that the Jews consider themselves "God's chosen people." That leaves everyone else to be considered "less than chosen by God." The Chinese call themselves the Middle Kingdom— meaning that they are at the center of the earth. Clearly everyone else is peripheral, in their view. The Germans were told—and presumably believed—that they were the Master Race. What did that make everyone else?

I have been told that the Filipinos—a Catholic people—have a charming myth about the genesis of human beings. According to the myth, when God decided to create Adam, He formed a bit of clay into the figure of a man and put him into the oven. Unfortunately He left him in too long and he came out burned to a crisp. He put that man down in Africa. Then He formed some more clay into another figure of a man and again put him into the oven. This one He took out too soon. He put this half-baked model down in Europe. He fashioned a third figure of a man and took him out when he was a beautiful golden brown. This one He put down in the Philippines.

Though we may all chuckle at this little bit of Philippine folklore, how is it different in kind from the Judeo-Christian notion that God made us in His image? Note too, if you will, the male chauvinism in the very term *His image.* No different in kind from the pre-Copernican view of the universe with the earth at the center.

While it is certainly true that virtually every group has this inflated view of itself and a somewhat dimmer view of everyone else, there are exceptions to that rule. People who have long been subjected to domination by other groups often come to accept the standards of beauty and other values held by the dominant group. Thus British values, dress, and manners have been accepted in parts of the world formerly ruled by them as the standard of excellence by which all others are measured. The same is true for French and Spanish cultures in areas they once dominated. In the United States, blonde is still the hair coloring that sells most, and many people suffer severe discomfort and considerable expense to have their noses clipped to Anglo-Saxon proportions (I've never heard of a case of someone having an operation to have a nose made larger for cosmetic purposes). Far more important for human behavior than these dominant attitudes toward beauty, however, are other belief systems and ways of viewing the universe—and themselves—that subject peoples may unknowingly have taken from the dominant group. The most debilitating of these beliefs may be the suspicion that "they"—often, in modern times, Europeans in Asia or Africa—are, in fact, superior to "us." This leads to a kind of ethnic inferiority complex on a very basic level which can dominate much of one's behavior in counterproductive ways.

That having been said, however, the evidence seems quite overwhelming that we tend to view our own groups as being pretty good, while we tend to view "them" less favorably. This is extremely important for successful communication, since as we have seen again and again throughout this work, we tend to trust messages received from one of "us" and tend to mistrust messages from one of "them." The more different or threatening we see "them" as being, the less we are likely to trust "them."

Much of the time those of us whose major identities are associated with majority groups are only dimly aware of some of our most important identities. That they are important in molding our attitudes, values, and behaviors there can be no question, yet, generally, most of us associate with other people who are so like us (indeed that is precisely why those identities are so important—they are constantly being reinforced) that we tend not to be conscious of them. We take them for granted. Think of the white, male, middle-class American who spends much of his time associating at work and at play with other white, male, middle-class Americans. Rarely would he become conscious of the importance of those four identities to his behavior. Yet we know that each of them profoundly influences how he thinks and behaves. But let him set foot into a predominantly black or Chinese neighborhood or onto an American Indian reservation, and instantly he becomes conscious of the color of his skin. Or let him have to deal with a group of upper-class white Americans, or a group of lower-class white Americans, and instantly he will become conscious of his class identity. Admittedly, the longer one stays in those "other" groups, the less conscious one is likely to become of the difference between oneself and the others. But that is because the way they talk, the way they think, and the way they act will eventually become less strange and more predictable. The same holds true for almost any identity one can mention. As long as we surround ourselves with others who share the same identities as we do—and most of us do exactly that—we operate more comfortably in our environment. Because it is more predictable and because it is so familiar we don't have to make a great many things explicit, and because it is so easy, we tend to think about it very little. As soon as we step out of that familiar environment, however, everything has got to be made explicit, and it takes a great deal more psychic energy just to get the simplest tasks accomplished.

As with the examples in the previous chapter on the relationship of stimulus to surroundings, when everyone else is just like us, we tend to fade into our surroundings and not notice ourselves. But surround us by "them" and suddenly we stand out sharply. What is more, context is all-important in determining who we perceive ourselves to be at any given moment. Regardless of ethnic background, Americans overseas are likely to see themselves as—and be seen by others as—Americans. At home, however, their identity as Americans tends to fade or to become less salient, and their identity as Polish Americans, Irish Americans, African Americans, or some other ethnic identity becomes more important in describing them.

The more threatening "they" are, the more sharply the differences are seen. For minority groups—whatever the minority—this is precisely the problem. They can try to surround themselves with "their own kind," but it may not be easy. Like it or not, they are usually forced to deal with the dominant majority. This situation is particularly so with the smaller minority groups. Most often their perception is that the majority is hostile toward them; thus (a) they are constantly reminded of their minority identity, and (b) they are being forced to exert a greater amount of psychic energy (required in dealing with "them") more often than majority people are forced to, simply by virtue of the numbers involved. This of itself is both anxiety-producing and tiring.

Have you ever wondered why most big cities have so many ethnic and racial neighborhoods? I think it is precisely because we prefer to be with the people who are like us. Sometimes it is quite conscious. When the immigrants were pouring into the big industrial cities in the northeastern United States in the late nineteenth century, they were drawn to those neighborhoods where people from the old country (in some cases even people from the same village or region in the old country) had settled before them. In the 1970s and 1980s "Little Saigon," "Japan Town," and African, Mexican, Cuban, and Central American neighborhoods sprang up in big cities across America. The things that drew them were shops where they could buy familiar foods, other people with whom they could converse in the mother tongue, and churches where they could worship in a familiar setting. Most important, these recent immigrants were drawn to the place where there were a lot of other people like themselves—people who shared their values and attitudes—so that for a part of each day they could feel comfortable. For too many hours of each day they felt very conscious of what made them different. In the evening they wanted to relax and feel at home. As increasing numbers of gay men and lesbians have "come out of the closet," they too choose to live in sympathetic communities. Thus you have the Castro Street district in San Francisco, Greenwich Village and Chelsea in New York City, and similar, if smaller, replicas in many big cities in the United States and Europe today.

Please note: I am not suggesting that all ghettos are voluntarily maintained. Quite the contrary. Class and race play a large part in separating people. Frequently real estate agents and mortgage lenders see to it that certain neighborhoods don't have too many African Americans, Hispanics, or others (frequently Asian Americans on the West Coast) move in. If too many "undesirables" somehow do manage to get into a neighborhood, "white flight" is likely to follow, which effectively creates a near total minority neighborhood. Note too, however, that even in these class- or ethnic-oriented ghettos, there tends to be a certain amount of voluntary "subghettoization." Not only do Hispanics not live with African Americans, but even more specifically, Dominicans tend to live with Dominicans, Salvadorians tend to live with Salvadorians, Mexicans with Mexicans, and so on.

Misperceptions in Conflict Situations

That "we" are good and "they" are less than good in a great many situations is an attitude anyone studying interpersonal, intergroup, or international relations must take into account. The student of intergroup or international conflict must also consider the likelihood that the more intense the conflict, the better *we* become and the worse *they* become.

In international affairs, particularly where national identity is strong, notice that *they* have "spies" while *we* have "intelligence personnel." Notice, too, that *we* have never declared an aggressive war; *they* fight aggressive wars while *we* fight wars of self-defense. From the German point of view it was Britain and France, after all, who declared war on Germany in 1939, merely because *we* Germans went to the rescue of other Germans being massacred and mutilated by the Poles.

During the Cold War, most Americans simply accepted the rightness of the American position that it was necessary to fight international communism whenever it challenged "the Free World." With the end of the Cold War, that xenophobic nationalism seems to have passed, and increasingly Americans seem to be looking inward and saying "a pox on foreign problems. Let the foreigners solve their own problems." Certainly there was no enthusiasm, in white America, for sending troops to Haiti or Somalia (actually there was considerably more support among African Americans) or to Bosnia. There was support for sending troops to get Iraq out of Kuwait, but that was because American economic interests (oil) were perceived to be threatened directly. Undoubtedly the image of bully Saddam Hussein attacking a small defenseless neighbor certainly also played a part in shaping American support for the war. In addition it was the kind of war Americans like: short and victorious, with few American casualties.

All the general problems of perception and communication inherent in any interpersonal, intergroup, or international relationship are invariably exacerbated in nearly direct proportion to the intensity of the threat perceived by the parties in a conflict situation.

It could be that the only real hope for those who would like to resolve group conflict is to have each of the groups in a conflict situation identify with some third, larger identity of which both form a part. African Americans and white Americans may be in frequent conflict, but if U.S. interests are threatened (as was felt to be the case in Kuwait), black and white Americans coalesce in their American identity and work together to fight a common foe. However, when the threat to the third, shared identity is removed, we may return to our old animosities. I am afraid that those who cherish the hope that one day all humans will rank their human identity above all other identities will be disappointed. Only an invasion from outer space would cause that to occur. Too many of us focus more on the differences that divide us than on the human qualities that we share.

> Premise 6. If we want to communicate
> effectively with one of "them," it is important
> to get to know their perceptions, attitudes,
> and values as well as their cultural language.
> The more like them we become, the easier
> communication with them will become. But
> it may make communication with "us" more
> difficult.

As I argued before, no two individuals share no similarity of perception, and thus we should be able to communicate at least on the most rudimentary human-animal level. I start from the axiom that no human communication is impossible. It is just more difficult with those with whom we share the fewest group identities. The more we get to know them, however, the easier communication becomes, and the better we come to understand their attitudes, values, and beliefs. We may not accept those perceptions as our own, but at least we will understand what they believe, and eventually we will learn how to communicate with them more effectively.

Throughout this work I have argued that if we want to communicate effectively with "them," it is important for us to learn their cultural language. We can do that most effectively by living among them and coming to know them well. One of the problems with that is that the longer I live among them and learn their attitudes, values, and beliefs, the greater the possibility that I will become more like them. At least, the more I speak their cultural language (which I must if I want to communicate with them), adopt their style of dress, mannerisms, and so on, the easier it will be for me to communicate with them, to be sure, but the less my own group is likely to continue to view me as one of "us."

Think of the people from the black ghetto who want to have an impact on the white middle-class establishment in order to make things better for their group. One of the best ways they can do that is by learning the white middle-class-establishment culture. The African Americans who do, and do it well, may indeed succeed in getting their message translated into terms the white establishment can understand and accept, but in the process they run the risk of being perceived by their own group as having sold out. Every black kid who originally came from "the street" but went to college faces this problem with his or her former peers.

The same holds true for foreign affairs officers who are sent abroad. In order to be effective they must learn not only the spoken language of the foreign country but the cultural language as well. The longer they are there, the more open to learning about *them* they are, and the more effective they could become in translating messages from our government to their government in language that they could understand and accept. The only problem is that if they are very successful in learning about the other culture, they run the risk of being perceived by *us* as having "gone native" and of being recalled. Indeed, no matter how successful any foreign service officer is at communicating across cultural barriers, most governments will send him or her on another assignment after four or five years, precisely because of the fear that if foreign service officers stay in one country too long, they will begin valuing the other culture and its beliefs over their own.

*Premise 7. Every individual must inevitably
be a member of a myriad of different perceptual and identity groups simultaneously.
However, one shares a higher degree of
similarity of perception and a higher degree
of group identity with some groups than with
others. Consciously or otherwise (usually
subconsciously), one always rank-orders these
identities. Not only is each individual's rank-
order unique, but that order varies as the
context (environment) varies.*

All of the identities we hold have some impact on our behavior. The more important the identity, the more it influences our attitudes, values, and beliefs, and the more it will influence our behavior, consciously or otherwise. Although the ranking of these identities can and does change with time and circumstance, to understand human behavior at any given moment it is important to know which identities are primary and which are only second- ary or tertiary in that particular circumstance, and how we rank the values of each of those identities (see figures 1.6 and 1.7 again).

Getting to know our group identities is very complex. That is because we are members of so many different groups simultaneously. Still one is not a member of an infinite number. By identifying the groups of which we *are* members, we also identify some of the groups of which we are not. If I am a man, I am not a woman. If I am middle-aged, I am neither young nor old. If I am middle class, then I am not poor.

It is an instructive exercise to try to list as many identi- ties as one can possibly think of. Having done that, one should then try to rank how important each of those groups (of which we form a part) has been in molding our per- ceptions. A list like this helps us identify who we are. By ranking the identities, in specific contexts, we begin to see just how important each has been—or continues to be—

in shaping our attitudes and values in those contexts. We may have great difficulty in ranking some of them, but that may be because we cannot think of them in the abstract but rather only in concrete situations. I know, for example, that my identity as an American is of great importance to me. I also know myself well enough to know that if there were ever to be a conflict between my identity as an American and my identity as a Jew, the former would certainly take precedence. That tells me something about how I rank each of those identities and how they affect my behavior. That is why I live in America and not in Israel. For one of my sons, however, that identity was reversed and he does live in Israel.

In premise 4 we discussed the fact that the more identity groups people share, the more loyalty they are likely to show to those people. While that is undoubtedly true, it did not deal directly with the question of *intensity* of identification. There is no doubt that we do not identify equally with all groups. Some are clearly more important to us than others. For some people, religious or ideological identification can be all-consuming. For others it may be family, class, profession, ethnic group, race, or nation. For still others it may be level or type of education that is most important for their worldview. Each one of us has some identities that are clearly more important for our behavior than others.

The late Richard Cottam, formerly at the University of Pittsburgh, has argued, not without some merit, that primary identities should be considered those for which an individual would sacrifice most of his or her time, money, and, if need be, life. He has argued that secondary identities are those for which the individual would sacrifice only some of his or her time and money. For a tertiary identity, argues Cottam, the individual would be willing to sacrifice only some of his or her time and perhaps a little money.

Whether those are the yardsticks that ought to be applied to measure the importance of particular identities or not, the point is well taken. People are often willing to kill and to die if they perceive a threat to the group that they define as being primary to themselves at any given moment. Thus for centuries identities like loyalty to a particular monarch, religion, ethnicity (often associated with language), and/or race (however defined) were (and in some cases still are) the primary identities for which many people have willingly died. More recently, identities like nationalism and ideology have become the primary identities over which people fight. For over a hundred years Europeans killed each other over Protestant versus Catholic identities, yet only a few centuries later Catholic Germans and Catholic French were quite willing to kill each other in the name of their "higher" loyalty to their nations.

In some ways nationalism itself is a relatively new identity. It started with the American and French Revolutions and spread over most of the rest of the world in the nineteenth and twentieth centuries. For many people it is the most important identity they hold. What makes its hold over people so strong is the fact that it often combines language, ethnicity, religion, and long-shared historic memory as one people attached to a particular piece of land. Given premise 4 (when people share a number of important groups, that reinforces identity), it is no wonder that nationalism has become such a powerful primary identity. In the early twentieth century, particularly, it was thought that ideologies like democracy and communism would overtake nationalism as the primary loyalty to which people gave their allegiance, but during World War I the United States was talking about making the world safe for democracy while being aligned (for a short time) with czarist Russia against imperial Germany. And in the mid-twentieth century, when communism was specifically supposed to transcend nationalist loyalties, the two communist giants, Russia and China—for primarily nationalistic reasons—seemed, for twenty-five years, much more likely to go at each other than against their supposed common enemy, capitalism.

With the new century upon us, the identities that seem to be sweeping the world are ethnic and religious nationalism.[7] One cannot help being struck, particularly since the end of the Cold War and the demise of the Soviet Union (and most of the other totalitarian communist regimes that ruled their countries), by the number of separatist, nationalist conflicts that have broken out. Armenia, Azerbaijan, Chechnya, Bosnia-Herzegovina, Croatia are all names on the front pages as this is being written. They have broken into conflict now because the totalitarian regimes which previously restrained it are gone, and the governments which took their place are trying to establish ethnically pure states. The battles are new. The conflicts are not. Many go back hundreds of years.

We saw this ethnic nationalism in the period between World War I and World War II, after the demise of the Austro-Hungarian Empire, particularly in the Balkans. With the end of the British and (to a lesser extent) French empires we also saw the reemergence of ancient hostilities between people who were not allowed to violently express their fear and hatred of each other under the old colonial system. But as those empires collapsed we saw Hindus and Muslims in India (not ethnic groups, but religious nationalists) rip that country into India and Pakistan. Later, Pakistan was torn by ethnic nationalism between Punjabi and Bengali, with the latter declaring their own state of Bangladesh. Other ethnic conflicts have erupted throughout Asia and Africa. In the early '70s it was Ibos and Hausa

---

[7] Samuel P. Huntington sees these forces as coalescing in the form of "civilizations," broad cultural identities (Arab, Western, Chinese) which Huntington believes will be the focal point of conflict in the future. See Samuel P. Huntington, *The Clash of Civilizations and the Remaking of World Order* (New York: Simon & Schuster, 1997).

in Nigeria. In the '90s it has been Tutsi and Hutu in Rwanda. As this is being written there are more than three dozen ethnic and religious conflicts raging around the world.

Neither religious nor ethnic conflicts are new. Some of these groups have hated each other for centuries. What is new is that many now feel they have to have their own ethnically pure, independent nation-states to protect their group identity.[8]

One final note about these primary identities: While it is the large group that more or less subconsciously decides which identity will take precedence in any historical period or context, there have always been individuals who will not go along with the group decision as to which identity should be ranked higher. Thus in every time period and in every context, some individuals have dissented from their group definition of primary identification and instead followed the dictates of their own personal identity ranking.

Clearly, only a few identities are primary, and rarely is one called upon to die for them. Most of the time we take these primary identities for granted and think very little about how they affect our daily lives. Being an American or Christian or white or middle class may very much affect the day-to-day behavior of most of the people who live in the United States, but, as I argued earlier, we are usually unaware of those identities until juxtaposed against some threatening "they."

One of the problems involved with the study of the effects of identity on behavior is context. At work—whatever we do—most of us dress, walk, behave, and generally communicate like the workers we are. With our parents we behave as we believe children should, with our spouses

---

[8] For a brilliant discussion of ethnic conflict see Donald L. Horowitz, *Ethnic Groups in Conflict* (Berkeley: University of California Press, 1985).

or lovers we behave like spouses or lovers, with our children we behave like parents, with friends we behave like friends, and with acquaintances we behave like acquaintances. Each of these contexts determines not only how we will behave, but also how we will communicate. Still, clearly, context determines which identity will take precedence and thus which will most influence our behavior. But context changes from moment to moment. In the same room can be our boss, our secretary, our parents, siblings, spouse, and children, and our communication with—and behavior toward—each will be different. What is more, we rarely get our behaviors mixed up. More will be said about role-related behavior later in this book.

The importance of context determining identity—and therefore behavior—cannot be overstated. Under what conditions will an international businessman behave like a businessman first and only secondarily as a national of his country? In what contexts does the head of an American religious voluntary agency operating overseas behave as a representative of her church, her organization, or her country? In what contexts did Henry Kissinger's identity as secretary of state take precedence over his identity as a German-Jewish-American? In what contexts did his other identities take precedence? Without knowing the man one might have predicted before he became secretary of state that he would be overly favorable to Israel because of his ethnic heritage. Yet that proved not to be the case. When he was dealing with diplomats the world over who had been his former students at Harvard, did he deal with them primarily as fellow diplomats or as their former professor?

While context is important in determining identity and therefore behavior, there is probably a blending that occurs on many occasions. The role of secretary of state may demand certain kinds of behavior—in broad outline—but the way those behaviors are played out will depend heavily on the unique blend of identities of the occupant of the office and his or her personality.

We do know that the identity that takes precedence in any given situation will dominate and determine a person's perception of the situation, which will further strengthen that identity—in very circular fashion. Perceptions do affect attitudes and values, which do contribute to and mold identities, which do affect behaviors, which in turn do affect our perceptions, attitudes, values, and identities. This is the circle of causality that was discussed in the previous chapter.

What we do *not* know is (a) precisely which affects which and in what ways, (b) how to accurately measure the relative ranking (importance) of either perceptions or identities at any given moment (they are so highly situation-related that they change from moment to moment), and (c) which is easier to modify.

> *Premise 8. It is not only possible but neces-*
> *sary to distinguish between individual,*
> *group, and national cultures.*

By individual cultures I mean the unique, learned, group-related perceptions (including verbal and nonverbal language or codes) stored in each individual's memory plus the highly individual ranking we make of the attitudes, values, beliefs, disbeliefs, and norms of behavior of the groups with which each of us identifies. Since no person is likely to be a member of all and only the same identity groups as anyone else or is likely to rank all of his or her identities exactly the same as anyone else does, the overwhelming probability is that no two individuals can be "culturally identical"—in other words, no two individuals are likely to perceive and rank their attitudes, values, beliefs, or disbeliefs identically. Further, since each person's experience in life is, and must be, different, so perforce, each person must be considered culturally unique. That is why it is not only possible but necessary to speak of each interpersonal communication as also being an intercultural communication.

Regardless of how strongly any of us identifies with any particular group, there will always be some aspect of that group's cultural attitudes, values, or beliefs from which we will deviate ever so slightly—at a minimum. Indeed, if we were to take the time and make the effort, each of us could construct an entire list of characteristics that distinguish us as individuals from the broad cultural groups of which we form a part. None of us is merely the product of the groups to which we belong. That is precisely what makes humans individually unique. And while that makes for a more rich, varied, and interesting world, it also makes generalizing about people and learning about intercultural communication that much more hazardous. But while we may each be unique, that uniqueness does know bounds, and the boundaries are usually those that have been prescribed by one or more of the groups with which each of us identifies.

By group culture I mean the symbiotic relationship that exists between a group as a whole and the individuals who comprise the group. A group, as such, does not have a data bank in which to record its historic memory outside of the data banks of each of the individuals who comprise the group. Nevertheless, the collective memory of the group (dispersed as it may be) cannot be overlooked. Every group *does* have a culture of its own. Every group *does* teach its members its own perceptions, attitudes, values, and so on. That is why at the outset we made that premise the most basic one of this entire work.

Yes, college students are a distinct group from high school or, certainly, elementary school students. But even more specifically, students who have gone to Harvard or Yale share a different set of perceptions, attitudes, and values than do students who went to Penn State or Michigan or Berkeley. People who work in the computer industry certainly do share a culture that most of us who do not could not possibly share, but again, it gets more specific than that. While technology may be erasing the distinction between DOS and Mac, the "we-they" animosity between those two groups is as great as almost any I know. It's almost acceptable among people who belong to those two cultures to call each other disparaging names. And IBM prides itself on having developed a "Big Blue" culture which not only provides an identity for IBM workers all over the world, but, more importantly, makes communication among them that much easier.

Aside from collective memory, by group culture, I refer here also to the aggregate ranking of attitudes, values, beliefs, and disbeliefs held by members of the group. There is little doubt that the perceptions of the dominant members of the group (however defined) usually count more heavily in the collective memory of the group than do the perceptions of the more peripheral members, but the predominant cultures of the rank-and-file membership of the group cannot be overlooked. One can think of innumerable cases (ranging from small social clubs through formal organizations like labor unions to whole countries) where the dominant members have been overthrown precisely because their value systems came to diverge significantly from the value systems of most of the other members of the group.

A nation is nothing more than a particular kind of group, as we shall see elsewhere. However, since every nation comprises many different identity groups, and since no nation contains within its boundaries all and only the same groups as any other nation, and since no nation occupies exactly the same environment as any other nation or has had exactly the same history as any other nation, every nation may be said to have a culture unique to itself. That would seem to imply that every international communication is also an intercultural communication, and that is correct in most situations. But because some people rank certain of their group identities (and group cultural values) more highly than they do their national identity in certain situations, sometimes international communications are *less* intercultural than are some communications within nations (that is, intranational communications.) More about that later. Here the intriguing questions for scholars to consider are: In which situations are specific group cultures more important in determining an individual's behavior and in which situations are national cultures more important? Actually this is no different from asking: Which group identity will take precedence in which contexts?

> *Premise 9. It is inevitable that individuals, groups, and nations will have internalized elements of several different, even conflicting, value systems simultaneously. They are able to survive and function under this condition primarily because:*
> a. *They are able to identify in different degrees—and at different levels of consciousness—with each of the value systems;*
> b. *Most simultaneously held group identities only rarely come into direct conscious conflict; and*
> c. *When two equally ranked identities do come into direct conflict, the individual, group, or nation will attempt to find some third identity that can accommodate, neutralize, rationalize, and/or synthesize those conflicting value systems.*

This premise is closely related to the theory of cognitive dissonance developed by Leon Festinger. The major difference is that Festinger uses the term *cognition* to mean more or less the same things I mean when I talk about attitudes, values, and belief systems.

His basic contention is that the individual will find conflicts in simultaneously held value systems psychologically disturbing and will strive to reduce those conflicts. He says:

> The presence of dissonance gives rise to pressure to reduce or eliminate the dissonance. The strength of the pressures to reduce the dissonance is a function of the magnitude of the dissonance. In other words, dissonance acts in the same way as a state of drive or need or tension. The presence of dissonance leads to action to reduce it just as, for example, the presence of hunger leads to action to reduce the hunger.[9]

While this is very much an encapsulation of Festinger's theory, it is the portion that is most relevant to this premise.

I have been arguing throughout this chapter that each of the groups with which individuals identify teaches its members its own cultural values. That being so, it follows that some groups to which the same individual belongs may teach totally different and/or conflicting values. Indeed, it is almost inevitable that this should be so. An individual is able to survive this conflict and function for three reasons.

First, we do not identify to the same degree (or with the same level of intensity) with each of the groups of which we form a part. (See premise 7.) The fact that one is an American, for example (primary identity), is much more important in molding our attitudes, values, and behaviors than would be one's identity as, say, someone whose parents were born in Germany (secondary identity). An enormous portion of the things one liked and desired and did for most of the hours of every day would be markedly affected and colored by one's identity as an American. On the other hand, that same person's identity as a second-generation German American would only affect some of his or her attitudes, values, and behaviors some of the time.

---

[9] Leon Festinger, *A Theory of Cognitive Dissonance* (Stanford, CA: Stanford University Press, 1957), 18.

When the two identities came into severe conflict (as they did for a few years during World War II), there might have been some conflict for some second-generation German Americans, yet many of the younger males enlisted in the U. S. military to show their loyalty to the United States.

Second, one can survive and function while holding two or more conflicting value systems—even if they are very nearly equally ranked—because they probably rarely come into direct conflict. On some broad level of generalization my identity as, say, a university professor may be equally ranked with my identity as a father, but context often dictates which set of values will take precedence. Most of the time the two simply do not come into direct conflict. When I am in the university I think and act like a professor. At home, on the other hand, particularly when my sons lived with me, I acted like a father. The sets of attitudes and values that are associated with each identity would be totally inappropriate in the other context. (Unfortunately we all know people who do rank their professional identities more highly and find that they have little time for their children.)

It can happen, of course, that two *equally ranked* identities will come into conflict. That leads us to the third reason people survive and function, which is really just a way of coping. If I had ranked my identity as a university professor completely equally with my identity as a divorced parent with custody of my children, I would have been hard-pressed to decide what to do if one of my children were sick and needed me at the same time that I was supposed to be at the university teaching a class. (This is not just a personal example. Probably thousands of single working parents make similar decisions daily.) If I ranked either of those identities more highly, there would be no conflict. I would teach my course or be with my child without a moment's hesitation because the unequal ranking would make clear what I *ought* to do. But if I had ranked them equally then I would have had a problem. One of the ways to get around that problem of equal ranking of identities in conflict is to find a third identity. For example, in the case just discussed, I might decide that my identity as a humanitarian required me to be with someone who was sick. Or I might decide that my role as breadwinner demanded that I not risk my job by being absent. Either way I would probably seek some third identity that would relieve me of the conflict. Most of the time these decisions are made totally subconsciously.

In the psychological literature under the heading of "psychosomatic illness," there is a classic example of what can happen when a person holds two conflicting value systems equally and simply cannot bring him- or herself to rank one over the other, or cannot find that third identity with which to escape from the conflict. The example cited is of a young Englishman at the start of World War I who apparently *equally* valued his identity as an Englishman and as a pacifist. Had he been able to value his identity as an Englishman more highly, he would have gone off to war to defend his country. Conversely, had he valued his identity as a pacifist more, he would have gone to jail for his beliefs. But because he did value both equally, he could not decide to act on behalf of one or the other. People in such a state can be said to be ambivalent. As with most people who are ambivalent—who cannot make a conscious decision—he allowed himself to be battered by circumstances. When he was conscripted he could not bring himself to refuse to serve. Instead he probably told himself that even though he was in the army, he would not carry a gun. When they told him he had to carry a gun, he probably told himself he would not use it. This type of rationalizing and refusing to make a conscious decision in favor of one identity or the other continued until it could continue no longer. The moment ultimately arrived when he was handed a gun, told that if the Germans started to advance he was to fire, and unfortunately for him, the Germans did start to advance. To have fired the gun at that point, and actually kill someone, would have been to allow his English identity to take precedence over his pacifist identity. Not to have fired the gun would have been to allow his pacifist identity to take precedence, but at the cost of being a traitor to his buddies and to his country.

Because he could not choose on a conscious level between these two identities, his body chose for him at a subconscious level. At precisely that moment he went blind! He was sent back to a hospital in England where he was subjected to every physical test known. A healthy pupil involuntarily contracts and expands with a corresponding increase or decrease in light intensity. His did neither. Accordingly it was determined that he had gone physically blind. Then on November 11, 1918, when the church bells all over England tolled the end of the war, the conflict that had produced his blindness was removed and he immediately regained his eyesight.

This is perhaps one of the most extreme examples in the literature of what can happen when someone is unable to choose between identities, but it probably only differs in degree from what happens to others in similar situations. We get sick or faint or find some other physical excuse not to have to choose.

Before we leave the discussion of this premise, let us look at another example, this time on a political level. In empirical research I conducted in Sri Lanka in the late 1950s I discovered that among the political elite there were three distinct identity groups: the "Westernized," the "traditional," and a third middle group, which I labeled the "emerging elite."

The Westernized political elite spoke, read, and wrote in English as their preferred language; had either studied in the United Kingdom or in Sri Lanka's equivalent of Eaton and Harrow; preferred to wear Western-style clothes; and, if given the opportunity, would have remade Sri Lanka into a tropical replica of Britain. The traditional political elite spoke, read, and wrote in Sinhalese as *their* preferred language; had studied largely in rural, traditional schools; wore traditional Sri Lankan dress most of the time; and, if given the opportunity, would have remade Sri Lanka in the image of the ancient Sinhalese kingdoms. The members of the emerging elite, on the other hand, were "double-value-oriented." They spoke, read, and wrote in *both* English and Sinhalese; they went to schools where they learned *both* Western and ancient Sinhalese history, culture, and values; they wore *both* Western and traditional dress; and, given their choice, they would have created a society that was economically and technologically as modern as Britain and culturally as distinctively Sinhalese as the ancient Sinhalese kingdoms. This third group did hold both identities equally and was trying desperately to synthesize their conflicting cultural values. At the time I wrote that book I was not certain whether their efforts at synthesis would succeed or whether ambivalence would win out. At this point in time while it is still not completely clear, it appears that synthesis may be winning. Despite a major civil war that has rocked the country since 1983, Sri Lanka has continued to develop economically but has done so in a distinctively Sinhalese fashion.

Premise 10. The environment in which a communication occurs can be a major factor in determining how effective one can be in intercultural communication.

The context of an encounter is quite important for how I am going to feel in an intercultural communication. If the context of the encounter is my environment, where I am surrounded by people who are very similar to me culturally, most of my attitudes and values will constantly be reinforced. I may find visitors in my midst who have different perceptions, attitudes, and values to be quaint, amusing, or interesting, but I am not likely to feel terribly threatened by their worldview. They will be the ones who are "different." If our meeting is merely casual, there is virtually no threat whatever. If I am going to have to work with them, that may be a little more difficult, but I can always console myself with the knowledge that given enough time they will learn how we do things here. It is *they* who will have to learn our perceptions, attitudes, and values.

When the encounter is in the other person's environment, however, it is a different story. It is I who will have to do the learning. The entire burden of trying to figure out those sometimes very strange attitudes and values (to say nothing of language) falls on me. What is more, in my own environment—precisely because I do have a relatively accurate approximation of the attitudes and values of most of the people with whom I must work (or if I don't, it is not too difficult for me to find out, since I know what to look for and what to ask)—I feel a sense of efficacy. I know how to get things done; therefore I have a sense of power. When I am in a foreign environment, however, not only does the burden of the learning fall upon me, but my very sense of identity—who I am and the rightness of what I value—is challenged. Not only is living and working in a foreign environment tiring, it is threatening precisely because it involves a challenge to that identity. Since I do not share the attitudes and values—and since I may not even be certain what they are—it is much more difficult to get anything done. Hence there is also a challenge to my efficacy, and I may very well experience a sense of powerlessness. What is more, if there is no one to reinforce my previously held values and attitudes, I may come to doubt their soundness myself.

We speak of some people going native in a foreign environment. What that means, of course, is an abandonment of one's own attitudes and values and the acceptance of theirs. I think that this is much less likely to happen if we are in that foreign environment with other members of our own groups whom we know and trust and with whom we identify. The reason that is so, of course, is that each of those people can reinforce the correctness of their own ranking of attitudes and values. When alone in a foreign environment—particularly when we are young and have not been thoroughly socialized into our own groups—there is much more likelihood of going native.

It is not simply working in a foreign country that can be difficult. Trying to work in any city other than our own can be surprisingly more difficult than one might expect. In my own city I know how to get from here to there. I don't have to look at maps or constantly ask directions. I know what sections of town are safe and which are not, and I don't inadvertently wander into the "wrong part of town." Even the pace—how rapidly people move—changes from city to city, as do the norms for the time one is supposed to arrive at certain kinds of social functions. Also, the way people are expected to dress at different professional and social functions varies from city to city within the same country. All of this must be learned by newcomers, and it can't help impeding their productivity and effectiveness—at least at first—if for no other reason than the time and effort that is required.

I would go one step further and argue that one's effectiveness may be somewhat impaired by trying to do business in someone else's office. If I go to a businesswoman's office it may very well be she who sits behind *her* desk, who calls upon *her* secretary to take notes, who can choose to divert her attention from me by answering *her* phone when it rings. The situation is reversed, of course, when she comes to my office. That is why it is not uncommon, when neither party in a negotiation is willing to give the slightest advantage to the other party, that meetings are sometimes arranged on neutral turf, where neither party is any more at home than the other. This is, of course, quite common in union/ management negotiations, as it is in negotiations among nations. Often the only way one party will agree to meet on the other's turf is if the next meeting will be on their own turf.

All of this is presented here merely to highlight the importance of environment to the effectiveness of any intercultural communication.

Premise 11. Because biological and environmental factors are ever changing, perceptions, attitudes, values, and identities are ever changing. Consequently, new perceptual and identity groups are constantly being formed, and existing groups are constantly in a state of flux.

The biological process is inexorable: We are children, teenagers, young adults, middle-aged, and old. Inevitable growth and decay cause constant changes in our identity. Yet these physical factors, as we have seen, account for only a fraction of our perceptions. Just think for a moment of the ever widening circles of new experiences and associations attendant upon physical growth. In the first years of our life particularly, but often considerably longer, if only one parent worked, we were surrounded by the protective cocoon of family. Rarely was the shell penetrated by an outsider, and when it was, most often the family acted as a shield between us and the intruder. Hence, it is not surprising that it is the family identity that has been the most basic and primary for most humans. As we learn to walk and talk our world widens, first to the houses and other children next door and then to those at the end of the street. The next big step comes when we are allowed to cross the street (with not too much traffic) by ourselves. Suddenly the physical expanse of our world has doubled— along with the different people in it. Next comes school. If crossing a street opened the world, going to school is equivalent to exploring the planet. No matter how restricted the neighborhood served by the school, there will be children in attendance from an array of cultural milieus. Suddenly we meet children of different economic classes, ethnic backgrounds, religions, and races. And the process continues. The further we go in school, the more diverse the backgrounds of our classmates become. Not only are we associating with people from a greater variety of groups but we are coming across increasing numbers of people whose experiences and ways of viewing the world differ more from our own. At first most of them seem terribly strange. After a while they seem less so. Just think of all the groups we may have become a part of in the process. We have learned to read, and that event alone exposes us to centuries of thought. Yet that is only a part of the learning experience. Beyond the academic there are sports, music, dance, and drama.

Still the process continues. Somewhere along the line we discover the wonders of sex and for most, eventually, that incredible institution called marriage. Suddenly we are a family ourselves, and wonder of wonders, parents. Then we watch what we were too young to remember, as our children go out and discover their own worlds. We can't help comparing how different our children's world is from our own. "We didn't have that when we were young." "The world was different back when I was growing up." Yet it is amazing: For all the differences we see, how very similar all children are.

Every culture changes, some more slowly than others. We are a part of so many different cultures in the course of our life, it is inevitable that some of the groups with which we identify will change more rapidly than others. Some will disappear entirely. Others are constantly emerging. It may be true that the more things change the more they remain the same, but change they do.

> Premise 12. While it is not easy to develop
> sharp intercultural communication skills, it is
> worth the effort to do so, if what you have to
> do in the course of your work or your life
> requires you to communicate effectively
> across cultural boundaries.

We in the West are culturally conditioned to accept machines and automation as ways to improve the productivity of labor. So, a number of years ago, when some agricultural specialists from the United States tried to help Sri Lankan peasants improve the output of their rice crops, they tried to introduce a simple gas-driven machine that transplanted rice seedlings over a dozen times faster than was then being done by young girls bending over and planting each seedling by hand, one by one. The experiment was a total flop, and experts couldn't figure out why. Only much later did someone raise with the foreigners the delicate subject that farmers believe their rice harvest will be enhanced if virgin girls plant the seedlings. The machines the Westerners tried to introduce were far too powerful for young girls to handle. Only when a Western agricultural specialist who was interculturally sensitive took the trouble to determine why the experiment had not worked was he able to come up with a solution that did: small machines that could be operated by these young girls.

Intercultural communication skills aren't something that one is born with, they are developed over years of practice and hard work and being in contact with people who are different from us. The more different the people, of course, the more practice we would need to develop those skills. The problem is that many of us just dismiss "them" as weird, when confronted with people whom we don't understand, or people who do things differently from the way we do them. Our instinct when talking to someone who doesn't understand our language is to speak louder. That obviously isn't going to help if the person doesn't understand the words, but somehow it makes us feel as though we are trying.

When confronting people who are different—and in an ever interdependent world there are increasing numbers of Asians, Hispanics, African Americans, and women in the workplace, to mention only the more obvious groups—white American males, who have been notoriously poor at understanding other cultures (Peace Corps notwithstanding), are increasingly going to need to learn how to communicate effectively across cultural boundaries. So are all of the other groups mentioned. To do that they must try to develop skills in communication across cultural divides.

I have argued throughout these pages that all of us have been parts of many different groups and group cultures throughout our lives. Shouldn't we have developed these intercultural communication skills by now? One might think so, but it doesn't work that way. The reason is that we have been socialized into those group cultures in such subtle ways as to be unaware of it. To become good intercultural communicators we have to consciously come to understand what culture is and how it affects us.

The first step in that process is to understand the impact of culture on everything we do and think. The second step is to realize that others have different cultures and are likely to do and think differently from us. The third thing to do is to try to suspend judgment about whether what others do or think is good or bad. Establish that their culture is different, then try to learn all you can about it. It is terribly important that we bring to the process as open a mind as possible. An open mind is not one into which any piece of garbage can be dropped and accepted without discernment. Rather, an open mind is one which understands, respects, and accepts differences. The open mind is curious about differences, but also discerning and able to pick out bits and pieces of experience with other cultures that are of value. It is also sensitive to how ideas from one set of cultural values can be translated to a different set of cultural values—as Sam Green did in Guatemala. Indeed, once we do understand what they are saying in another culture, one of the most difficult things about intercultural communication is finding just the right way to translate what we want to say into communication which reflects values they can understand.

Finally, one needs to understand the communication process itself, where the breakdowns are most likely to occur, and what we can do to protect against them. We need to discover the most likely areas of intercultural communication breakdown and come up with innovative solutions. In most cases we can, but it takes a lot of thought, innovation, and frequently just plain hard work.

Propositional Summary for Chapter 2

Perceptual group: A perceptual group is a number of individuals who perceive some aspect of the external world more or less similarly but do not communicate this similarity of perception among themselves. Technically they are not really a group if they do not communicate among themselves. As soon as they do communicate about their shared perceptions, they become an identity group.

Identity group: An identity group is a number of people who perceive some aspect of the external world more or less similarly and recognize and communicate this similarity of perception.

Spiraling of communication: Other things being equal, the higher the degree of similarity of perception that exists among a number of individuals, the easier communication among them is likely to be, and the more communication among them is likely to occur. Conversely, where there is little or no communication among individuals, there tends to be a decrease in similarity of perception, which in turn tends to make further communication more difficult.

Sharing of identities: As the number and importance of identity groups that individuals share rises, the more likely they are to have a higher degree of group identity. That is, the more overlapping of important identity groups that an individual shares with other individuals, the more important the particular group of people is likely to be to him or her.

Recognition of identity: Any "we" (identity group) comes into much sharper focus when juxtaposed against any "they" (a different identity group). The moment we are juxtaposed against some other group, we have no choice but to become conscious of that identity. This is particularly so if the other group is perceived by us to be hostile or threatening.

Getting to know "their" perceptions: If we want to communicate effectively with one of "them," it is important to get to know their perceptions, attitudes, and values as well as their cultural language. The more like them we become, the easier communication with them will become. But it may make communication with "us" (our own group) more difficult.

Ranking of identities: Every individual must inevitably be a member of a myriad of different perceptual and identity groups simultaneously. However, one shares a higher degree of similarity of perception and a higher degree of group identity with some groups than with others. Consciously or otherwise (usually subconsciously), one always rank-orders these identities. Not only is each individual's rank order unique, but that order varies as the context (environment) varies.

Individual, group, and national cultures: It is not only possible but necessary to distinguish among personal, group, and national cultures. Personal cultures are those unique, learned, group-related perceptions stored in the memory bank of each individual. Since no person is likely to be a member of all and only the same identity groups as anyone else, or is likely to rank all of his or her identities exactly the same as anyone else, the overwhelming probability is that no two individuals can be "culturally identical"—that is, each individual is likely to be culturally unique.

Group cultures are those symbiotic relationships that exist between a group as a whole and the individuals who comprise the group. Every group does have a culture of its own. Every group does teach its members its own perceptions, attitudes, values, and so on.

A nation is nothing more than a particular kind of group. Since every nation is made up of many different identity groups, and since no nation contains within its boundaries all and only the same groups as any other nation, and since no nation occupies exactly the same environment as any other nation or has had exactly the same history as any other nation, every nation may be said to have a culture unique to itself.

When values conflict: It is inevitable that individuals, groups, and nations will have internalized elements of several different and possibly conflicting value systems simultaneously. They are able to survive and function under this condition primarily because

a. They are able to identify in different degrees—and at different levels of consciousness—with each of the value systems;
b. Most simultaneously held group identities only rarely come into direct conscious conflict; and
c. When two equally ranked identities do come into direct conflict, the individual, group, or nation will attempt to find some third identity that can accommodate, neutralize, rationalize, and/or synthesize those conflicting value systems.

Communication environments: The environment in which a communication occurs can be a major factor in determining how effective one can be in an intercultural communication.

Cultural change is inevitable: Because biological and environmental factors are ever changing, perceptions, attitudes, values, and identities are ever changing. Consequently, new perceptual and identity groups are constantly being formed and existing groups are constantly in a state of flux.

The Communication Process: It Is Not Possible to Not Communicate

3

I t is simply *not* possible to not communicate. I know of no more basic statement about the communication process than that. We may not have always communicated what we wanted to, or thought we were communicating, but we cannot not communicate. If I say nothing in a particular situation, I have communicated something to others, whether I intended to or not. If I had said a great deal, or just a little, in that same situation, I would also have communicated something; again perhaps not necessarily what I intended to communicate, but something. There is nothing I can do or say—or not do or say—that doesn't communicate something to someone. The same words I utter or body motions I make may communicate completely different things to different people at the same time, but I can't help communicating something to everyone who is listening or watching. All of us are engaged in communication *100 percent* of the time, twenty-four hours of every day. That communication may not necessarily be conscious or be with another person, but we send off and simultaneously receive messages all of the time. Merely walking down a crowded street requires the taking in and sending out of an incredibly large number of messages simply to avoid bumping into other people. We do that continuously in our own cultures, only rarely having an accident. The reason we so easily avoid bumping is that we and the other people walking in the street are all simultaneously sending and receiving messages. We have learned so well how to send and receive these messages that none of us is consciously aware of how we do it. Nevertheless we are still sending and receiving them. But just because we cannot avoid communicating doesn't mean that the people with whom we try to communicate will necessarily understand what it is we are trying to communicate. Allow me to illustrate with two personal anecdotes.

Many years ago while traveling in India, after having spent a year studying in Sri Lanka, I had an experience that I think illustrates the complexity of all intercultural communication. It is important for the reader to know that in Sri Lanka people don't shake their heads the way people do in most other cultures to signal yes and no. In most of the world one indicates yes nonverbally by nodding the head up and down. A horizontal motion of the head from left to right in most places normally means no. In Sri Lanka that is not the case.[1] If one wants to signal yes

---

[1] Porter and Samovar tell us that Sri Lanka is not the only place where people gesture no nonverbally in a different way. "...an Abyssinian is apt to express no by jerking the head to the right shoulder; a Dyand of Borneo may express it by contracting the eyebrows slightly—and Sicilians express no by raising the head and chin." Richard E. Porter and Larry A. Samovar, "Communicating Interculturally," 22, and see also Roman Jakobson, "Nonverbal Signs for 'Yes' and 'No,'" both in *Intercultural Communication: A Reader*, 2d ed., edited by Samovar and Porter (Belmont, CA: Wadsworth, 1976), 235-40.

or okay nonverbally, one slowly moves his or her head horizontally from left to right and right to left. Indicating no also involves moving the head horizontally, but it is done more rapidly. Having spent a year in Sri Lanka, I had adopted the Sri Lankan pattern without being aware that I had done so. (Few of us are consciously aware of how many of the local mannerisms we pick up when we have lived in a place for a while.) Anyway, upon arriving in what was then called Benares, India, I wanted to rent a rowboat to take a trip down the holy Ganges River. Since my knowledge of Hindi (the local language) was limited to *Nimasti* ("hello") and *ek, doe, teen* ("one," "two," "three"), I knew that my communication with the boat owner would have to be primarily in sign language. I had done pretty well at it until we came to the question of price. With some difficulty I finally conveyed to him that I wanted to know "how much?" He held up three fingers and said, "Teen rupee." In English I responded "okay" and without realizing it simultaneously shook my head slowly from side to side, Sri Lankan fashion. He responded by holding up two fingers and said, "Doe rupee." Instantly I realized what had happened and reverted to my American way of nodding my head up and down to indicate that I accepted his offer.

Okay. But that was in India between people who clearly were not from the same culture. Now move closer to home. Haven't all of us, at one time or another, made some gesture to someone we knew well (and who we assumed was "one of us"), taking it for granted that our meaning would be understood as we intended it to be understood, only to discover that the exact reverse was read into the gesture? For example, in my own case, being of Eastern European ethnic heritage, I learned to hug men whom I know and like when I greet them. I do that often. But when I tried to hug a colleague I had come to know and like who was of Anglo-Saxon heritage, I'm afraid he was most offended by my behavior.

As I have argued all along, the reason misunderstandings occur at home among people who are like us is that they are not part of all of the groups to which we belong, and we are not part of all the groups with which they identify.

What those little incidents have taught me is that if one wants to communicate more accurately with another human being, one had better try to consciously develop intercultural communication skills—that means trying to recognize and get to know both the verbal and nonverbal languages of as many as possible of the groups to which the other person belongs.

What I'd like to do in this chapter is to systematically go through the steps in the communication process—as I see them—and point out to the reader the complications added to that process by trying to communicate accurately with people from cultures other than our own.

Before we do that, however, we ought to have a very clear idea about the purpose of communication.

The Purpose of Communication: "Read My Lips" Doesn't Always Mean Understand What I *Really* Mean

As I noted in chapter 1, the human being is perhaps the most social of all animals. He or she must interact with other humans merely to survive. The earliest interaction that occurs is between a newborn infant and its mother. The child has needs that have to be met in order for it to survive. In order for the child to have its needs attended to, it must let them be known. As we grow older our needs become more complex, but still if we are to have them met by others, we have to let those others know what they are.

Almost all human communications are attempts to achieve goals. The goal may be as simple as wanting to buy two tickets to the theater, or as complex as trying to prevent terrorist bombings. Regardless of the complexity of the message, consciously or subconsciously the sender is always trying to achieve a purpose by sending the message.

The purpose of studying intercultural communication is to make it more effective. The reason it is important to communicate effectively is so as to be certain that the message the other person receives is as close as possible to the way it was intended when it was sent. The more accurately the receiver gets the message, the less likelihood there is for conflict (over the wrong things) and misunderstanding, and the more likelihood there is of the sender's achieving his or her purpose.

Let me be specific about my bias on this matter; I do not believe that "better communication" is a panacea. At every level of analysis conflict has persisted and probably always will. I am convinced that to the degree that interpersonal, intergroup, or international communication can be facilitated (a) there is likely to be less misperception and fear of others and (b) at least the actors can be more certain, if they are in conflict, that they agree on what the conflict is about.

It is a basic tenet of this work that communication is a process. As such it is continually operating, through feedback, with the environment and with everyone and everything in that environment. It is an ongoing process that never ceases until we die. It is applicable regardless of the level of analysis. The same process operates whether one considers intra- or interpersonal communication, intra- or intergroup communication, or intra- or international communication. Of course, the specifics of how that process operates change as one changes the actors and settings, but the process remains constant.

While I wouldn't say that "to reach better understanding between people" is the only reason people communicate (sometimes we consciously try to deceive), I would say that most of the time when people do communicate, they come away from the exchange knowing a little better what the other person is like or understanding better what the other person was trying to say than they would have, had they not communicated.

It is because of communication that it is possible to transmit the ideas of one time and place to another and from one generation to another. That is what makes culture possible. If it were not for communication, there could be no such things as groups or cultures.

Aristotle characterized the communication process as being concerned with "who says what to whom with what effect." Not a bad beginning for the first known attempt to deal with the communication process in a scientific manner. In fact, it was so good that it has survived for almost twenty-five hundred years.

As we shall see, human communications are so complex that they can never be entirely accurate. That is, no one can ever convey to another *exactly* the idea that one intended. At best, one can come close. At worst, one is forced to give up the attempt. (Or perhaps still worse, one thinks that he or she has communicated accurately only to discover later—or never to discover—that in fact, one has not communicated accurately at all.) I have on a shelf in my office a sign that says: "The greatest problem of communication is the illusion that it has been achieved."

I paint a bleak picture of the difficulties inherent in human communication not to discourage the reader from trying. Quite the contrary. Experience has shown that as long as we recognize the difficulties involved, we will not automatically assume that we are communicating well but, on the contrary, will make a more conscious and concerted effort to communicate accurately and thereby: (1) probably communicate better, (2) probably not become as easily frustrated at the amount of effort required to communicate accurately, and (3) be more selective in our choices of when it is important for us to make that effort and when it is not. Further, by recognizing the steps involved in the process we will be better able to attempt to control and correct those steps that we can effect, in order to improve our communication skills. Yes, communication is difficult, but by understanding why it is difficult and at what steps breakdowns are most likely to occur, we enhance enormously our ability to communicate more effectively. Since there is almost no human endeavor one can imagine that does not require effective communication, the whole range of human interaction—at the interpersonal, intergroup, and international levels—can be improved by better understanding and coping with the communication process.

The Communication Process Dissected: Remember, It Is Neither a Frog Nor Humor— It Will Survive

Among specialists in the field of intercultural communication there seems to be general agreement that intercultural communication is merely a subset of the broader field of communication. While I believe that is true, I'd like to turn it around and argue that since all human communication is intercultural, at least to some degree, the study of intercultural communication can provide fruitful direction to guide the study of human communication. Forgive me if this sounds arrogant, but I am absolutely convinced that many people in the general field of human communication simply have not been perceiving the problem from the most useful perspective; and once they do, great strides in the study of human communication will be made.

If one is to improve communication at any level of analysis, it is important to understand clearly how the communication process operates. Accordingly I present here my own model of the communication process. Models are ways of thinking about problems or processes that exist in the real world. They are neither right nor wrong. Some are just more useful than others. I immodestly think mine is very useful.

Figure 3.1 Interpersonal Communication Process

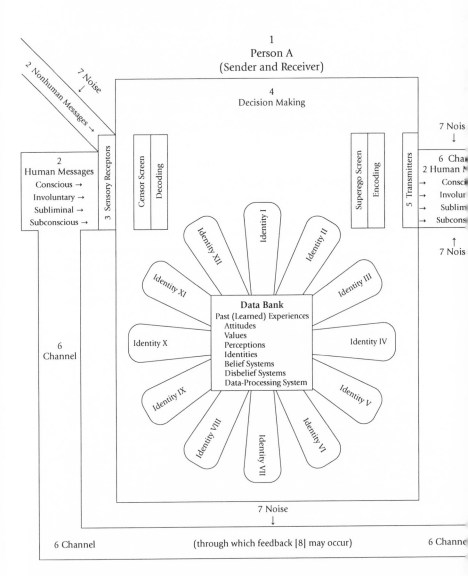

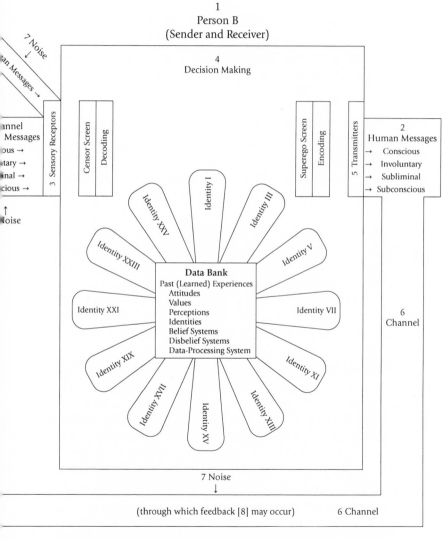

1
Person B
(Sender and Receiver)

Adapted from Singer, *Intercultural Communication: A Perceptual Approach*, 1st ed. (Englewood Cliffs, NJ: Prentice-Hall, 1987), 70.

I have presented my model here (figure 3.1) with numbers and letters added so that the reader can follow it as I discuss each step in the process in some detail. After we have discussed each of the steps in my model, I will complicate things still further by introducing Dean Barnlund's model of the communication process. In no way does his model contradict anything that I will say here, but it does add a refinement and a sense of the ongoing nature of the process, which my model alone may not adequately capture.

1. Senders and Receivers

Since I am interested primarily in human communication, I take the individual as my basic unit of analysis in this chapter. In the next I will use the same model, modified, to look at both groups and nations as well. To the degree that the model presented here discusses communication between people, it is a model of interpersonal as well as of intercultural communication. More will be said of that in chapter 4. Here I want to focus on the communication process as such.

One is both the sender and receiver of communications *at all times.* People are constantly sending *and* receiving messages simultaneously. There is no way they cannot. There is a Russian proverb that says: "You can't listen with your mouth open," but the fact is, you can. You listen with all of your sensory receptors, even while your mouth is in overdrive. At the very same time you are reading these words you are reacting: consciously or subconsciously, verbally or nonverbally. Thus, you are continually sending off messages as you receive them. Conversely, in a face-to-face conversation, even as I talk I am picking up not only the messages you may be sending but also thousands of other bits of information from the environment. Whether, or how, I convert those bits of information into messages that I can understand will be discussed shortly. Here it is simply important to note that neither our sensory receptors nor our transmitters ever cease to function until we die.

In the previous chapters I stressed what makes each individual unique. However, we cannot lose sight of the fact that as long as both senders and receivers are human, they share many traits. Not the least of those common traits is that everyone has the same number and kind of sensory receptors and transmitters. While each may operate differently for each of us—and some of us may not even have the use of one or more of them—all of us have receptors and transmitters. Further, individual differences aside, these receptors and transmitters operate in essentially the same way. Having said that, we must not lose sight of the fact that each individual is unique, both physically and experientially. Therefore, inevitably there will be differences between individuals. The more different sender and receiver are, the harder one has to work to overcome those differences.

2. Messages: Anything That Stimulates Some Nerve Endings in the Brain

Message is a communication term used in the strict sense to mean any stimulus that can be perceived by the nerve endings in any of our sensory receptors. Each "bit" of data that fires even one or two nerve endings in any of our receptors can be viewed as a message. More commonly we think of a message as being a pattern of perhaps hundreds of thousands of discrete bits of data that make up an intelligible whole; but depending on the circumstances, the individual bits themselves can be viewed as being messages. The stimuli by themselves have no meaning. People attribute meaning to the stimuli, thereby transforming them into messages. Because no two individuals can attribute exactly the same meaning to the same message, no two individuals can communicate 100 percent effectively.

As I noted above, each of us attends to messages—stimuli—twenty-four hours a day. Although for most of those hours we are attending to stimuli from nonhuman and internal sources, they are stimuli nonetheless. The door closing in the next apartment, the wind blowing the trees, the light coming in the window, our stomach informing us that we need food—in short, everything that is picked up by our nerve endings—are messages. Even when we sleep, we are receiving stimuli from the internal and external environments and unconsciously reacting to them. If the room gets too cold or too warm, while remaining asleep we adjust the blankets accordingly. If a particular topic is being discussed in the next room, the topic may find its way into our dreams. And if the message is loud enough (a car backfiring, perhaps), intense enough (perhaps a full bladder), or important enough (the baby crying), we might wake from our sleep to attend to the message. In the course of every hour of every day from the moment of birth, a human is bombarded with hundreds of thousands of discrete bits of information—stimuli of one sort or another that reach our sensory receptors.

Obviously we cannot attend to all of those messages equally because (a) if we did, there would be no way that we could concentrate on any specific message, and (b) we have not been trained by past experience to recognize the meaning of all of the different messages that bombard us.

Nonhuman messages: You don't hear the air conditioner until someone turns it off. Unquestionably, the greatest number of messages we receive every moment of the day are from nonhuman sources. Aside from seeing the words on these pages with your eyes, simultaneously the millions and millions of nerve endings on the surface of your skin have been reacting to the temperature in the place where you are sitting as you read this. Your ears are reacting to noises being made by movement around you. Your nose is picking up the variety of odors that may be present in your surroundings. You may not have been conscious of any of those messages until I mentioned them, but they have been there all along. More will be said in a moment about how we cope with the large quantities of data we receive simultaneously. Here it is important for us just to recognize the many sources of stimuli (messages) that surround us, even when we are alone in a quiet room.

You may never have thought of an odor as a message, but every place has an odor peculiar to itself. The room in which you are sitting as you read this is giving off odors different from those in any other room. A hospital smells different from a dentist's office. A room smells different from a meadow. A meadow in the tropics smells different from one in colder climates. Odors are often low-intensity messages, and if we work around the same smells all of the time, we become oblivious to their existence. But they are there. Go to an unfamiliar place, and you are often struck by the strange smells—until you have been there long enough not to even be aware that they are there.

Messages are also being sent by everything in one's environment, merely by virtue of the fact that they are there. When we become used to them, however, we are aware of them only on a subconscious level. Take them away suddenly, and we may become consciously aware of their absence.

Before this chapter is completed we hope to have made the reader aware of the bewildering number of messages—nonhuman and human—that each individual must choose to either attend to or ignore. Sometimes, of course, no matter how hard individuals may try to ignore certain nonhuman messages (so that they may concentrate on other things), it is impossible to do so. The heat or cold in the room may be so intense that it is simply impossible to think about anything else. The level of noise outside can be very high, but so long as it is fairly constant it is possible to adjust our screening devices to overcome it. But when it is unpredictable—sometimes very loud, sometimes very quiet—it becomes difficult to ignore. We can read where the light source is dim, but if the light gets bright one moment and dim the next in unpredictable fashion, reading becomes impossible.

Human messages: Verbal and nonverbal. The human animal is a most complex creature, continuously sending out a multitude of messages simultaneously. Some are conscious, but many more are involuntary, subliminal, and/or subconscious.

For the moment grant me that humans transmit perhaps dozens of messages simultaneously with all parts of their body. The problem then becomes: To which message does one attend? Think for a moment of the young child who verbally sends the message, "I don't have to go to the bathroom," while nonverbally she has her legs crossed and is turning red in the face. To which message does the parent attend? As the child grows, her ability to control and/or mask involuntary or subconscious messages increases enormously, thus making it often much more difficult to decode precisely what it is that the person is trying to communicate, or trying not to. The child in this example, of course, is trying to ignore the very loud message she is receiving from her body in order that she may continue to attend to whatever it is that she is doing. It is only when the internal message becomes so "loud" (intense really) that the child can no longer ignore it—or the parent intervenes—that the child will finally attend to her bodily needs.

Available evidence indicates that no one is completely successful at camouflaging most messages. Yet everyone is communicating so many different messages at the same time (even if one is not trying to mask them) that it is difficult to know to which messages one should attend. When you are talking with only one other person, are you listening to just what he is saying? Or are you also noticing the way he is saying it? The way he is dressed? The way he is standing? The deodorant he is using—or not using? The way he combs his hair? The look in his eyes? The list could go on and on. The fact is that you attend to *all* of those messages simultaneously—on at least some level of consciousness.

The process is complicated still further when the sender is trying to keep certain messages hidden—as everybody does at least some of the time. One of the major problems with trying to camouflage or hide certain thoughts is that they may be received by the other person as an entirely different message from the one being hidden. Thus because one cannot, or will not, articulate clearly and openly what the message is that she or he is trying to hide, the receiver often picks up some little hint of something and attributes meaning to that hint that could have nothing to do with what the sender was thinking. For example, suppose I had received some information that someone in my family was quite ill, just before I left for a party. I might feel that I didn't want to cast a pall over the party and, therefore, decide to keep the information to myself. If I were worried about the information I had just received, it would certainly affect my behavior and conversation although I had decided to keep it confidential. People at the party might interpret my behavior as disinterest in them, when in fact I was just preoccupied.

Why it is that a person feels that some messages must be camouflaged or not sent will be dealt with elsewhere. For now it is important for us to recognize that while we may not understand the meaning of the multitude of messages we receive from the people with whom we come in contact, we almost certainly will pick up something.

This gets considerably more complicated when the person with whom we are trying to communicate belongs to a culture that is quite alien to us. He or she will be sending off a host of conscious and subconscious messages—and we will be sending a different host of messages back—but neither of us may be able to pick up those messages because we don't understand the codes. Worse, perhaps, we may think we are picking up one message when in fact the message being sent is a different one. (Recall the shaking of the head mentioned at the beginning of this chapter.)

Subliminal messages: You didn't know you saw it, but you did. Aside from the work of psychologist Wilson Bryan Key, who takes a very strong stand on the importance of subliminal messages (literally, beneath the threshold, or limen, of awareness) to behavior, the work of those in what is known as neurolinguistic programming (NLP) as well as my own work in intercultural communication leads me to believe that subliminal messages may be much more important for human behavior, and particularly for intercultural communication, than are conscious perceptions.

Ask a male homosexual, for example, what it is he looks for in order to be able to identify another homosexual. Certainly gays can spot each other far more easily than heterosexual males can spot them. When asked, however, the homosexual will respond that he doesn't know how he knows, he just does. Sometimes a homosexual will tell you that he can tell by looking into another person's eyes. That is a very interesting response given what we know *scientifically* about involuntary reactions of the pupil of the eye. Berelson and Steiner report on a study done by E. H. Hess in which homosexual men, heterosexual men, and heterosexual women were asked to look at a series of pictures while optical machinery measured the dilation and contraction of the pupils of their eyes. What they found was that when the subjects were shown pictures of nude men (presumably well-built), the pupils of the eyes of the homosexual men and of the women tended to dilate measurably, while the pupils of the eyes of the heterosexual men remained unchanged. When pictures were shown of nude women (also presumably well-built), on the other hand, the pupils of the heterosexual men dilated measurably (interestingly, so did the pupils of the heterosexual women, but not to the same degree as did the heterosexual men's), while the pupils of the homosexual men actually contracted measurably.[2]

There is simply no way that anyone could be *consciously* aware of several millimeters' dilation or contraction of the pupil of the eye. Yet for centuries poets and lovers have

---

[2] See Bernard Berelson and Gary A. Steiner, *Human Behavior: An Inventory of Scientific Findings* (New York: Harcourt, Brace and World, 1964).

"known" that it is possible to read affection or attraction in someone's eyes. Scientists finally devised a way to measure what others have known for centuries!

A more recent study of communication styles among Arabs argues that Arab politicians like PLO leader Yasar Arafat wear sunglasses, even when indoors, so that others do not have the ability to "read reactions" in their eyes.[3] Can anyone honestly believe that eye-pupil movement is the only previously undetected signal people send off? Every dog knows that no two humans smell the same. People are not always as aware as are dogs. Indeed, most nonverbal behavior is so much below our level of consciousness that we may simply not know it exists, but it does.

Subconscious messages: You send and receive them all the time. Subconscious messages, like subliminal messages, are below the level of consciousness. They are ideas, thoughts, feelings about which we are unaware on the conscious level. We know they are there because they will come out in dreams, hypnosis and psychotherapy. The famous "Freudian slip" lets us know it is there, even though we might deny it completely.

In his classic study of nonverbal communication in intercultural situations, Edward T. Hall introduced us to the notion of distance and time as nonverbal messages, which are certainly subliminal. He pointed out that North Americans are comfortable standing somewhere between twenty-one inches and four to five feet from another person when discussing something (the more impersonal the subject matter, the greater the distance required), while Latin Americans and Arabs prefer standing no more than a foot apart if the subject is the least bit personal. When a Latino invades the personal space of a North American, the latter becomes extremely uncomfortable and is likely

---

[3] Gary R. Weaver, ed., *Culture, Communication and Conflict: Readings in Intercultural Relations*, 2d ed. (Needham Heights, MA: Simon & Schuster, 1998).

to step back to reestablish a "normal" distance. The Latino, uncomfortable with the greater distance, is likely to move closer to reestablish a desired comfort level, to which the North American responds by withdrawing still further, interpreting this invasion of personal space as aggression, while the Latino and Arab are likely to interpret the move away as rejection.

Similarly, North Americans take the idea of punctuality very seriously. If I say I will meet you at a certain time, you expect me to be there by no more than a few minutes later than I said. In fact, though, if I am a few minutes late, an apology on my part is in order. Latin Americans and Arabs simply don't view time the same way. An hour or two delay past when they were expected would not be uncommon. A North American who didn't know this probably wouldn't have waited.[4]

Additional research on subconscious involuntary nonverbal messages was done some years ago by a group of neurolinguistic programmers. Their work, NLP, stems from work done in hypnosis and therapy, and while I believe that the claims made by this group may be highly exaggerated, their findings cannot be ignored by scholars or practitioners in the field of intercultural communication.

The neurolinguistic programming scholars argue that *physiologically* people favor certain sensory receptors over others, both as a way of taking in data from the outside world and as a way of accessing data once they are stored internally. They believe that by observing subtle body movements one can determine the sensory mode being used at the moment and also the individual's preferred mode of processing data. That is, they claim that regardless of culture, some people will prefer to access data with their eyes, while others favor the ears, and still others access and/or process data with their feelings, and that if

---

[4] Edward T. Hall, *The Silent Language* (New York: Anchor/ Doubleday, 1973).

one observes carefully enough one can tell which mode is being used. They claim that it relates directly to right- and left-lobe domination of the brain, and brain-lobe dominance is not culture-related.[5] In other words, people who are right-handed—indicating left-lobe dominance—will generally move their eyes up and to their left when they are trying to visually remember something. Their eyes will involuntarily move up and to their right when they are trying to visually construct an image. Left-handed people will do the reverse. According to the NLP people, not only do our eyes involuntarily move in certain predictable and different directions when we access visual, audio, and kinesthetic experiences, but also our breathing is different, and our posture and muscle tone change. They claim these changes in breathing and muscle tension cause changes in our voice tempo and tonal quality. If these scholars are correct in their findings—and there is every reason to believe they are—then all of us have been involuntarily sending out subconscious messages constantly about how we process information without knowing we were doing it.

Interestingly, the NLP people argue that some tasks are better accomplished by certain sensory strategies than by others. They point to the fact that the better spellers use visual recollection to achieve their goal. Also, each of us seems to favor one sensory mode of behavior over others. If we listen carefully, we will hear people tell us about their sensory preference. Some will tell us they "see" what someone else is trying to say, while others will "feel" that someone else is either right or wrong, and still a third type will tend to "hear" what they are saying.[6] What is more, we do

---

[5] The only exception the NLP people have found thus far are the people from the Basque region of Spain, which leads them to believe that those people share a genetic trait that no other group of people in the world known to the NLP people share.

it almost completely subconsciously and involuntarily—although the NLP people claim that with practice we could make them conscious and control those preferences and shift them at will. This is important because they argue that we relate more easily to someone who organizes sensory data the way we do. In other words, if we want to be more effective communicators we need to teach ourselves to communicate in a number of different sensory styles, learn to observe other people's preferred styles more closely, and then communicate with them in the style they prefer. That is, they would argue, people who keep telling you that they "see where you are coming from," whose eyes go up to either the left or right when you ask them a question, whose shoulders are tense, and whose breathing is shallow and high in the chest are visual people. If you can respond to them in their own sensory language, the NLP people argue, then the person with whom you are trying to communicate will relate to you as "one of us" on a subconscious level, and that will make you a much more effective communicator. The content of your message will be much more readily accepted. Notice the NLP people are not addressing themselves to message content. Rather, they address themselves to the way messages are communicated. The subliminal sensory code, if you will. Interestingly enough, once you have read the NLP literature you may find yourself constantly attending to those subliminal messages that you hadn't even known people sent.

---

[6] Caution to the reader: You may not have the preference you think you do. I used to think I had a visual preference because I often need to see something in writing before I understand it. Yet after reading about neurolinguistic programming, I now realize that when I look at something I don't "see it," but rather I sound out the words and therefore "hear it" in my head as I read.

The body of NLP work is much more complex than I have been able to present here, and I urge readers to become acquainted with it, if they are not now. What is truly fascinating about it from the perspective of intercultural communication is that until I became familiar with their work, it would never have occurred to me to group people by the sensory receptors they prefer to use to access the world, yet that is precisely what the NLP people do. While I do believe that their claims about what this type of communication can accomplish seem highly exaggerated, in no way do I doubt that they are on to something very important in communication in general and for intercultural communication in particular. For regardless of which other cultures someone may be a part of, if we can tune in to that person's involuntary sensory-preference style of communicating, we may be building one more bridge to effective communication.

The significance of subliminal and subconscious perceptions to intercultural communication is immensely important primarily because (a) so many stimuli are probably subliminal, and (b) they are below the level of conscious awareness so we don't consciously know they are there—and thus they are difficult to deal with.

Let us stay with these two points awhile. Key argues that the overwhelming majority of the stimuli that bombard our sensory receptors are subliminal. The evidence he presents is persuasive, and finally he argues

> ...the conscious mind merely adapts itself to the basic program established in the unconscious; *no significant belief or attitude held by any individual is...made on the basis of consciously perceived data.*[7]

---

[7] Wilson Bryan Key, *Subliminal Seduction: A Media's Manipulation of a Not So Innocent America* (New York: Thomas Y. Crowell, 1968), 16 (italics in original).

In effect, what Key is saying is that the attitudinal and value frames through which all sensory data are processed may themselves be established on the basis of unconscious or subliminal data. If he is correct in that assertion—and I believe that he is—then it becomes particularly difficult to get people to establish different perceptual frames, precisely because they do not know—consciously—what caused them to establish those frames in the first place. This relates directly to what I was talking about earlier when I discussed core beliefs.

3. Sensory Receptors: Eyes, Ears, Nose, Tongue, Skin, and More

Since the time of Aristotle we have believed that humans have five basic senses and the sensory receptors that enable us to use those senses: sight, sound, smell, taste, and touch. Modern research indicates that there are many more. For example, we have an internal kinesthetic sensory mechanism that allows us to determine which way is up (at least we can in the earth's gravitational zone) even if all other sensory receptors are nonfunctional. Key argues that there are over thirty known senses and that more are being discovered all the time. The eyes, ears, and so forth are the organs that first record external messages, but those messages have to be sent back to the brain where they are processed. Depending on our cultural conditioning and our unique individual experiences, different people can react very differently to the same stimulus. (Think of the example of the young woman who ate the fried caterpillars.) What is more, there clearly are receptors in the brain that pick up and monitor the internal messages our bodies send.

The notion that each of our senses operates independently of each other is a Western concept. Eastern thought and tradition teach that all of the senses are integrated, each affecting the others. Thus for an Asian meal, not only are the appearance, texture, and smells of the food thought to be important to the way food tastes, but the total dining environment—decoration of the room, sound level, temperature of the room, emotional climate—is thought to influence the flavor of the food. Of course, when we think about it, we realize how true that is.

It sometimes happens that through disease or accident one or more of our sensory receptors is damaged and becomes inoperative. When that happens there is an extraordinary human ability to compensate by relying even more on other sensory receptors or on the same kinds of receptors in different parts of the body. For a blind person, hearing, smell, and touch become much more important and refined receptors of sensation than they are for those of us who have vision. For the person who loses the ability to feel sensation in certain parts of the body, other parts seem to compensate. None of us is really aware of how acute each of our sensory receptors actually is or can be until we are forced to rely more upon certain ones than we would in ordinary circumstances.

Physiologically we are not born with equally acute sensory receptors. That is, in some individuals some receptors are undoubtedly more acute than in others. Some of us have especially acute vision, others have a better sense of hearing, and so on. Probably because of that physiological bias in favor of certain receptors over others, we tend to favor our stronger receptors. That is, we learn to rely more upon them. Moreover, although there are almost certainly some experiential factors involved, we recognize that some people have an ear for music, as we say, while others are tone-deaf. Some have an eye for color or form, while others seem to be oblivious to visual stimuli. Allow me here to repeat a story that a colleague told me.

The colleague and his family had occasion to visit Mexico City for the first time. They were put up at a hotel in the heart of the downtown district. When they reached their room, their older teenage son, who was studying to be an artist, ran to the window and said, "Wow! Look at the spectacular view of the city from here." Moments later their younger son (who had been out of the room until then), who plays several musical instruments, ran to the same window and said, "Dad, just listen to the sounds of the city from here."

Of course this relates directly to the work of NLP. But the fact is that some cultures do favor certain receptors over others. The example cited above may help explain why "art culture" people are different from "music culture" people. Similar examples could be found for other visual cultures (such as dancers, hairdressers, or fashion designers) as opposed to cultures in which words and/or ideas are more important (as for example with writers, lawyers, or philosophers). All of those examples, however, may depend more on conditioning than on physical acuity of the sensory receptor.

4. Decision Making: You Can Respond or Not Respond, But You Must Make a Decision

For every single bit of data picked up by our sensory receptors, a decision has to be made by us with regard to it. Is it to enter our consciousness, remain subconscious, or be ignored? Is it to be merely stored or acted upon immediately? If it is to be acted upon, how? There are a number of processes at work in each of those decisions, and while for the sake of analysis we shall discuss them one at a time, it should be remembered that they are operating simultaneously and at incredible speed.

Censor screens: Pay attention to this, not that! Obviously, we cannot attend equally to all stimuli to which we are exposed. For one thing, not all stimuli reach the sensory receptors at the same level of intensity. That is, some sounds are louder than others, some images are clearer than others. All things being equal, the louder sounds and the clearer images—the more intense stimuli—would probably be transmitted to the brain by the sensory receptors before the less intense stimuli. But things are not always equal. Some stimuli are so important or so salient to us that regardless of intensity, we are likely to pick them out first. Conversely, some stimuli are so repugnant to us or so difficult for us to handle that regardless of intensity, we are likely to pick them out last, if at all.

The first range of decisions the brain has to deal with is what appears at first blush to be a simple ordering device: What do I focus attention on, and in order to do that, what do I block out? It is simply not possible to attend to all stimuli equally. Nothing gets our undivided attention. As you drive your car home, you focus your attention on the other cars on the road, pedestrians crossing the streets, stop signs and lights, and driving conditions in general. But that does not mean that you are totally unaware of the sounds of the music coming from your car radio, the temperature in the car, the vibrations the car may be making, familiar people who may be on the sidewalk as you pass, the ache in your bones, or your awareness that you have to be home by a certain time in order to attend more fully to something else that you must do. If it were not for this ability to temporarily screen out some or even most stimuli, it would not be possible to focus our attention on anything. And as we know from computer technology, we can deal with even the most complex problems, requiring perhaps millions of discrete decisions, just as long as we can handle them one at a time, in proper order.

Although this censor screen does permit us to focus our primary conscious attention on one activity at a time, consciously sending most other inputs to subconscious storage for the time being, it does more than that. The censor screen is not something we were born with. *What we are born with is the ability to construct such a screen.* Just how that screen is to be constructed, which stimuli it will let through, and which it will block out is *both* a physical and a learned phenomenon. It is physical in the sense that some of us are born with certain of our sensory receptors being favored over others. It is learned in the sense that each of our group cultures has taught us what we ought to see and what we should expect to see. Thus in the process of being socialized into some groups and not others, we have learned what we should consider important and thus should attend to, and what is not important and is therefore to be relatively ignored. If we have not learned certain things (such as a particular alphabet), stimuli relating to those things will be perceived merely as nonsense symbols or will be disregarded entirely.

The existence of identities—and of the belief and disbelief systems that are associated with those identities—may be crucial to what is admitted and what is excluded. If I were a devout Hindu, I would be much more likely to admit messages pertaining to Hinduism and the associated beliefs that I held (like the unquestioned belief in reincarnation, with what it implies) and to screen out other identities and other belief systems that I did not hold. The same process would be true regardless of which identities were most important to me. Someone who works in the women's clothing industry sees a woman and may be immediately conscious of what she is wearing. A dermatologist might well notice her skin. A shoe salesperson might notice her shoes, while a lecher is more likely to see only her figure. Two women from the same town—one a Republican, one a Democrat—read the same morning newspaper. The Republican reads everything the Republican candidate had to say the day before, both because it is relevant to her and because it is automatically worth knowing about. If she noticed that the paper also contained a speech by the Democratic candidate, she probably wouldn't bother to read it because she knows full well that the Democrat would *not* have anything of value to say. And if our newspaper-reading Republican were to read the Democrat's speech, what she would find would be reinforcement of her preconceived belief that the candidate was a fool. Clearly, the higher I rank certain identities, the more likely I am to attend to their messages before I attend to other messages relating to other identities that I rank lower. The opposite side of the coin, so to speak, of selective attention is selective inattention. We consciously or subconsciously *do not attend* to those stimuli to which our culture has not trained us to attend.

As we have seen, learning occurs in the group one happens to be born into or that one happens to come into significant contact with. Each group teaches somewhat different responses to the same stimuli. Learned responses become part of the culture of the group. Since each group teaches its own culture, two people from entirely different groups observing the same stimuli could respond so differently in some cases that one might wonder whether, in fact, they were responding to the same stimuli.

The censor screen helps us see what we expect or want to see. It also helps us to avoid what we don't expect or don't want to see. More than fifty years ago Gordon W. Allport and L. Postman conducted an experiment that graphically illustrated the effect of stereotyping on perceptions.[8] In the experiment a large number of Americans were shown a photograph of what appeared to be a scene in a subway car. In the scene two men are standing, one black and well dressed and the other white and wearing working clothes. They appear to be having a confrontation of some sort. The white man in the picture is holding an open razor of the type men once used to shave with. Each person was asked to describe the picture to someone who could not see it. The second person would then describe to a third person what had been described to him or her. The third person, in turn, would describe it to a

---

[8] Gordon W. Allport and L. Postman, *The Psychology of Rumor* (New York: Holt, Rinehart & Winston, 1947), as reported in Otto Klineberg, *The Human Dimension in International Relations* (New York: Holt, Rinehart & Winston, 1964), 42. Although the concept has not changed, for a more recent discussion of stereotyping see Richard W. Brislin, *Understanding Culture's Influence on Behavior* (Fort Worth: Harcourt Brace, 1993), particularly 171-79.

fourth, and so on through six or seven people. In over half the cases reported by Allport and Postman, the razor changed hands from the white to the black man, and the black man became the one who was poorly dressed. Indeed, in some cases the black man was reported to be "brandishing" the razor or "threatening" the white man with it. As Otto Klineberg points out, "This does not mean that half the subjects reacted in such a fashion, since one shift in a rumor chain might be reproduced by those who followed. It does mean that in 50 percent of the *groups* this phenomenon was observed."[9] In the study the distortion was avoided in only two groups: among African Americans, for what were assumed to be obvious reasons, and among young children, who had not yet learned the stereotype. However, when this experiment was repeated approximately twenty years later at a black high school in New York City, as much distortion occurred among African American students as had been reported among whites in the original study.[10] One possible explanation may be that black students participating in the experiment had subconsciously accepted the predominant white stereotype of African Americans.

These experiments illustrate two principles involved in any communication process. Most obvious, and what is most pertinent for any discussion of intergroup communication, they show the transmutation of sensory data to conform to expectations. But they also illustrate that in any process of communication, the more steps a message must go through from its original source to its intended recipient, the more distortion is likely to occur. I have not seen a recent update of the Allport and Postman study using the same picture, but I suspect that the most significant change among whites in the intervening years would be that now they

---

[9] In Klineberg, *Human Dimension,* 42.

[10] This second experiment was reported to me in a personal communication by a student who took part in that experiment.

would report blacks carrying knives—not razors.

The point is that whites tend not to see the large percentage of black males who are well dressed or who are not carrying knives. Instead, if whites read about or see one African American on television with a knife, not only do they attend to it, but it also reinforces their preconceived belief that "blacks carry knives." We elect to attend to some stimuli and elect to screen out millions of other stimuli that we are not prepared to see or do not want to see. We must do that simply to be able to function. If we did not, the cacophony of stimuli to which we are exposed would be so overwhelming that we could not cope. But we should also be aware that while doing this allows us to focus our attention and to get things accomplished, it also distorts reality enormously. For each of us reality becomes not what is really "out there," but rather only those relatively few bits of "reality" that our censor screens have admitted into our consciousness. The remainder go unattended or at best are stored in our subconscious.

Decoding: "One if by land, two if by sea".... In this statement the fellow on the "opposite shore" had to know not only what to look for, but also what the signal meant, if any communication was to take place. Unless both the sender and the receiver of the message understand the same meanings of the code or the language used, little communication, or none, will occur—or worse, miscommunication will occur instead.

If I stand by the shore and watch the waves break on the beach, all I see are waves breaking on the beach. But if a trained oceanographer stands on the same beach and watches the same waves break, she or he can tell a great deal about the tides, storms at sea, and more. That is because she or he knows what to look for and I don't. She or he knows the codes.

If I write the word *cmoλ*, anyone who knows how to read Russian will know immediately what it means. But to anyone who does not know that code it might just as well be a nonsense syllable. When I write the English *rappel* or *belay,* people who have engaged in rock climbing—but only they—will know what I mean. To be sure, people who do crossword puzzles, play Scrabble, or are simply very well versed in the English language may know the dictionary meaning of those words, but only those who climb and descend regularly and share the same love of heights and adventure can really know their meaning.

Meanings are not transmitted; symbols are. Symbols serve as stimuli to elicit meaning in the person receiving the stimuli. One of the reasons it is possible for us to decode messages as well as we do is that communication does not occur in a vacuum. There is always a context in which communication takes place. What is more, regardless of the broad national differences among people, the people communicating in a given situation probably have at least some group identities in common. They may be in the same line of business, the same age, married, of the same education level, and so on. Interactions are most frequently between people who have several group identities in common.

The point is that each of the groups of which we are a part will have taught us its own special verbal and cultural languages, attitudes, values, and ways of perceiving the world—in sum, the group codes—and only if we know those codes well can we understand messages relating to that group identity. What is more, each of the codes we have learned is stored in our data bank. Thus as soon as any of our sensory receptors pick up a stimulus, it is immediately checked through the literally trillions of bits of data we have stored to determine if we know what it means. If we have ever learned the code, we will be able to decode the stimulus, at least on a subconscious, if not a conscious, level. We do not forget codes once they have been learned; we simply lose the ability to call them into conscious memory unless they were very well learned initially and/ or are periodically reinforced at the conscious level. People will tell you that when they were young they spoke a certain language but that they have since forgotten it. Yet under hypnosis it turns out that they can often be induced to speak the language they consciously do not remember.

Part of the decoding process is learning how to listen and watch. In the United States the presumption is that if you want to communicate with someone else, the burden of figuring out how to do so effectively rests with you. After all, it is you who wants to communicate, not the receiver of your message. In Japan and some other parts of Asia the exact reverse is the case. In those cultures the burden of understanding the communication rests on the receiver of the message. It is his or her responsibility to figure out what it is the sender is trying to communicate. In part this difference in perspective may be the result of cultural perspectives within the respective societies. In the United States we tend to think we are being ignored or misunderstood if people don't ask questions. In Japan, which has a much more hierarchical society, it would be a sign of disrespect (and ignorance) to ask questions.

Both extremes are, I think, just that—extreme. Being a white American social scientist, I can't help believing that the burden of being understood rests with the communicator. I also recognize the value and importance of learning how to listen in any communication process. For one thing, the whole point of feedback is to try to interpret what images are in the other person's head. If we don't listen carefully when they speak, we will never be able to calibrate our message so that the other person can understand and possibly accept it; we will never develop the intercultural skills we need to become good communicators.

Learning how to watch is probably considerably more important than learning how to listen. Messages that can be observed with the eyes are particularly important in decoding subconscious messages that the sender may be transmitting. This is particularly true in light of the work of the neurolinguistic programmers reported earlier. The kind of clothes people wear has already been touched upon. What about the way they walk, sit, or use their hands? How far or close do they stand when they talk to you? Do they position themselves perpendicular (with shoulders more or less pointed toward the other person) to you or parallel (with chests facing each other more or less parallel)? Do they look you in the eye when they speak? Do they bite their nails? What are their other nervous habits? The answers to these and other questions about a person's nonverbal behavior help us to achieve much greater insight into other people than verbal communication alone would convey. The trouble is, we have to learn what these nonverbal messages mean to the people sending them. Certainly not all of these nonverbal messages mean the same thing in every culture, and it is very difficult to observe these nonverbal behavior patterns in cultures foreign to our own, since we don't really know what the norms of nonverbal behavior are. By watching we can begin to find out.

Studies reveal that there are some basic differences between black and white Americans regarding distance, positioning, and eye contact. The African American male seems more comfortable at a closer distance than does the white American male, but whereas the white American will tend to stand parallel to the person to whom he is talking, enabling him to look the other person directly in the eye, the African American tends to position himself perpendicular to the person with whom he is communicating and thus tends to avoid eye contact. These same studies reveal that in general, blacks (both male and female) tend to avoid eye contact much more than do whites.[11] One

---

[11] See the study by S. E. Jones and J. R. Aiello in *Journal of Personality and Social Psychology*, cited in Stanley E. Jones, "Integrating ETIC and EMIC Approaches in the Study of Intercultural Communication," in *Handbook of Intercultural Communication*, edited by Asante et al.; see also Kenneth R. Johnson, "Black Kinesics: Some Non-Verbal Communication Patterns in Black Culture," in *Intercultural Communication* 4th ed., Samovar and Porter, 259-68.

can begin to see how important this can be in intercultural communication between, say, a white teacher and a black student. Out of cultural habit and preference, the African American student listens best by not looking directly at the speaker but rather at some neutral object like the ceiling or out the window. White teachers, unaware of this cultural difference, tend to assume, since white students avoid eye contact only when they are *not* paying attention, that black students must not be paying attention most of the time.

On the same subject of eye contact, it was reported to me by several Nigerian students that in northern Nigeria (where most of the population is traditional Muslim) it is a sign of disrespect to look directly into the eyes of a superior. Thus when northern Nigerians come to this country to study, their efforts to display respect for their teachers by avoiding eye contact may be interpreted as lack of attention or deceptiveness. Conversely, when Americans (both white and black) go to northern Nigeria, whites more than blacks, but both groups more than Nigerians, try to look their superiors directly in the eye as a mark of their attention and respect, only to be perceived as being disrespectful and discourteous.[12]

In *Beyond Culture,* Edward T. Hall reports on work being done in the field of synchronized body motion.

> People in interaction either move together (in whole or in part) or they don't and in failing to do so are disruptive to others around them. Basically, people in interactions move together in a kind of dance, but they are not aware of their synchronous movement and they do it without music or conscious orchestration. Being "in sync" is itself a form of

---

[12] Personal communication to the author by former Nigerian students.

> communication. The body's messages (in
> or out of awareness), whether read
> technically or not, seldom lie, and come
> much closer to what the person's true but
> sometimes unconscious feelings are than
> does the spoken word.[13]

The work being done in the field is truly remarkable. The problem is that the evidence is overwhelming that each group teaches a different pattern of body movement and synchronization. What is fascinating, however, is the evidence that as people begin to learn how to react to each other, over time they become more in sync with each other.

Once again, the important thing to remember about the codes—whether verbal or nonverbal—that each of the groups of which we are a part teaches is that they make communication much easier for people who are a part of the group—who know the codes—and very difficult for those who do not know them.

Human data bank: So far there are no computers as sophisticated. There is no question that the data bank we carry around in our heads is the world's most complex, most sophisticated, and fastest information-storage-and-retrieval system. Our most sophisticated computers, as amazing as they are, simply cannot begin to compete. To be certain, they can do computations much faster than we possibly could in our heads, but they have nowhere near the storage capability nor the efficient retrieval system of our brain. Researchers in the field of artificial intelligence are trying, but they are not there yet, despite Big Blue's occasional defeat of Kasparov across the chessboard. Nor, of course, are computers yet capable of reasoning on as wide a range of topics as is a human, or of feeling emotion.

In figure 3.1, I have drawn the data bank at the center of a cluster of different identities. Each of the petals in the

---

[13] Edward T. Hall, *Beyond Culture* (New York: Anchor/Doubleday, 1976), 71–72.

drawing represents one of the groups with which the individual identifies, as it did in the drawings of value structures presented earlier. This was done to remind the reader that in the person-to-person communication model presented here, the individual is a composite of all groups—and group identities—to which he or she belongs.

Stored in our data bank are:

- All the past experiences we have had, as well as the attitudes toward those experiences that we held at the time of the initial experience and the attitudes we have developed since;
- An awareness of the groups with which we identify and the shifting ranking of those identifications from context to context;
- The complete belief systems (and disbelief systems), attitudes, values, and modes of perception that each of the groups of which we form a part has ever taught us;
- A knowledge of our needs, drives, desires, and urges—in short, information about everything contained in our id;
- The memory of what behavior patterns are expected of us in each conceivable situation—our superego—and also the memory of the rewards that each group of which we are a part bestows for behaving in those prescribed ways, as well as the punishment they are likely to distribute for violation of those patterns;
- The peculiar combination of inherited and learned traits called personality or temperament which makes us each unique;
- A learned series of probabilities as to the likelihood that any particular action will produce a specific effect; and perhaps most important;
- Something equivalent to computer software we have learned (or downloaded!) which is unique for each of us and which tells us what to select from the universe of data "out there," as well as providing a program to help us process the data once it is selected.

In sum, our data banks contain not only information about everything we have ever learned or felt and a sense of who we are, defined in large part by the groups with which we identify, but also information about how to go about learning what we do not yet know.

Clearly, no two people in the world can possibly have the same information, attitudes, and values stored in their personal data banks. They simply are not part of all and only the same groups as anyone else. That is why every communication is—and must be—to some degree intercultural. Indeed, the very best that can be hoped for is that two individuals can have some more or less similar codes and values. Obviously, the more similar the data stored in their banks, the easier communication between them is likely to be. The more different the data, the more difficult communication is likely to be. A good intercultural communicator recognizes these differences and attempts to determine what is in the mind of the person being communicated with, rather than assuming—as most people do—that what is in my mind must also be in the mind of the other person. It never is.

Just as a chain is only as strong as its weakest link, so too a communication is only as accurate as its most inaccurate step. *The major problem in any communication process is the dissimilarity of data stored in the data bank.* Thus it is probably the storage of data that is more responsible for miscommunication or lack of communication than any other step in the entire process. That is why the last two chapters were devoted to helping us understand the kinds of things that get stored in our data bank and how these things then determine so much of what we see and how we behave.

Superego screen: Want versus ought. In order to describe what I mean by superego screen, allow me to present a simplified guide to Sigmund Freud. Freud argued that thought processes consist of three parts. The *id* consists of those animal drives and urges in us that crave instant gratification—food, water, safety, power, affection, and sex; what we really want and want now! (The sexual urges Freud called *libidinal urges*—coming from our libido. What made Freud so unacceptable to his Victorian contemporaries was his insistence that all people have these—including the sex drive—even as infants.) As we are socialized into the group norms, we learn how to suppress (either repress or sublimate) those urges for the sake of group cohesion. No group could survive if every member sought instant gratification of every urge regardless of the needs or wishes of other members of the group. These constraints on our behavior Freud called the *superego*—what we *ought* to do or want. Caught between what we really want and what we have been taught we ought to want and how we ought to get it, the individual develops a compromise self-image—the *ego*—which attempts to balance the inner drives and outer constraints. We speak of someone with a strong ego as having a clear picture of what he or she wants and needs and knowing how to deal with superego constraints on those needs in order to achieve his or her objectives. Conversely, someone with a weak ego is intimidated by society's "oughts" and is unable to admit to anyone, self included, that the needs and desires exist. Admitting to these needs may produce feelings of guilt for having them.

Clearly, as animals, regardless of who we are or where we were born, most of us will have similar animal needs, although for any number of different reasons—some physical, some learned—some needs will be stronger in some of us than in others. Just as clearly, each society or group has developed its own set of behaviorally acceptable norms for dealing with those needs. Thus the compromise self-image of each person has to be different. This is no small matter in facilitating communication between people socialized by the same group norms. It becomes a gigantic barrier to communication between people socialized into different sets of norms or "oughts."

Most groups have done their work of socialization so

well that most of us—at least on the conscious level—have learned to deny to ourselves that we have urges that we are not supposed to have. The urges are there, of course, but at the subconscious level. We know they are there because they can be articulated under hypnosis or in dreams or in therapy. And because they are there, despite all of our conscious efforts not to communicate to others that they are, invariably they inadvertently get sent out to others as messages. Most often our superego is strong enough to prevent them from being consciously expressed, but my own suspicion is that they "leak out" at least on a subliminal level despite our best efforts to contain them. To prevent the expression of these instinctive urges, every human constructs what I call a superego screen. By that I mean a filter we impose between the instinctive animal reactions we have to certain stimuli and the actual reactions we allow ourselves to have. I call it a superego screen precisely because it contains the information we have learned from our identity groups about what reactions to stimuli are expected and accepted. It helps us translate those inner urges into external communications that will be acceptable to the groups that are important to us.

A middle-class black hearing a racial slur in an exclusively white setting may actually want to react by punching the person who made the remark, but the superego screen filters that reaction and the message that comes out is likely to be much more moderate. A closet homosexual hearing a joke about a "queer" may also want to hit the person who told the joke, but because he may not want to reveal his true identity, he may laugh along with everyone else. Anyone sufficiently angered by something someone else may have done or said may momentarily feel capable of murder, but—when the superego screen is functioning as it is supposed to—instead, a much more socially acceptable response is substituted.

So it is with every stimulus we perceive. No matter how we might like to react, on the basis of past experiences, impulses, needs, or what have you, our reactions are tempered by the filter of the superego screen to make our reactions more socially acceptable than they would otherwise be.

Encoding: You have to learn how to quack if you want to talk to ducks. I have this Gary Larson cartoon on the door to my office.

The Far Side   **by Gary Larson**

The Far Side © 1983 Farworks, Inc. Used by permission of Universal Press Syndicate. All rights reserved.

Having decided what response would be appropriate to a particular stimulus in a particular circumstance, we still have to decide how to encode the messages we want to send. Accordingly, we must check our data bank for information about the intended recipient of the message. The more we know about that individual, the easier it is for us to choose a code in which to send our message. That is, if I know that the intended recipient of my message understands English, English will be an appropriate code for me to use in sending the message. But if I know that the person with whom I am trying to communicate does not understand English, and I don't know any of the languages he or she does understand, then I have no choice but to encode my message in some nonverbal language. The problem is, of course, that if I don't know other people's verbal languages the probability is not terribly high that they will understand my nonverbal language either.

We needn't refer merely to linguistic codes here. The same holds true for all other group identities. If I want someone to understand my message, I simply must translate it into a cultural language the other person understands and accepts. Regardless of the message we want to send, if we want it to be acted upon favorably, we had better know the cultural values of the people with whom we want to communicate and how to encode our message in terms that they can understand. That means really getting to know them.

5. Transmitters: Our Whole Body Is a Transmitter

By this time it should be quite clear that we send messages with our entire body. Each part of our body is capable of transmitting messages. What is more, it should also be clear that we send out many messages simultaneously—through our eyes, face, head, hands, skin, and muscles. To the degree that we can use all, or most, of our transmitters to communicate the *same* message simultaneously, we will

certainly be more effective in getting our message across.
The reason is that redundancy is an important part of effective communication. The more of the other person's
sensory receptors we can stimulate with the same message, the more likely that person is to understand the message the way we meant it to be understood. The problem
is, however, that there are only a very few times when we
succeed in concentrating our thoughts so completely that
our subconscious is also geared to sending the same message. Remember that at all times—even while we are trying to concentrate on sending the same message—we are
also receiving messages, and some of those messages we
receive will undoubtedly distract us from concentrating
on the message we are trying to send. Indeed, we simply
can never concentrate entirely on sending the same message precisely because part of our brain is always reserved
for dealing with involuntary internal bodily communications and functions, while another part is reserved for
monitoring all of our sensory receptors. Given that, however, the more we can concentrate on sending the same
message with as many of our transmitters as we can mobilize, the more effective our communication is likely to be.

Conscious messages: Here's what I want to say. Let us start
with the messages an individual consciously decides to
send. We can use our voice box to send verbal messages.
Not only can we control the content of the message, but
we can also control the tone to achieve our purpose. I can
say "No," or I can say "No!" My tone of voice can add the
emphasis that an exclamation mark conveys in writing.

As for nonverbal messages, whole books have been
written about how we express ourselves with our body.
The clothes we choose to wear in different situations,
whether men shave or do not shave, the way they comb
their hair and how long or short they choose to keep it,
whether they wear tattoos or nose rings, the kind, color,
and amount of makeup a woman chooses to wear—or
not wear—whether she wears tattoos or nose rings, all

transmit messages to other people about how we choose to be perceived. The reasons we choose to dress as we dress or groom as we groom are usually subconscious, of course, but the decisions we make with regard to these things are often conscious.

We can write our messages, play them on musical instruments, or send them via smoke signals. The range and magnitude of ways in which we can send conscious messages is enormous. Probably the major limitations on how we send conscious messages are the constraints of the situation (whether the intended receiver understands the languages we know), the distances involved, the number of people to whom the message is being sent, their attitudes toward us, the context in which the message is being sent, and the limits of our imagination.

The trouble is that very often, even on the conscious level, we are sending not just one message but several simultaneously. Probably that is because our mind operates far more rapidly than our ability to communicate. So that while we are saying one thing with our voice (sending a message) to one person, we may be saying something else (sending a different message) to that same person by our body movement and still something else (another different message) to a third person standing nearby. Put aside the other transmitters for a moment and consider only the verbal messages. Here again, the words may be saying one thing but the tone of voice or the speed with which the words are delivered may be saying something entirely different. Often when we really don't mean the words we are saying, we try to compensate by overly reinforcing the deceptive message by concentrating on our deception, thus not acting natural and thereby defeating our intention to deceive. It is very hard to act natural consciously, because most of the time that we are really being natural we are not conscious of the way in which we are sending messages. It is a little like walking. Once we have learned how to do it, we do it without thinking about what we are doing. When we try to be consciously aware of how we are walking, we become clumsy and unnatural in our movements.

Involuntary messages: "God I wish I didn't blush." As in walking, once we have learned to communicate, many of our messages are sent by involuntary reactions. Someone says something funny and we can't help laughing. We see something we don't like and our whole body shudders. Both these examples deal with learned involuntary responses to stimuli. They are messages in that they say to others how we are responding. Because they are learned, it means that everyone may learn somewhat different responses, and we must be very careful when we interpret these that we are doing so correctly. Because we respond involuntarily in a certain way to a certain stimulus does not mean that everyone has been taught to respond in the same way. Some of us tend to think of crying on the death of a loved one as being an involuntary response. Others of us have grown up in cultures that teach that one is never to display extreme emotion publicly. Both crying and laughing may be involuntary responses to stimuli, but we *learn*, through the groups into which we have been socialized, which is appropriate in which situation. In some cultures smiling or even giggling can mask embarrassment or anger. Not *all* involuntary responses are learned, of course. Some are nothing more than involuntary reflexes to protect us from harm, like quickly withdrawing our hands when we inadvertently touch something hot, or blinking as something approaches our eyes.

We really cannot control involuntary responses to stimuli, but please note that in many cases, which stimulus produces which involuntary response is learned. Sweating and perhaps shaking in situations where we are nervous may be involuntary messages we send, but the stimuli that make us nervous are learned. The same for blushing when we are embarrassed or turning pale when we are frightened. Often we would dearly love to be able to control those responses so as not to let other people know how we feel, but most often they elude our conscious efforts at control.

The number of involuntary messages we are capable of sending is, of course, vast. For one thing they are not all the same for everyone, even in the same culture groups. For another, different cultures teach different involuntary responses. To cap it off, not all of them are known.

Subconscious messages: Things I don't know I know. Because of the work done by Sigmund Freud and those who have followed him, I doubt that anyone today would seriously question either the existence of our subconscious mind or the fact that we send many messages without being conscious of the fact that we are sending them. Every once in a while thoughts that we are having on the subconscious level intrude into our consciousness. The famous "Freudian slip" (when we say aloud what we were thinking on the subconscious level) forces us to recognize this. Indeed, there is little doubt today that the greatest bulk of our thinking processes occurs on the subconscious level. It also seems pretty clear today that it is a good thing for us that it does. It would be too difficult for us to cope consciously with the vast number of thought processes that seem to be going on inside our brain simultaneously.

But if those thought processes are going on in the brain, it seems fairly clear that some indication of those thoughts will be communicated by us, somehow. Whether the person observing will be able to receive correctly what is being transmitted is another question entirely. But we will probably be communicating something.

Not every message we send is transmitted with enough intensity for the receiver to pick it up at the conscious level. Most often the message being sent—whatever it is—is too weak (in terms of intensity of stimuli) to be *consciously* perceptible. Subliminally, however, there is no doubt such messages are being sent and received.

Although I do not have hard empirical evidence, I am fairly certain that most subconscious messages are transmitted subliminally. It would seem to me to be logical that this should be so. In the first place I am not certain that we are sufficiently practiced to be able to control subconscious messages. It seems to me that it may be somewhat analogous to the use of certain muscles of our body. They are there, and they function at an involuntary or subconscious level all the time. But before we can gain conscious control over their use we are required to put in a great deal of effort training ourselves in control over them. The number and location of those muscles is extraordinary. Most of us at one time or another have engaged in an activity that is outside our normal range of physical behavior, and if we do it long enough, the muscles involved can hurt the next day, whereupon we are likely to say, "I used muscles I didn't know I had till now." More to the point, however, we have many transmitter muscles of which we are totally unaware. Indeed, the NLP people have shown how obvious these involuntary subconscious messages become, once we know what to look for. I am certain that we use them continually, but we have no idea—on a conscious level—that we do. Precisely because we are unaware of them, my suspicion is that the vast majority of messages we send are sent subliminally.

6. Channels of Communication:
Messages Can Only Flow Where Channels Exist

Every message in every communication must be sent over a channel. Without a channel there is no way for a message to travel. In the case of one individual talking to another, the channel is the air through which the sound travels. In the case of a broadcast, the channel is the airways. In e-mail communication, the channel is a computer with a modem. If in the first case the sender whispers and the intended recipient is too far away to hear the message, no communication has occurred. If in the second case the intended recipient does not have a radio or does not have it turned on or tuned in to the correct frequency at the time of transmission, no communication has occurred. If in the third case the address is wrong and the message never gets delivered, again no communication has occurred. One of the major problems in the communication process—but often one of the easiest to overcome—is the lack of sufficient channels of communication. The so-called hotline between Moscow and Washington was set up during the Cold War years precisely so that there would be a direct channel of communication between the leader of the Soviet Union and the president of the United States over which messages could travel, if those leaders chose to use it. That, of course, is a different problem. We can set up all of the channels of communication we want, but if the people the channels were intended to serve choose not to use them, no communication will take place. Still, having the channel there is one of the first steps to effective communication, and, in itself, the existence of the channel communicates a willingness to exchange messages. Once the channel exists there is, at least, the possibility that the parties will use it. Since certain groups may have a cultural preference for one type of channel over another, it is likely that our message would be attended to more seriously if we knew their cultural preference and transmitted our message over it.

For example, since relationships are so important to them, most Latin Americans would prefer a face-to-face communication over a telephone conversation no matter how trivial the message. North Americans, on the other hand, frequently prefer telephone, fax, or e-mail messages precisely because, at least in part, they take up less time than a face-to-face meeting would. Someone who is interculturally sensitive would adjust to those differences and act accordingly.

Another point that should be made is that if it is important that there be open communication between two persons or two places at all times, it is probably wise to be certain that there exist a number of different channels, so that in the event one channel gets blocked (for whatever reason) or temporarily does not work, another channel will be available. For example, trying to get a message through on a telephone will fail if a storm has knocked down the telephone lines; but if there is a direct radio link, messages can still get through.

In the previous section I argued that people use many transmitters to send the same message simultaneously, which is good because it helps to get the message across as the sender intended it to be received. That works best in face-to-face communication, of course, because all of the channels are available for each of the messages to travel through, so that the receiver's sensory receptors can be stimulated by every message being sent. One of the reasons telephone communication is so unsatisfactory is precisely that, although the sender is transmitting nonverbal messages along with the verbal, the only channel being utilized to transmit the message is the channel to convey the verbal message. Hence, the other messages are likely to be lost or distorted and the full communication is not being picked up by the receiver for lack of sufficient channels.

But even if the channels between sender and receiver are adequate to the messages being sent, there are still difficulties to overcome.

7. Noise: An Open Fly Makes Lots of Noise

In every communication system there is what the communication specialist calls noise. Noise is anything that interferes with the transmission of the message. It might be a baby crying and drowning out the voice of the sender in a face-to-face conversation, or the gum the speaker was chewing while he was talking, or a beautiful sight that caught the eye of the intended recipient and distracted her attention at the moment the message was being sent. Or it might be some nonverbal body movement perfectly acceptable in one's own culture but offensive in another. In the example I used at the beginning, my open fly made so much noise that none of my students heard a word I was saying. In the example where the airways are the channel, the noise might be the electrical storm that interferes with the airwaves, or the jamming of certain frequencies that some governments practice, or the accent of the speaker that causes the recipient to pay more attention to the speech pattern of the speaker than to the message. In the example of written communications, noise could be the poor handwriting that makes the message illegible, or the rain that smears the address and makes the letter undeliverable, or the psychological state of the recipient at the time of receiving the letter that prompts him to throw it away unopened.

Sometimes there is something in our minds that is so important or so all-consuming that we are simply not able to concentrate on anything else. That, too, constitutes noise with regard to communication on any other topic.

Although a problem, noise is one of the easiest problems in the communication process to overcome, provided we take it into account and then compensate for it. If the heating system or the traffic outside or anything else is making noise, we simply have to speak louder to overcome the noise level. If our message was interrupted by any one of the noises mentioned thus far in this section, all we have to do is be aware of the problem and take steps to rectify it.

Not all problems of noise in the system can be overcome completely, however. Sometimes differences in attitudes or values or other cultural differences constitute noise in a communication system. The lack of trust that often exists between individuals, groups, or nations can constitute noise in the communication process. Someone from group "us" may not be able to hear what someone from group "them" is saying, not because the intensity of the message is too low or because of the lack of linguistic or other codes, but rather because the mistrust between them and us is so great that virtually nothing "they" said would be received by "us" as it was intended. That constitutes noise. Often the mistrust between the parties is so great that no direct communication can occur. In those cases the only way to establish any communication is through some neutral third party whom both trust, through whom at least some communication can occur. In those kinds of situations there can probably be no direct communication until at least some modicum of trust can be established so that the level of noise in the system is reduced.

In short, not all noise can be dealt with by increasing the intensity of the message or by removing the cause of the noise.

8. Role of Feedback in Communication: "Is This What You Mean?"

Perhaps the most important method for overcoming the deficiencies of the communication process is feedback—the return to the sender of data about the results of his or her communication effort. Feedback is built directly into some communication systems, particularly that of face-to-face communications. If the receiver of a message in a face-to-face communication does not understand some portion of the message being sent, she or he can immediately convey that lack of understanding to the original sender, who can then attempt to correct the deficiency. This is precisely why face-to-face communication can be so effective. But we are constantly getting feedback from the environment as well. Earlier in this chapter I said I wanted to add Dean Barnlund's model of the communication process as a refinement of my own. Here is the place to do that. The reason I feel that Barnlund's model is important is that feedback from both the environment and individuals is such an integral part of it. Also it conveys better than my own, I think, the continuous nature of the communication process.[14]

Barnlund starts with a hypothetical case of a single person (Mr. A) sitting alone in a doctor's office. There are three sets of cues Mr. A can and does attend to simultaneously: what Barnlund calls public cues, private cues, and nonverbal behavioral cues. Mr. A assigns meaning to these cues (decodes them). He also transforms (encodes) these stimuli to which he attends into "neuro-muscular sets," which in turn are available to others in the form of verbal and nonverbal cues.

The public and private cues themselves can be any stimulus, verbal or nonverbal, to which Mr. A can attend. To be a public cue these stimuli must be "part of, or available to, the perceptual field of all potential communicants." Private cues are stimuli that are not automatically available to anyone else (for example, the fact that there is a pain in his stomach, or the memory that he has an appointment in an hour that he must keep). Whether public or private, both types of cues in Barnlund's model must have been created prior to the event under analysis and must remain outside the control of the persons under observation.

Nonverbal behavior cues are the behaviors of Mr. A himself—seeing his own reflection in a mirror, straightening his tie, or changing his position in the chair. They differ from public and private cues in that they are initiated or controlled by Mr. A himself, whether consciously or unconsciously. To all of these cues Mr. A can and does assign positive, negative, or neutral values based on his prior conditioning. But he does not attend to them simul-

---

[14] The Barnlund model is taken from Dean C. Barnlund, "A Transactional Model of Communication," in *Language Behavior: A Book of Readings in Communication*, edited by Johnnye Akin, Alvin Goldberg, Gail Myers, and Joseph Stewart (The Hague: Morton, 1970), 44-61.

taneously. Instead, he selects from the plethora available as his attention or gaze shifts from one to another. Barnlund points out that given the opportunity, the individual will probably attend to those stimuli to which he has assigned positive meanings and values rather than attend to meanings to which he has assigned negative values.

From Barnlund's description, the reader should get a sense of the richness and complexity of *intra*personal communication alone. Remember, no other individual has yet been introduced into the model. This communication and steady flow of feedback are occurring from within the individual and between the individual and the environment.

As soon as another individual is introduced into the model (Mr. B in Barnlund's model), the picture gets infinitely more complicated. In the first place, the other individual has the option to attend (or not to attend) to all of the public environmental cues that Mr. A was exposed to. He will assign different meanings to many of those cues than Mr. A did, to be sure, but the same public stimuli are there for anyone to attribute meanings to. He will also bring with him his own set of private cues to which Mr. A will have no more access than Mr. B has access to Mr. A's private cues. More important for the study of intercultural communication, however, each will try to attend to the verbal and nonverbal behavior cues of the other, attributing meaning to each of the cues based on his own past experience, attitudes, and values rather than on the other person's. What is more (and this is the reason I have included this in the feedback section rather than elsewhere), each person will begin to regulate the cues he provides for the other, each may recognize (Barnlund says *will* recognize) the possible meanings the other may attach to his actions, and perhaps even more important, each will attempt to interpret his own acts as if he were the other. In other words, Mr. A will interpret any act of Mr. B's through his own cultural filter. If Mr. B shakes hands (or doesn't shake hands), Mr. A will assign a meaning to that act based on what Mr. A knows that act means in his own culture. It would almost never occur to Mr. A to wonder whether that act might mean something entirely different in Mr. B's culture unless, of course, Mr. A was interculturally sensitive.

While there may be problems with Barnlund's model, I like it because it conveys the sense that the communication process is an ongoing, continuous one rather than a series of discrete events and also because it represents the incredible complexity of that process. Add to that how much more difficult it becomes (1) when the two individuals in the exchange do not share a great many cultures in common (and therefore will attribute different meaning to the same cues) and (2) when more than two people are involved.

Let's leave Barnlund's model now and take a look at an exercise that Harold Levitt devised many years ago to demonstrate the necessity for feedback in communication.[15] In that exercise a volunteer is given a sheet of paper with six or seven rectangles drawn on it. The drawing is the message, and the volunteer is asked to communicate that message to a group of people who will attempt to draw it from his or her instructions as precisely as possible. The exercise is done twice: once without any feedback and the second time with feedback. Almost invariably, without feedback no more than 20 percent of the people (and usually considerably less) are able to approach correct representation in their drawing of the placement of the rectangles on the page. With feedback—that is, with participants asking as many questions as they feel are necessary in order to draw it correctly—between 50 and 90 percent are able to make a very close approximation of

---

[15] Harold Levitt, *Managerial Psychology*, 2d ed. (Chicago: University of Chicago Press, 1964), chap. 9.

the correct placement of the rectangles. The exercise with feedback usually takes *at least* twice as long as the same exercise without it, but the results in terms of precision of communication are obviously worth the extra time.

One of the more interesting things about the experiment is that when the sender estimates, immediately after attempting to communicate without feedback, how many in the audience got the message more or less accurately, the sender almost always overestimates the number he or she believes to have received the message correctly. Invariably the sender thinks he or she has communicated quite well. Similarly, if the audience is asked immediately after they have completed the exercise, without feedback, how well they think they have drawn the rectangles, they too overestimate their degree of success. Many more people think they have done the drawing accurately than actually have. Now, if no feedback were built into the system, both sender and receiver would believe they had communicated quite well, even though they had not. Only when the exercise is repeated, introducing feedback, do both sender and receiver begin to estimate realistically how well or poorly they are communicating.

An even more interesting aspect of this exercise is that it is one of the only examples I know where one can actually compare visually the message as it was sent and the message as it was received. In recent years I have taken the drawings done in my classes without feedback and put them up on the wall on one side of the room, separating into two columns those by students who said they had done the drawing correctly and those by students who said they had done it incorrectly. On the other side of the room I have put on the wall all of the drawings that were done with feedback, dividing them in the same way. Through this procedure some startling facts became obvious:

1. The overall contrast in the degree of correctness between those drawings done with feedback and those done without becomes immediately apparent.

2. The variety of opinions on how correct *correct* really is also becomes apparent. Invariably there are some drawings by students who said they had done them incorrectly that are far more correct than other drawings by those who said they had done them correctly. Similarly, there are always some drawings in the "correct" section that are far more incorrect than many of the drawings hanging in the "incorrect" section.

For me this is a striking example of how badly we generally communicate most of the time, even when the message is culturally neutral and far from threatening. If we can't communicate accurately how to draw approximately six rectangles on a page among educated adults who are more or less culturally homogeneous, how can we ever hope to communicate accurately with someone with totally different perceptions, attitudes, values, and belief systems?

Rectangles drawn on a page in a particular arrangement is a relatively unambiguous message. The more ambiguous or abstract the message becomes, the less accurately it is likely to be communicated. If culturally similar people have difficulty communicating among themselves how to draw rectangles, how can people who are culturally heterogeneous possibly communicate about subjects like democracy, justice, equality, or social change?

More than anything else, what repeated use of this exercise (in any number of different cultural settings) has taught me is that when I ask people if they understand what I have said and they nod their heads yes, all I can be sure of is that the muscles that connect their heads to their necks are in good working order.

What depresses me most about the implications of this exercise is that most of the time we tend to attempt to communicate without feedback or at least without adequate feedback. There are a number of reasons why this is so:

1. Communicating with feedback often takes at least twice as long (sometimes much longer), and none of

us has the time to use feedback in every communication we attempt.

2. The process of giving feedback, aside from being time-consuming, is exhausting. When I ask the people who have volunteered to do the exercise how they feel when it is over, "tired," "drained," or "exhausted" are the words I hear most often. None of us has the physical or psychological energy that would be required to communicate with adequate feedback all the time.

3. Most of us, I'm afraid, would rather *not* have the feedback on how well or poorly we have communicated. We would, I think, rather just assume that we have communicated well and let it go at that.

4. Mass communication systems such as television, radio, newspapers, and magazines simply do not have direct feedback built into their systems. They can tell if their number of viewers, listeners, or readers drops, but there is little or no direct way that they can know how their audience has perceived the material they have put out. When you consider that most people learn about events around the world—of vital importance to their well-being—almost exclusively via the mass media, one is forced to pause and wonder how accurately they can possibly be getting the message.

Having said this, however, I must add a positive note. Difficult as the communication process may be, the fact is that all of us communicate all of the time. We may not do it as well as we could, but we do it. What's more, we do it at times with people who share few of the perceptions we hold. In other words, difficult and complex though the process may be, we do it constantly, so we know it is not impossible. Understanding these complexities should not paralyze us; rather, knowing how complex the process is, we should approach it somewhat more realistically than we have previously. Just doing that could automatically make us better intercultural communicators.

Propositional Summary for Chapter 3

It is not possible to not communicate: Everything we do or don't do, twenty-four hours of every day, communicates something to whoever is there to observe us. We may not be communicating what we intended to communicate, or we may not even be conscious that we are communicating something, but communicating we are.

The purpose of communication: Virtually all human communications are attempts to achieve goals. The goals may be as simple as wanting to buy two tickets to the theater or as complex as trying to prevent terrorist bombings. Regardless of the complexity of the message, consciously or unconsciously the sender is always trying to achieve a purpose by sending it.

Communication is a process: Communication and feedback to and from the environment and everything in that environment is a continuous process that only ceases when we die.

The same communication process operates at all levels of analysis: It operates whether one considers intra- or interpersonal communication, intra- or intergroup communication, or intra- or international communication. The specifics of how that process operates change as one changes the actors and settings, but the process remains constant.

Senders and receivers: Since this work focuses primarily on human communication, the individual is the basic unit of analysis. The individual is simultaneously sender and receiver of communication. There is no way one cannot be.

Messages: Message is a communication term, used in the strict sense to mean any stimulus that can be perceived by the nerve endings in any of our sensory receptors. Each discrete "bit" of data that fires even one or two nerve endings in any of our receptors can be viewed as a message. More commonly, we think of a message as being a pattern of perhaps hundreds of thousands of bits of data that make up an intelligible whole, but depending on the circumstances, the individual bits themselves can be viewed as messages. The stimuli by themselves have no meaning. People attribute meaning to the stimuli, thereby transforming them into messages.

Nonhuman messages: Unquestionably, the greatest number of messages we receive, every moment of the day, are from nonhuman sources. The eyes pick up everything within their line of vision; the nerve endings on the skin react to temperature as well as touch; the ears pick up the sounds around us; the nose picks up a variety of smells—all at the same time. We may be receiving messages only subconsciously, but we are receiving them nonetheless.

Human messages, verbal and nonverbal: The human animal is continuously sending out a multitude of messages simultaneously. The vast majority of the messages we send are nonverbal, and we are most often not aware that we are sending them. Everyone is communicating so many different messages at the same time (even if they are not trying to mask them) that it is difficult in the extreme to know to which messages one should attend.

Subliminal messages: Subliminal means beneath the threshold, or limen, of awareness. Subliminal messages are that vast number of messages we send and receive without being conscious of the fact that we are either sending or receiving. The work of the neurolinguistic programmers has focused primarily on the nonverbal messages all of us send and receive all of the time.

Sensory receptors: Sensory receptors are those body mechanisms that allow us to take in information from the external environment. While Aristotle identified five senses—sight, sound, smell, taste, and touch—modern research indicates that there are many more.

Decision making: For every single bit of data picked up by our sensory receptors, a decision has to be made by us with regard to it. Is it to enter our consciousness, remain subconscious, or be totally ignored? Is it to be merely stored or acted upon immediately? If it is to be acted upon, how? There are a number of processes at work in each of those decisions, and it should be remembered that they are operating simultaneously and at incredible speed.

Censor screens: Obviously we cannot attend equally to all of the stimuli to which we are exposed. Some stimuli are so important or so salient to us that regardless of level of intensity, we are likely to pick them out first. Hence, the first range of decisions the brain has to deal with are what to focus on and what to block out. That process is taken care of by our censor screens.

Decoding: Meanings are not transmitted, symbols are. Decoding is the process by which the individual checks his or her data bank to determine the meaning, if any, he or she has learned to ascribe to a particular symbol.

Human data bank: The data bank in everyone's brain is the world's most complex, most sophisticated, and fastest information-storage-and-retrieval system. It contains not only information about everything we have ever learned or felt, but also information about how to go about learning what we do not yet know.

Superego screen: To prevent the public expression of our most primitive instinctive urges, every human constructs for him- or herself what I call a superego screen. It is a filter we impose between the instinctive animal reactions we have to certain stimuli and the actual reactions we allow ourselves to make. I call it a superego screen because it contains all of the information we have learned from our identity groups about what reactions to stimuli are expected and accepted by those groups.

Encoding: Encoding is the reverse of decoding. It is the process by which we decide what symbols to use to present the particular message we want to send. Normally we choose those symbols that we believe the recipient of our message will be able to decode.

Transmitter: Our entire body is a transmitter of messages—our voice, eyes, face, head, hands, skin, muscles. Each part of our body is capable of transmitting messages. To the degree that we can use all or most of our transmitters to communicate the same message simultaneously, we will certainly be more effective in getting our message across.

Conscious messages: Conscious messages are those we consciously choose to send. They can be verbal or nonverbal. The range and magnitude of ways in which we can send conscious messages is enormous. Probably the major limitations on how we send conscious messages are the constraints of the situation, the distances involved, the number of people to whom the message is being sent, their attitudes toward us, the context in which the message is being sent, and the limits of our imagination.

Involuntary messages: Involuntary messages are those messages we send that we cannot control. Both crying and laughing may be involuntary responses to stimuli, but we learn through the groups into which we have been socialized which is appropriate in which situation.

Subconscious messages: Humans send messages without being consciously aware that we are sending them. Although I have no empirical evidence to substantiate it, I am fairly certain that the vast majority of all the messages we transmit are subconscious.

Channels of communication: Every message in every communication must be sent over a channel. Without a channel, there is no way for a message to travel. One of the major problems in the communication process—but often one of the easiest to overcome—is the lack of sufficient channels of communication. Once the channel exists, there is at least the possibility that the parties will use it. Without the channel, the certainty is that no communication will occur.

Noise: In the communication sense, noise is anything that interferes with the transmission of a message. Every communication system contains noise. Noise is another of those problems in every communication system that is *relatively* easy to overcome—provided we know it is there.

Role of feedback in communication: Perhaps the most important method for overcoming the deficiencies of the communication process is feedback—the return to the sender of data about the results of his or her communication effort. Communication with feedback often takes at least twice as long as communication without it, but the difference in degree of similarity between the message sent and the message received tends to rise sharply when feedback is introduced.

Communication at Different Levels of Analysis: Organizations, Groups, and Nations Don't Communicate, People Do

Communicating at Different Levels:
Individual, Group, National

Organizations, groups, and nations don't communicate, people do—in the name of the unit they represent. Thus, in a sense, at every level of analysis, all communication among people is, on the one hand, interpersonal communication, that is, people talking to people. On the other hand, people change roles, depending upon whom they are talking to, and with that role change comes a completely different form of communication. A male chief executive officer talking to his female secretary does not communicate the same way as when he is talking to his male peers on the board of directors, to a potential customer on the golf course, to his friend at the gym, or to his wife and kids at home. All of these may be interpersonal communications, but the power relationships are different in each, and the role which the CEO sees himself playing will alter the kind of communication that occurs. Is he speaking for himself or for his organization? If he is speaking for himself, which self is he speaking for?

In this chapter, I will examine how communication operates at each level of analysis. What must be kept in mind, however, is the level we are examining. The actors change at each level: How they perceive their own roles and how they perceive the roles of the people with whom they are communicating changes from level to level.

The Role of Power in Communication: Power Is Both Relative and Contextual

If all communications have a goal or purpose—conscious or otherwise—then to one degree or another all communications become, in part, an attempt to exercise influence. It would be an overstatement to say that all human behavior is power-oriented. It would not be an overstatement to say that there is an element of an attempt to exercise influence in all human behavior. Even if that attempt to influence you is only to get you to understand my message the way it was intended, that itself is a form of influence. The part of behavior that is power-oriented is that part that attempts to exercise influence over others or to prevent others from exercising influence over us.

I use the terms "power" and "influence" in the broadest sense to mean how people, groups, and/or nations try to get what they want from other people, groups, and/or nations. How do they go about trying to fulfill their needs, goals, and values? What happens when the individual's needs are not the same as the needs of the group or of the nation?

As used in this book, power is a relative term. It is the ability both to influence others to behave in a manner desired by the one wielding the power and the ability to prevent others from exerting influence on one's own behavior. Is power, then, the same as influence? Not quite. Power is the *ability* to exercise influence and the *ability* to prevent influence from being exercised over oneself. Whether the individual, group, or nation will choose to use the power it has in a given situation is another point entirely. Some individuals, groups, and nations—at different times and/or in different contexts (for whatever reasons)—may choose not to use the ability they possess. But if they have that ability to exercise influence—whether they use it or not—then I consider them powerful. If in fact they do not have the will to use the power they have—as distinct from ability— that is a different matter. In that case I would argue that, to the degree they are lacking in will (everything else being held equal), their power is diminished.

People, groups, and nations tend to try to maximize their power in order to get what they want or to prevent others from being in a position to influence them. To the degree that representatives of groups or nations are chosen (by whatever process) to be leaders, they are chosen because their constituents believe that those individuals will protect and/or advance the interests of the group. If the leaders come to be seen by the people they are supposed to represent as not exercising maximum influence to obtain desired group goals, those leaders are likely to be replaced by others considered more capable of doing the job. The union leader who is perceived by the rank and file as accepting too many of the demands of management runs just as great a risk of being replaced by a more militant leader as does the head of a company or government when he or she is perceived by the stakeholders or constituents as not representing *their* interests. Even military dictators have been overthrown when enough of their constituents became disaffected.

Nations seem to be the entities that make the broadest definition of what are legitimate ways to exercise influence. Every religion in the world and every state has some sort of "thou shalt not kill" prescription written into its basic law. One may not kill another person from the same nation merely because one believes it is in one's own interest to do so. But if one kills as a soldier, to achieve what is believed to be in the national interest, there is rarely any punishment. Under certain circumstances, such as in time of war, if one of "us" kills enough of "them," instead of being punished, he or she will be considered a hero and may even get a medal. However, coercion (of which killing is the most extreme form) is only one way of exercising influence. Every day of every year, every individual, group, organization, and nation exercises at least some influence over other individuals, groups, organizations, and nations, and only rarely do they rely on coercion as the means of achieving their ends.

Because there are many different ways in which influence may be exerted, there are many different manifestations of power. One speaks of the power of the pen or the power of the purse or the power of an army. But power is contextual. That is, the pen, or the purse, or the army is powerful only if it is used in an appropriate context. A brilliant, logical discourse may influence the behavior of people who hear it in the quiet of a lecture hall, but it could not possibly have any impact on them if they were in the midst of a battlefield. They simply would not be able to hear it. Conversely, in a world where increasing attention is paid to the battle for the human mind, guns, rockets, and nuclear weapons may be totally inappropriate as instruments of power in a great many contexts. Yet for many individuals and small terrorist groups, this is their way of letting the world know they exist.

Individuals, groups, and nations have power, in part and under some circumstances, because of their ability to coerce, but in *greater* measure and in many *more* circumstances they have power because they are able to *persuade* other individuals, groups, or nations to want the same things they want. And most often persuasion takes noncoercive forms.

To present arguments in a way the other party can understand and accept as being in his or her or its own best interest is perhaps the most common and most effective form of persuasion. That is why a chapter like this is essential in a book on intercultural communication. Successful communication with another individual, group, or nation means, if nothing else, that you were able to *persuade* the other to understand your message the way you intended it to be understood. If you have convinced others to do or think something you wanted them to do or think because you were successful in convincing them that it was in *their* interest to want the same thing you wanted, you have been successful indeed. Clearly, the more different culturally the other person, group, or nation is from you, the more difficult the process of exercising that influence will be. If I am doing something only because I feel you are forcing me to, I will probably do it only halfheartedly in the first instance, and the moment your back is turned I probably won't do it at all. But if I am doing something because I am convinced that it is in my own best interest to do it—or because it makes me feel good—you can be certain that I will do it with persistence and perseverance.

Sam Green's experience in Guatemala (see page 50) presented earlier is a perfect example of that. He put the government's message into language the Indians could understand.

Another example I can cite occurred early in 1987, at the height of the Tamil-Sinhalese ethnic conflict in Sri Lanka. At the time I was deeply involved in trying to find a peaceful solution that both sides could accept. The conflict had reached the stage where I was convinced that the mass of ordinary people on both sides wanted peace and would settle for compromise short of what they might otherwise desire. I had become convinced that politicians on both sides were pressing the war for political reasons. I was in the country doing research on the problem, trying to think of something that the then president of Sri Lanka might consider worth the price of compromise. After all, he was an independently wealthy man, from a very respected family, who had been a successful politician all of his life and had now achieved the pinnacle of political power. He knew as well as I, however, that history would be his final judge. An idea finally hit me. I did some research and discovered that professors of international affairs, as well as parliaments of the world, were eligible to nominate candidates for the Nobel Peace Prize. When I met with him, I told him of my intention to nominate him for the Nobel Prize, if he could bring about a peaceful resolution to the conflict. That was in February of 1987. When I returned to the United States, I was asked to testify before a congressional committee looking into the conflict, and I told them of my plan. In July the Sri Lankan president and the then prime minister of India, Rajiv Gandhi, came up with an agreement which was meant to bring peace to the island country. It didn't, but as soon as the agreement was announced, the U.S. Congress did nominate both heads of state for the Peace Prize. On reflecting on why it didn't work, I realize now that no one thought about offering the head of the Tamil separatist movement something that he might have wanted more than an independent Tamil homeland. He was not even given the prestige of being one of the signers of the agreement, hence he had nothing to gain by accepting it—and he didn't.

Let's now go from matters of state to the totally trivial. A few years ago I had some houseguests for an extended period of time. I had shown them where things were, how to handle little quirks in the house, and some house rules that I wished them to honor, one of which was to clean the lint trap in the clothes dryer when they were done with it. For some reason that was the one they ignored, and I found myself getting more and more annoyed every time I went to put my clothes in the dryer and found a dirty lint trap. Since this was so trivial I felt stupid making an issue out of it, yet

I found myself growing increasingly annoyed over the months. One day I happened to be in the basement when they were doing laundry and said: "I don't know whether you have noticed, but the design of this dryer sucks (which was absolutely true). They put the lint filter on the inside, just under the opening of the door. Every time you take your clothes out you get lint all over them. The only thing I have found helpful is to clean the filter *before* I take the clothes out. It doesn't work 100 percent, but it sure helps." I never found a dirty lint filter after that.

Are these examples of manipulation—trying to get people to do what you want? Of course they are. But as I have been arguing all along, most communications are attempts to get people to do things you want. My argument here is that if you want to be successful at it you have to put the message into terms that are meaningful to them.

What many scholars and practitioners fail to see is that power rests as much or more on the ability to persuade as it does on the ability to coerce. Influence can be, and often is, exercised without the persons being influenced being aware that it is happening. Certainly people will do what others want within limits in order to gain access to the things (material or nonmaterial) they desire. That is why in relations between weak and powerful individuals, groups, or states, coercion is for the most part not necessary to achieve the long-term policy goals of the more powerful. As early as 1934, Charles E. Merriam wrote:

> Power is not strongest when it uses violence, but weakest. It is strongest when it employs the instruments of substitution and counterattraction, of allurement, of participation rather than of exclusion, of education rather than of annihilation. Rape is not an evidence of irresistible power in politics or in sex.[1]

---

[1] Charles E. Merriam, *Political Power* (New York: Collier Books, 1964), 179.

An attractive instrument of power is anything, material or nonmaterial, possessed by one individual, group, or nation that another desires and seeks to obtain by doing what the possessor wishes. Of course, there are limits on what one will do in order to achieve certain goals, but those limits are relative and contextual. In order to achieve a higher education—if that is perceived by the individual as important and/or desirable—one may sacrifice a great deal (leisure, money, time), but rarely will one sacrifice his or her family.

If someone is hungry and another person produces more food than he or she can consume, the hungry person is much more likely to pay the price the one with food asks (which means doing what the person with food wants) rather than to use violence. The hungrier an individual, group, or nation is, the higher price it will pay to get the needed food. A moderately hungry man is not likely to kill in order to obtain food, but a starving man is.

This is not to say that coercive instruments never work. They do—particularly in the short run. But they often create enduring hostility, which may be more damaging to the long-run interests of groups than any apparent short-term gain may have been worth.

While there is no space in this edition to enter into a detailed discussion of the components of power, I have found it useful to look at five basic components, most of which can be applied on the individual, group, or national levels.[2] The first component I considered was wealth, both material and human. Does the individual, group, or nation have the material resources—be it money, machines, or whatever—to accomplish its goals? As for human wealth, what are the talents and skills available? The second component was organization, both formal and informal. "In unity there is strength" is not just a cliché, it is an

---

[2] For a more complete discussion of the components of power, see the first edition of this work.

absolute fact of power. The better organized or more co-hesive the group or country, the more powerful it will be. The third component was information, both basic and specific. Does the individual, group, or nation have the information it needs to function effectively? It's not only the quantity of information it has that is important (it could suffer information overload), but also does it have the right and timely information it needs to achieve its goals? Status, both ascribed and acquired, was the fourth component I considered. What is the status of the indi-vidual, group, or nation, both in its own eyes and in the eyes of others? Finally I looked at will, both conscious and subconscious. Does the individual, group, or nation have the will to survive and prosper? Certainly the greater the will (everything else held constant), the more likely its goals will be achieved.

Until now very few communication specialists have been prepared to deal with the power aspect of the com-munication process. On the other hand, most political scientists have failed to recognize the importance of cul-tural differences in the situations they study. *It is one of my most deeply held convictions that the study of intercultural com-munication informs the study of political behavior. It is also my contention that a study of communication that ignores the power dimension of any relationship is missing a critical element.*

Intra- and Interpersonal Communication

Intrapersonal Communication: "Know Thyself" Really Makes Good Communication Sense

When I first came across the term *intrapersonal communica-tion*, I didn't like it at all. My first reaction was: Most of us don't talk to ourselves, so why use a term like that? Hav-ing thought about it and worked with the concept for some years, I have come full circle and now believe it is the most important part of the communication process over which we do have some control.

There seems to be an incredibly large gap between the enormous amount of information about ourselves stored in our subconscious and the amount we are able to bring to *conscious* awareness. What is more, we seem to be surprisingly poor at listening to and interpreting the multitude of messages our bodies continuously send. To be sure, I can recognize the signals when my body tells me that it is too cold or too warm or whatever. When I recognize the signal, I can respond to it or not. If I decide to respond, it is I who makes the conscious decision to either turn down the air conditioner, move to a warmer place, or put on a sweater.

What is more, there is always a plethora of conflicting internal messages that continually bombard us, to which we simply cannot attend simultaneously and to which we sometimes decide not to attend. "I'm cold," "I'm hungry," "I'm tired," "I'm thirsty," says the body. "Forget it for now," you say. "The teacher has assigned this chapter tomorrow, and like it or not I am going to sit here and read it before I attend to anything else." Any of these messages could become so loud and create so much noise in our internal communication process as to give us no alternative but to attend to it. For instance, our eyes have a way of closing when we are tired that effectively puts an end to our reading.

While most of us would not normally think of any of this discussion as intercultural, from one perspective it is. That is, there is going on within us a competition for attention among our various identities. The fact that you sit and read these words instead of going out, perhaps to party with friends, means that, at the moment at least, your identity as a student (if that's what you are) is taking precedence over some other more socially oriented identity, and you are doing what a student is supposed to do. Sometimes, however, it is important to attend to those other identity needs first so that you can turn your attention, without internal noise, to tasks which may be more demanding.

Most of our needs, goals, and values are, of course, subconscious and remain so most of the time. We simply cannot bring everything into conscious awareness simultaneously—nor should we. We couldn't function if we did. On the other hand, we are able to function and pay attention to things that engage us, or which we enjoy doing, because our unconscious is taking care of so many of the functions our bodies must attend to. Some researchers have argued that at any given moment the human mind has the capacity to deal consciously with "7 plus or minus 2 chunks of information."[3] That is, as we turn our conscious attention from one thing to another, either from our external environment or from internal signals, something must drop out of consciousness, at least temporarily. No problem there. The important question, however, is whether we can call into conscious awareness those attitudes and values that have so subtly been put there while we were growing up. Therapeutic and hypnotic evidence indicates that we can. But therapy and hypnosis are extreme methods of getting at the information. It seems to me that some rather intense and honest introspection may be able to achieve at least some of the same results. Having once brought these attitudes, values, beliefs, or whatever into conscious awareness, we can deal with them one way or another. Once we realize what they are, we may decide to change them or keep them exactly as they are, but at least our decision will be conscious.

It is purely axiomatic to argue that the more we know about ourselves, the more effective and accurate our communication is likely to be, all else equal. The interesting thing to note is how much less we know about ourselves than we think we do. How well do we know what we are really trying to achieve every time we try to communicate or what our own personal and group cultures actually are?

---

[3] Robert Dilts, et al. *Neuro-Linguistic Programming: The Study of the Structure of Subjective Experience*, vol. 1 (Cupertino, CA: Meta Publications, 1980), 54.

In a useful conceptualization of how individuals communicate, Joseph Luft and Harrington Ingram developed what they called the Johari Window to help analyze human interactions.[4] (See figure 4.1.) Luft and Ingram argue that in every communication there is an "open area," which includes information known both to ourselves and most other people. On the personal level this might include such public information as our height, gender, and approximate age.

Figure 4.1

	Information Known to Self	Information Not Known to Self
Information Known to Others	Open	Blind
Information Not Known to Others	Hidden	Unknown

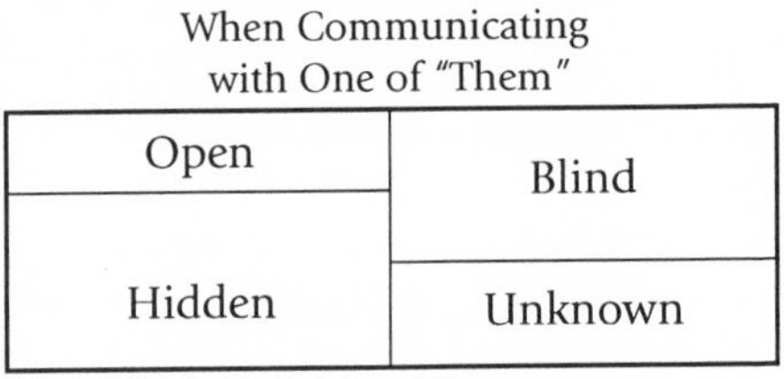

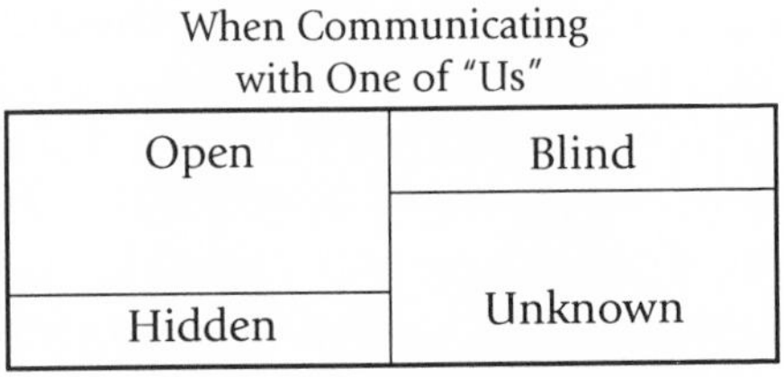

When Communicating
with One of "Them"

Open	Blind
Hidden	Unknown

When Communicating
with One of "Us"

Open	Blind
Hidden	Unknown

---

[4] Adapted from *Group Processes: An Introduction to Group Dynamics*, 3d ed. by Joseph Luft. Copyright © 1984, 1970, 1963 by Joseph Luft. Reprinted by permission of Mayfield Publishing Company.

The "blind area" contains information that others know about us but of which we are not ourselves aware. This might include such things as nervous habits or prejudices we might have that are obvious to others but not to ourselves. We are even frequently blind to how others perceive our personality.

In the "hidden areas" are those things we know about ourselves that we usually try to keep hidden from others, usually information about ourselves of which we are not very proud. Individuals, groups, and nations all have a great deal of information they try to keep hidden. Just think for a moment of some of the things about yourself which you try to keep hidden from most people. The "unknown area," of course, contains information about ourselves that neither we nor others know is stored there. This frequently includes much about how our core beliefs were formed.

In the Luft and Ingram model the space taken up by these four areas changes depending upon our relationship with the persons or groups with whom we are communicating. We tend to have a much larger hidden area and a much smaller open area when communicating with one of "them"—a person or group with whom we do not share a great many identities and therefore whom we know only vaguely or really don't trust. The less one identifies with or trusts certain people, the less one is likely to want to reveal about oneself. That is because of our fear that they might use the information they have about us against us. On the other hand, we are much more likely to be open (to have a large open area) when communicating with someone who is one of "us"—that is, someone we know well and do trust.

To the degree that an individual wants to operate more effectively, it seems to me that the blind and unknown areas have to be greatly reduced. That has nothing to do with others. That has to do with getting to know ourselves. To the degree that there is information stored in those areas about which we are unaware, we will be less effective communicators. To the degree that we are able to become conscious of what is stored there, we are that much more likely to become more effective intercultural communicators and may even become happier people.

Getting to know, consciously, *how we perceive others* may be as important to successful intercultural communication as getting to know our own perceptions. I am *not* referring here to getting to know their attitudes and values. That is important, of course, and we will discuss it shortly. Rather, I am referring here to getting to know how *we* perceive others—including the motivations we attribute to others. For example, if I have biases against people who are short or tall, black or white, Catholic or Jewish, Tutsi or Hutu, or Republican or Democrat, I ought to be consciously aware of that *before* I try to communicate with them. If those biases are there—and we would be less than human not to have some—then I think we ought to make them conscious, at least to ourselves. Because America was a racist, sexist, homophobic, and anti-Semitic society, particularly while I was growing up, it is likely that I am somewhat racist, sexist, homophobic, and anti-Semitic myself. Knowing that enables me to fight those feelings, but in order to fight them I have to consciously recognize that they exist, probably in the inner core of my belief system. We may not be able to erase some of those biases entirely, but making them conscious can help us to examine them more rationally and ask ourselves on what they are based and whether they have enough merit to be retained, or whether we might not want to revise them.

Not all of these expectations are biases in the true sense of the word. Rather, they are incorrect attributions we make about how *they* are likely to think or behave in certain situations. Indeed, there is an entire field of study within social psychology called attribution theory. What this branch of learning examines is the motives we attribute to others—correctly or incorrectly—in order to explain their behavior.

There is nothing that another person does or does not do to which we do not attribute *some* motive. If someone from our culture extends a hand, we simply assume that the motive is to shake hands, and we react instantly by extending ours, without having to think consciously at all about "why he did that." It is precisely because we have learned so well to interpret the expected behavior of our own groups that we can function so easily with other people from those same groups. On some level of consciousness we think we know very well why *we* do what we do. The problem is that we have no yardstick but our own with which to measure why those from another group do what they do. Thus we tend to judge them by the wrong measures, and of course, we are more likely to be wrong than right. All of us can think of examples, I am sure. One that comes to my mind was the year my son, who has lived more than half of his life in Israel, came to visit me in the United States. I was about to go out shopping, and I asked him if he wanted to join me. He was talking on the phone at the time I asked him, and instead of answering in words he gave me a nonverbal sign extending his fist, palm down, and then thrusting out his fingers. I took the sign to mean "go," so I did. When I got back, he asked me, rather irritated, why I hadn't waited for him. I said I thought he had told me to go. "No, I told you to wait." he said. Only after we reconstructed what happened did we both realize that I had attributed exactly the opposite meaning to his hand signal than he had intended. We both laughed. We attribute attitudes and motives to others not necessarily because these attitudes and motives are correct but rather because we think they are correct. We simply cannot help thinking that they are correct if we are unaware that different people have different attitudes and values. Thus *it is our perceptions of them* that will determine our attitudes and behavior toward them rather than what they are like or what their motives really are.

Interpersonal Communication: Getting to Know You

Since every individual is culturally unique, every communication involving humans is, and must be, to some degree intercultural. In no way is that a problem. I am convinced that simply recognizing the fact can help us communicate much more effectively. For once we recognize the intercultural nature of all interpersonal communication, we can then apply everything we know about intercultural communication to making those relationships more effective.

We simply cannot remind ourselves too frequently that everyone is culturally unique and that the perceptions and identities I have in my head are probably not the perceptions and identities that are in the heads of the other people with whom I must deal. Just reminding ourselves of this will force us to try, by whatever means possible, to determine just what it is that is in the other person's head. Interestingly enough, to the extent that we are nonjudgmental and can communicate to others that we will accept them no matter what their attitudes and values, the more likely they are to reveal more of those attitudes and values to us. That's the kind of thing that makes for effective intercultural communication. I am also convinced that one of the reasons Mr. Rogers's television program has been so successful for so many years is that he really does convince kids that he truly likes them just the way they are.

The more different the value structure of the other person is from our own, the more difficult communication will be. It is always hard to understand why the other person does not see things the way we do. But regardless of how different the values may be, it is better to get them out into the open and look at them consciously than to allow them to go unexamined, thereby creating noise in the communication system.

As with everything else I have discussed in this work, the more we understand our own and the other person's cultures, the more effectively we will be able to communicate. The less well we understand them, and the less we deal with them on a conscious level, the more difficulties and miscommunications there are bound to be in any relationship. If it is important enough for us to communicate, then there is really no choice but to spend the time and effort to try to understand the other person's perceptions, attitudes, values, and beliefs so that we can have some common codes through which to communicate.

In chapter 3, I presented a model of the communication process. If you go back and look at figure 3.1 you will see that it is really a model of the interpersonal communication process: one person communicating with another. The groups with which each person identifies will be different—and, therefore, so will their perceptions be different—but that is what makes any interpersonal communication also an intercultural one.

It seems to me that regardless of context or level of analysis, if there is another human with whom I want or need to communicate, I can do so most effectively by determining those group identities we share and then start to build from there. And while I am certain that most of us do this intuitively, what I am suggesting is that we make the effort more systematic and more conscious.

The place to start, it seems to me, is by first identifying the people with whom we are trying to communicate. What do I know about them? Using the Johari Window model, there will be some things about them that are "open" and that therefore I will know immediately, or at least I will have some first impressions that will have to be checked later. Just looking at other people will establish quite a few of their identities. From the way they dress and talk I will probably be able to make some judgments regarding their level of education, their class background, and the like. I will probably be able to detect from their accent or dialect not only the country they are from, but also the part of the country (assuming, of course, that I am familiar with the language they speak and their country as well).

If they are from my own country, I might be able to identify the city they are from. I might also, merely on the basis of their physical characteristics, be able to tell the ethnic group to which they belong. Now, one has to know the country from which the other person comes fairly well to be able to establish so much within the first few minutes of conversation. This illustrates at the outset why it is easier to communicate with someone whose cultures we know than with someone whose cultures we do not. If we know what to look for, we can decipher the codes immediately. Not knowing the codes makes it that much more difficult.

Aside from those immediately apparent "open" and "blind" bits of information about the most obvious identity groups to which the other people belong, which we pick up instantly, a few minutes of conversation could reveal their names (which will further help me identify their ethnic groups), their occupations, whether they are married or have children, where they went to school, what they studied, and a host of other specific identities. A series of questions no more personal or probing than is normally acceptable at a cocktail party in the United States reveals enough about the other people for me to determine whether I am interested (a) in pursuing the conversation any further and, if I am, (b) in exploring further those identities or experiences we share in common. The "Oh, you lived in Boston, too" or "Gee, I love to sail, also" establishes those first identities we share in common, which can sustain the conversation through its first minutes. There is nothing magical about any of this. All of us do it all the time, whenever we meet a new person. We do it so quickly and so subconsciously that we don't think about what we are doing. I believe, however, that if we were to make the process more conscious, we would be more thorough and might ask better questions, the answers to which are important to know if we want to communicate more effectively with this person. Be careful though. It doesn't apply in all cultures. In American culture people want to know what you do. In other cultures they frequently want to know what family you are from. If you have started asking questions of someone from another culture and the person is reticent in answering, maybe you have asked the wrong questions, and should change course. Similarly, you may find that people from certain other cultures will ask how much money you make, how much you paid for your house or car, and so on. You may not want to answer these personal questions, in which case it is quite appropriate for you to change the topic.

Assuming that we do want to continue the conversation by establishing which group identities we share with the other person, we are "building bridges," so to speak. That is, we establish common identities, in effect, to say to the other person "Hey, you are one of us," or perhaps more important "I am one of you." What we are really doing by establishing these common identities, where we find them, is building trust. The more "we" groups we can establish between us, or at least the more important these groups are to both of us—the more trust will be established. Aside from our earlier discussion about the importance of trust in communication (see chapter 2), recall from our discussion of the Johari Window model that the more trust is established, the larger the other people's open area becomes. Thus to the degree that we establish these "we" linkages, we can probe deeper and deeper and get to know more about the other person's attitudes and values. We may not know which identities are most important to our newfound acquaintances—meaning that we may not know how they rank the attitudes and values we suspect them to have, on the basis of what we know about other people of the same identities—merely by a few minutes' worth of conversation. But if we think about it for a moment, it is startling how much we can know about other people in a very short time. The first conversation with another person will in no way tell us all we need to know to communicate effectively, but it may establish whether there will be a second conversation. If enough common identities and interests are established, the likelihood is that there will be.

It often happens that many of the people we have to work or associate with are people with whom we do *not* share a great many similarities of either identity or perception. Still we must work with them. As we saw in chapter 3, it is much less difficult to communicate with someone with whom we do share many common codes. But if communicate we must, it probably pays for us to probe in order to find whatever common identities may exist. The more we can find, the more bridges we will have built toward the other person.

If we are going to be in a work relationship with someone whose value structure is different from ours, it is important to the successful completion of our tasks—whatever they may be—to understand the other person's values as well as we can. We don't have to accept those values as our own, but we had better understand them and try to accept them nonjudgmentally. That is why so much work is being done today on what has become known as "cultural diversity in the workplace." You may not like "them," but frequently the law, and/or increased profits, if it is a business, require you to work with "them." Similarly, to the degree that our own attitudes and values conflict with the other person's, there are times when it can be useful to bring those differences out into the open and other times when we may want to keep our own concealed. That is a matter of strategy, but we had better know what those differences are.

Cultural Diversity:
Who Are All These Strange People?

Let's stick to this question of cultural diversity for a moment. Originally it became an issue in the United States when civil rights laws were passed in the 1960s and 1970s to combat the effects of years of racial segregation. "Affirmative action" originally was shorthand code for hiring minorities—particularly African Americans. Somewhere along the line women got added to the list of groups of people that companies were supposed to hire. This inclusion of women coincided with the breakdown of the nuclear family. Divorces were on the rise, and more women needed to find employment. At about the same time there were changes to the laws on immigration, and increasing numbers of Hispanics and Asians were also entering the workforce. Suddenly predominantly Anglo-Saxon Protestant males, who had dominated the American workforce from the beginning, were being forced to work alongside people who were very different from them. Although federal, state, and city governments did the most to adjust the imbalances in the workforce, corporations also started hiring increasing numbers of these "different" people. Let's make no mistake about it, however: They did so, initially, because they had to. It was the law. Only later, after the difficulties of the initial adjustments had been made, did corporations, in particular, come to realize that this diversity in the workplace was an asset. Instead of looking at things from one perspective, over time the infusion of different perspectives was adding to increased innovation at the workplace and better outreach for sales to groups which were until then ignored. Some examples might illustrate the point. Had Hispanics within the Chevrolet corporation felt empowered (meaning, had they felt that what they had to say mattered), one of them might have been able to tell upper management that their idea of selling a new model of car called the "Nova" under that name in Latin America wasn't a particularly good one, since in Spanish *nova* means "no go." Eventually Chevrolet got the message, but not until after they had spent a fortune trying to market a car whose name said it wouldn't go.

Then there was Chiclets trying to sell in Latin America

packages of chewing gum in boxes of a size affordable to the mass of U.S. consumers but not the vast numbers of poorer Latin Americans. But once the company listened to a Mexican marketing person and began packaging the gum in smaller, affordable boxes, Chiclets sold like wildfire. Today the business world is increasingly aware of the need to adapt marketing and other corporate strategies to the different cultures of both their employers and their customers. The lesson American managers are learning is that, among other things, intercultural awareness leads to the realization that "we" can do a much better job of selling to "them" if we can identify them as one of "us."

With the increasing number of diverse people entering the workforce, one would think that the workforce culture would change and become more diverse. That may be happening, to some degree. Certainly the literature said it would. But there is another factor at work which I recognized one day in my course on intercultural management. An African American woman, who was studying for her Ph.D. and who had been working in industry for a number of years, was giving a report on just this subject. The course was taught at night to accommodate people who were working, as was she. As she spoke on how the corporate world was changing, I was struck by her appearance. She had her hair tightly braided and made into a bun in back. Although very feminine, she was wearing a blue blazer with a matching skirt. Instead of a blouse, she wore a man's button-down shirt and tie. She spoke perfect middle-class standard English, and her vocabulary was very much the vocabulary of corporate America. In the midst of her talk I said to her: "You know what? Corporations haven't changed to accommodate the influx of new diverse groups, rather you have become a white male." She was a little startled by my comment, and we all talked about it for a while, and what we came up with was the operation of the same phenomenon as was noted in the United States generally. The majority of people who live in the

United States today are not white Anglo-Saxon Protestant males, but they were the ones who established the norms to which everyone else who came later was expected to conform. Similarly in American industry, they too were the ones who established the cultural norms, and to get ahead one is expected to assimilate. That certainly is changing somewhat, but it is changing more slowly than one would have expected, and the reason probably is that old norms die hard. For better or worse, people have assimilated, and these assimilated folks are going to be looking for people like themselves to work with. Hence the ones promoted first, and most often, are going to be the people who are the most like the people doing the promoting.

Steps in the Communication Process: How Many Steps Does Your Communication Have to Go Through?

Let us turn now to another important rule in communication: *The more steps a communication must go through to reach its intended destination, the more likelihood there is of distortion. The more culturally different the individuals involved are, the more likelihood there is of distortion.* With all of the difficulty *any* two individuals have in communicating effectively, pause a moment and reflect on what happens to a message each time another person who is culturally dissimilar is added to the process. For the sake of argument let me say that we are sending one message through five different people: Alice, Bob, Carol, Dave, and Emily.

Let us also say that the message will be passed in a face-to-face communication, with feedback in each case, from Alice to Bob, then from Bob to Carol, then from Carol to Dave, then from Dave to Emily. Let us suppose that each individual shares many of the identity groups with the person from whom he or she is receiving the message. Let us also suppose that there is trust in each of the two-person communications and that each person is going to work very hard to relay the message as exactly as he or she possibly can. Remember that there can be no more effective communication than a face-to-face, two-person communication in which the individuals share a large number of identity groups and in which there can be instant feedback (both ways) over a multiplicity of channels. There simply is no situation in which better communication can occur. Given all of that, even if we assume that there would be only a 10 percent distortion in each transmission of the message—which is probably a very optimistic assumption—there would still be at least a 40 percent distortion factor by the time the message reached Emily. Unfortunately for the communication process, in some circumstances the picture may be even gloomier than that: The decrease in the amount of message transmitted at each step may increase at an exponential rate. That is, if we assume that 10 percent of the message could be lost in the transmission from Alice to Bob, we have to assume that 20 percent *of the original message* could be lost in the transmission from Bob to Carol (the initial 10 percent from Alice to Bob plus an additional 10 percent from Bob to Carol); 40 percent could be lost between Carol and Dave; and by the time Emily receives the message from Dave, 80 percent of the original message could have been lost. Remember also that we are talking here about communication among people who are more or less culturally homogeneous. The more cultural differences we add, the more distortion there is likely to be. Just imagine trying to explain, through an interpreter, to a villager from rural India who has never seen electricity, how a microwave oven, a computer, or any other electric appliance we take for granted works.

Thus it is one of the most basic rules of communication that if one wants to minimize distortion (it cannot be eliminated), one must try to send the message through as few steps as possible, preferably on a face-to-face basis, between people who know and trust each other. This is simply a law of parsimony. Having said that, however, we will have cause in a moment to demonstrate instances in which it pays to violate that rule in order to ensure the message gets through.

Networks: It's Not What You Know, It's Who You Know

How many times have we heard the expression, "It's not what you know, it's who you know that really matters"? The fact is that there is a great deal of truth to that statement. But it's not just the people you know that is important. Equally important are the people your friends know. That is what constitutes networks. *Networks of people whom we know and trust are among the most important channels through which messages flow.* Probably the most important channels of communication for human behavior are the networks of people who know and trust other people. People are persuaded to buy a certain product, vote for a certain candidate, or do or think all sorts of things largely because of the personal influence that is exerted—sometimes subtly, sometimes not—by people we know and trust.

We have already seen that the most important network in the life of most people is the family. Beyond the immediate family, in a great many cultures, the next most important group is the extended family or kinship groups. In Western cultures that is less true. There, it is often people we call friends or acquaintances whom we know and trust. In either case, however, these people are capable of influencing us (and we, them) because we know and trust them. In either case it is trust that makes the system work.

Before we look at some illustrative cases, let us consider the extent of these personal-acquaintance networks. We are constantly reminded of how small a world it is every time we meet someone who knows someone else we know. Indeed, we keep saying that the world is con-

stantly "getting smaller." At M.I.T. a number of decades
ago researchers decided to investigate that proposition seriously to determine accurately just "who speaks to
whom?" Underlying that research was a basic hypothesis
that if one were to go through enough steps, everyone in
the world would be interconnected in an informal communication network with everyone else.

At least since Magellan, if not since Alexander the Great
and before, merchants, warriors, students, proselytizers,
and travelers—and in our own day, anthropologists, mis-
sionaries, Peace Corps volunteers, and people who surf
the Internet—have gone out to virtually every community
in the world, tying each of those communities (at least
indirectly) with the others. What is more, because of the
multiplicity of identity groups one can think of and the
inevitable overlapping of people from all over the world
in many of the same identity groupings, this becomes increasingly possible. Conceptually it is possible to imagine
small remote communities being totally isolated from the
rest of the world, but for the most part we are forced to
conclude that, in fact, linkages probably do exist among
nearly all the groups in the world. A picture of the linkages probably would look something like figure 4.2.

Figure 4.2

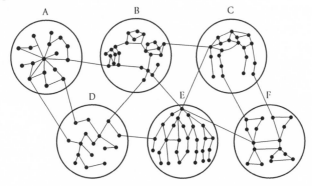

As soon as one person from A (say Athens) traveled to B (say Babylon) and got to know only one person from Babylon, he was instantly tied to Babylon's communication network and thus—going through enough steps—was within easy communication distance to everyone in Babylon. That is not to say that our traveler from Athens got to know everyone in Babylon but rather that the person in Babylon he did get to know spoke to other people in Babylon and knew many of them well (in my terms, was part of many identity groups in Babylon). Those people in turn were each part of their own network of acquaintances and identity groups with whom they communicated easily, and so on, so that, in fact, everyone in Babylon was linked by communication networks with everyone else in Babylon.

Having logically established the communication interconnections that exist in the world, the M.I.T. group directed its attention to the number of steps required to reach everyone within a given country and then the number required to reach everyone in the world. They established that anyone in the United States—sending messages exclusively through personal acquaintances—could reach anyone else in the United States in six steps, at a maximum, and that anyone in the world could reach anyone else in the world in fourteen steps.[5]

Figure 4.3

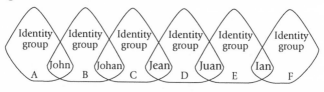

---

[5] Ithiel De Sola Pool, "Communication Systems," in *Handbook of Communication*, Pool et al., eds. (Chicago: Rand McNally, 1973), 3-26. It is from this work that the concept used in first the play, and then the 1993 film, *Six Degrees of Separation*, is taken.

Let us consider again the impact of face-to-face communication among individuals who are "one of us"—in other words, who share some identity group in common with us. Consider figure 4.3. John, who is a member of identity groups A and B, may want to pass a message to Johan. Because they share common membership in group B (and thus presumably speak B's language and value B's belief systems), they may be able to communicate at a relatively high level of understanding. Further, because both are members of group B, there is likely to be a higher degree of trust between them than there would be if they were not both members of the same identity group. Having received the message from John, Johan can transmit the same message to Jean because Johan and Jean are both members of group C. John would have had difficulty communicating with Jean because he wouldn't necessarily speak C's language or share C's values, attitudes, or perceptions. What is more, as a C, why should Jean trust an A like John?

Assuming relatively equal socialization into each of the groups, Johan, being bicultural (a member of both groups B and C), would have no more trouble communicating with Jean than he had with John. But whereas he communicated with John in B language, he would communicate with Jean in C language. (I don't necessarily mean only verbal languages here.) Similarly, the same message could be passed on to Juan by Jean, speaking D language, while Juan passed the same message to Ian in E language, and so on.

Earlier, I argued that the more steps a communication must go through before it reaches its destination, the more distortion there is likely to be. Thus I postulated the rule that one should go through the minimum number of steps possible in any communication in order to minimize distortion. That rule is certainly correct. But now we are faced with another rule that says that communication between individuals from groups who trust each other is likely to be much more accurate—and accepted—than between individuals from groups who do not. Faced with two rules that are equally correct but contradictory, how do we know which one to follow? We don't know, for all situations. Each situation may be different, and we just have to use common sense to know which rule is more applicable. For example, if the groups concerned really distrust each other significantly or are totally different in their values, then it is probably a better bet to take our chances with the distortion and communicate through individuals who at least trust each other. After all, if John and Jean don't know each other's language or don't trust each other, very little communication will occur anyway. It is better to use an intermediary who may distort somewhat but who at least will be trusted enough by Jean to get a hearing and who will get the message in a language (cultural or otherwise) he understands and presumably can relate to. Indeed, all of the literature in communication indicates that this is the most effective way to get messages accepted from one cultural group to another. Within a group of people who know and trust each other, on the other hand, eliminating extra steps is probably the best course of action.

The good communicator knows that it is better to take the chance of some additional distortion creeping into the message—by adding an extra step somewhere in the process, if necessary—than to take the chance that the message will stop at a hostile, or less than trusting, receiver. If the sender of the message is really interested in seeing that message reach its ultimate destination, it doesn't matter that another step is added.

Empirical tests have repeatedly shown that people who attribute a statement to someone they trust are likely to believe it, while if they attribute the same statement to someone they distrust, they tend not to. No surprise there. That is the kind of result one would expect to find, but the implications of this result are far more important to effective interpersonal communication than one might expect.

What is implied, at least in part, is that in some, if not most, communications the message itself may be less significant than the attitude of the receiver toward the sender. If we trust the sender, we tend to trust the message. If we distrust the sender, we tend to distrust the message regardless of content.

What is the significance of all of this to interpersonal communication? The significance is that *the more* intracultural *we can make any interpersonal communication, the more effective it is likely to be.* Sometimes that may mean trying to build bridges of trust to another person by identifying—and strengthening—the bonds created by group identities we may share. That means constant probing, an openness, and a willingness to understand—and accept as valid for the other person—values and attitudes with which we may be in complete disagreement, to accept the validity of another person's beliefs and recognize that ours are not as absolute as we once thought. Openness on our part will ideally be met with at least increased openness on the part of the other person. With openness can come increased understanding, thus serving to strengthen and accelerate the spiral of trust and enhanced interpersonal communication. It also takes a great deal of very hard work.

Environmental and Historical Impact on Groups: Ireland and India

Sometimes it is not at all clear how decisions are made. Sometimes decisions just seem to happen. Allow me to present some examples of how environment and history can have impact on groups and how they can react. Environmental and historical factors often have a major impact on the perceptions and behavior of groups. Either the group deals with them—consciously or subconsciously—or it dies. This is as true for private corporations, fraternities, and universities as it is for whole societies. I think that the more conscious any group can make these environmental and historical constraints, the better able the group will be to cope with its environment. For some—perhaps many—groups, however, these factors are rarely looked at consciously. Let me give just one example of an environmental factor—life expectancy—and see how two different groups (in this case whole societies) dealt with it but not in a conscious way, to the best of anyone's knowledge.

Life expectancy in Ireland during the nineteenth century hovered somewhere around fifty years of age. In those days the country was a land of relative deprivation. There was not a lot of food to go around. It has been said that in the nineteenth century Ireland's major export was people. The Irish are predominantly very religious Roman Catholics. One of the implications of that identity is that artificial birth control is wrong. Catholics are taught to value the natural process of procreation. Given that cultural value, how did the Irish cope with the problem of overpopulation? No one really knows when the group confronted this environmental problem, but somewhere along the line they did. And the way they did so was rather clever, I think. Somehow it evolved that it was inappropriate for Irish women to marry before the age of thirty or so. Take the biological reality that women can have children roughly between the ages of thirteen and fifty. That would be thirty-seven childbearing years. (Leave aside the 63-year-old woman who, not long ago, gave birth through artificial insemination. That is a late twentieth-century creation.) Given that artificial birth control is not acceptable to the Irish, if Irish women married young, think of the overpopulation problem that Ireland would have had. To the best of our knowledge, no group of elders or other authority figures sat around and said, "Look here, we have a problem, you know, and if we don't make it culturally unacceptable for women to marry before the age of thirty we will be in serious trouble." No, it just doesn't work that way. Rather, cultures evolve and change to meet environmental needs, or they perish—and many do. Now contrast that with India.

India in the nineteenth century was even more economically deprived than was Ireland. It was so bad that average longevity at the turn of this century was approximately twenty-eight years.[6] Faced with that environmental reality, if India had adopted the same "acceptable" marriage age for women as the Irish did, the society would have perished long ago. Instead, faced with Indian reality, somehow it evolved that the preferable age of marriage for an Indian woman was around twelve or thirteen. That way, not one precious potential childbearing year was lost. If the woman couldn't expect to live beyond twenty-eight, at least she had fifteen or so good years in order to propagate the species. And since more than half of all the children she had were certain to die before the age of five, not one of those precious years could be wasted if Indian society was to survive.

Please don't misread these examples. I am not saying that these societies—or anyone in them—made conscious decisions on how to deal with their environmental reality. Rather, I am saying that the cultures adapted to their environment, and that if they had not, they might have perished. While I realize these are extreme cases, I present them because they illustrate my point, which is that every group is confronted with environmental realities. Every group must deal with those realities in one way or another, or it will perish. Some groups may not adapt as well as others. There is no rule that says every group must survive. Throughout history many have not.

Intra- and Intergroup Communication

Groups: What Are They?

The first thing that has to be said in any study of communication within or between groups is that groups, as such,

---

[6] I recognize, of course, that the figure was so low because of the high infant mortality rate, but that in no way affects my argument.

don't communicate, people do, either collectively or in the name of their groups. Thus in a very real sense, all intra- and intergroup communications are at some level also interpersonal communications.

Perhaps because some formal groups such as organizations, corporations, bureaucracies, and nations have a legal identity separate from the people who comprise them, we sometimes forget that it is, after all, people who do the communicating for them. Thus if we want to communicate more effectively, either within groups or with other groups, we had better get to know as much as we can about the people with whom we will be communicating. Regardless of how much we may know about their group, it is imperative to know as much as we possibly can about the personal perceptions of the people with whom we must actually communicate. With which groups do they identify most closely? To what degree do their attitudes and values deviate from the attitudes and values of the groups of which they form a part?

Go back to figures 1.8 and 1.9 in chapter 1. At the center is the individual. The individual is a part of all of the cultures that surround him or her. In the discussion in chapters 1 and 2, the assumption was that most of those cultures represented were large identity groups, but actually some of them undoubtedly are small groups and formal organizations of which the individual forms a part. One will be as small as a family. One will be as large as a nation. When the officials of two corporations sit down to negotiate, the fact that they are both members of the identity group called fathers or husbands or urbanites or any of a hundred different identity groups they share is useful information to have. But presumably in the context of that specific encounter their different role identities as officials of a particular organization will become their primary identity, and therefore, their behavior is likely to represent the culture of the organization or group they are officially representing more than any other. Other individuals representing the same two organizations or groups, but bringing to the situation different identities and values, would surely behave somewhat differently, but the organizational or group culture would still dominate their behavior in that situation. That may be true in many instances, but in many intercultural cases it doesn't happen that way. Two businesspeople who clearly have an interest in working with one another may not do so merely because they share that interest. One may want to get to know the other as a person first, to establish a relationship and start building trust. The other, perhaps an American, may want to get down to business right away, and may even hope to sign a contract after the first meeting. Not likely in most of the world.

It has sometimes been argued that if we had women heads of state instead of men, there would be less tendency to go to war to settle disputes (a) because women are less aggressive than men, (b) because they are more inclined to nurture than men, and (c) because their identity as mothers would make them less likely to risk the lives of their children and the children of others in battle. So far, however, at least four of the women who have served as prime ministers of their countries—Golda Meier of Israel, Margaret Thatcher of Great Britain, Indira Gandhi of India, and Sirimavo Bandaranaike of Sri Lanka—have chosen military solutions to national and international disputes as readily as their male predecessors did. Clearly none of them was going to let her identity as a woman and mother interfere with doing what she perceived any prime minister in her position would do, and that was to fight.

Next let's try to get a better handle on what we mean when we talk about groups. Groups come in a plethora of types and sizes. They can include everything from a nuclear family to a country of hundreds of millions of people. Their purposes can be as diverse as making love or making war. Therefore, before going into a discussion of intra- and intergroup communication, it is important for us to differentiate those characteristics that groups have in common.

What is more, many of the different characteristics of groups will have a profound impact on the type of communication they attempt and the way communication occurs both within and between groups.

While every group has an identity, not every identity group is a group in the formal sense. That is, identity groups do not necessarily make decisions, maintain boundaries, or perform the other functions that most sociologists claim all "groups" are supposed to perform. An informal group may develop on the basis of some shared identity, and the people involved may begin to perform some of those functions, but as I have used the term thus far, identity groups per se are abstractions at a higher level of analysis.

As soon as a number of persons get together to perform any function, they have become at least an informal group. Every functional group has goals, and an informal group is no exception. Often those goals are unstated and implicit. They can be as informal as a group of friends who get together periodically to study or chat over coffee. Sometimes an informal group is so informal the members are not even aware that a group has been formed. In any event, whatever the goal, and however implicit or subconscious it may be, in order to achieve that goal, certain functions have to be fulfilled. At a minimum, arrangements must be made about where and when to meet. This implies that there has to be some direct internal communication within the group. Those channels may be sporadic and informal, but they are channels nonetheless. As soon as those channels become so formalized as to require different individuals or subgroups to perform specific tasks to carry out group functions, I would argue that they have become formal groups or organizations.

What I am proposing here is a categorization of groups based on the kind of communication patterns that exist. The major distinction between groups, viewed this way, would be their primary mode of communication. If they rely solely on informal communication channels to perform group functions, I would call them informal groups. If they have available to them routinized and formal channels of communication to perform those functions, I would call them formal groups or "organizations." However, it must be realized that both formal and informal groups use informal communication channels where they exist, but since informal groups have no regularized channels of communication available to them, they must rely solely on informal channels. As soon as formal channels develop, no matter that they sometimes use informal channels as well, they have become (by this definition) formal organizations.

I would consider the staffs of various institutions, such as schools, hospitals, libraries, fire departments, or bureaucracies, also to be formal groups. Whether the fire department is volunteer or paid need not concern us here. Neither should whether the institution is public or private. All of the institutions I have mentioned here have formal, regularized, and possibly prescribed channels of communication.

By viewing groups this way we can compare different groups and ask the same kinds of questions of them all. We can ask the same questions about groups of friends, workers, veterans' organizations, unions, private corporations, public bureaucracies, national states, and international organizations. Every group, from an informal association on up, has by virtue of this definition certain functions that must be performed. Two of the things that distinguish groups, then, are (1) *which* of those functions they perform, and (2) *how* they perform them. By this definition, every group has goals, which reflect or embody its values or the values of its members. The values and ranking of values that each group reflects is one of the major characteristics that distinguishes one group from another. The preferred ways in which groups perform the functions needed to achieve their goals also distinguish one group from another.

How are decisions made within groups? That, of course, depends in part upon the kind of group it is. Quite logically, informal groups make decisions informally, while formal groups usually have specific rules and regulations for how decisions are to be made. Simply by definition there could not be any formal procedure for decision making in an informal group, whereas there is usually a formal provision for a formal group.

Regardless of whether the group is an informal or formal one, and regardless of what the procedures for decision making are supposed to be, in practice most decisions in most groups are made by elites of that group. Indeed, it is the ability of some people to make decisions which have impact on other people that makes them elites in the first place. Regardless of the type of group one considers, that is the definition of elites: people who have the ability to make decisions which affect other people. The more impact they have on others, the higher on the elite pyramid they probably are.

Those who exercise the most influence over the greatest number of people I call primary elites. Those who exercise somewhat less influence over fewer people I call secondary elites. And finally, those who exercise just a little influence over still fewer people I call tertiary elites. But all of them have the ability to exercise influence—they have power. More will be said about elites and decision making below.

Intragroup Communication:
How Do We Communicate among Ourselves?

Recall from our discussion of premise 8 in chapter 2 that group culture is that peculiar symbiotic relationship between the collectivity and the individuals who comprise it. Their collective culture becomes the group culture at the same time as the group culture becomes, in part, their personal identity. Hence to get to know the culture of any group one has to know the perceptions, attitudes, values, identities, beliefs, and disbeliefs of the members of the group.

In the diagram of the communication process between individuals presented in chapter 3, the "petals" surrounding the data bank represented the identity groups to which individuals belong. In the model of the communication process within groups presented here (figure 4.4), the "petals" represent the different people in the group. Note that no two groups are likely to have all and only the same members. Each of the individuals in the group brings to it his or her own perceptions, attitudes, values, identities, beliefs, and so on. Collectively, the people who make up the group have a group memory and are the carriers of the group culture. "This is how we do things." "This is how things ought to be." The people who are there now learned it from those who were already there when the individual joined the group, and those individuals taught it to those who came later.

The individual, by his or her very presence in the group, changes the group somewhat. The smaller the group, the greater the impact a single individual can have on it. Still, every individual has the potential to impact even the largest groups. On the other hand, the individual him- or herself is changed by the group—at least in the context of that group. I may act one way at home or with friends, but there is no question that I act differently at work. And the reason this is so is because there is a culture of accepted behavior at work that is different from the culture of accepted behavior at home or with friends. Indeed, there are different accepted behavior patterns with different groups of friends.

Recall that the same person is part of many groups simultaneously. Thus, each individual in the group is not only constantly being socialized into the culture of this group, but at the same time is (a) bringing the cultural values of other groups to which she or he belongs into this group, and (b) bringing the cultural values of this group into his or her other groups.

It is a complex process, ongoing all of the time. Just as we are constantly sending and receiving messages simul-

Figure 4.4 <u>Intragroup</u> Communication Process

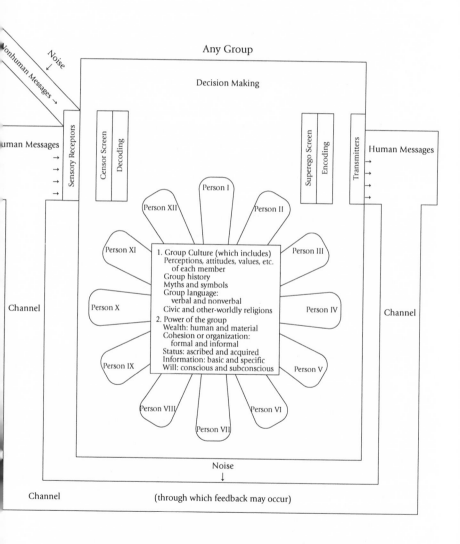

taneously, all of the time, similarly, we are simultaneously bringing other group values into this group and sending out this group's values into the other groups to which we belong. It is not a conscious process, but clearly, there is no way we could not be doing so.

While each individual in the group brings to that group his or her own perceptions, attitudes, values, and so on, the group has *its* own collective perceptions, attitudes, values, identity, beliefs, and so on that are distinct from those of the individual. Hence as we argued in earlier chapters, every group has its own culture.

Every group also has a history, and that history has an impact upon the group. Sometimes that impact is more pronounced than others. Ford has always been primarily a family-owned company. General Motors has not. While both are auto manufacturers, I'm told the culture of each is markedly dissimilar because of that historic difference alone.

Further, every group has myths, which it more or less believes, symbols to which individuals in the group have special responses, and its own unique language.

Finally, the power the group possesses, in each of its components, may well determine what the group can and cannot do in relation to other groups.

Once it has been determined who the members of the group actually are, then we can explore questions like: Who are the leaders of our group? What are their attitudes and values? Are the values of the leaders the same as the values of our group rank and file? (It is usually values of the dominant individuals within the group that become that group's values, though frequently not all members of the group buy into those values.) What are the attitudes of the members of the group on critical issues affecting the effective functioning of the group? Answers to these questions and others like these will tell us a great deal about how well the group is functioning and, perhaps, what can be done to help it function better.

A group has the sensory receptors of its members to

pick up information coming from the outside and to filter it. Because each person's filters are different, each one receiving information will perceive it differently. In some informal groups all the members get information, though they may not all share it. In more formal groups specific individuals are given the responsibility of monitoring information coming in from outside the organization. That is where the censor screens are applied in many organizations. Any organization would drown in information overload if it didn't have a censoring mechanism that kept out irrelevant information. The trouble is that frequently information important for the organization to have is *inadvertently* kept out. Presumably the individuals designated to monitor information would have been trained to look for, and understand, the messages that are important to the organization. Unfortunately for many groups, they aren't always adequately trained, and they miss important messages that they should let in. Or sometimes they just don't know how to decode the information that did come in. After all, groups and organizations also must decode messages.

In formal organizations, at least, there must exist some sort of formal mechanism for making all sorts of decisions. Some are as trivial as deciding what to do about a particular bit of information that may have come in, like next week's meeting has been canceled. Others are as important as whether to introduce a new product or to go to war—depending on the kind of organization it is, of course. Formal organizations are organized to make decisions at all levels. In any group it is the elites, whether primary, secondary, or tertiary, who make those decisions. In some formal organizations they are called "top management," "middle management" and "line management." No matter what they are called, they exist in every group. More will be said about elites below.

Once a decision has been made, it has to be communicated. I hold that the same kind of Superego Screen that operates on the individual level also operates on the group level. That is, while the source may not be libidinal, at least formal groups recognize that they can't always respond to stimuli as they might like to. "Oughts" operate within groups, just as they do within people. In particular, formal organizations want to present a certain "public image" and, therefore, may not do certain things they might otherwise like to do.

Having finally decided on what message to send, or action to take (which is after all a kind of message), they have to encode that message in language they believe the intended recipient can understand. Hence organizations too have encoding functions. And they have various kinds of transmitters through which to send their messages.

In examining the group one must ask not only whether the appropriate components of power are present, but whether the group has the ability to access and use them. Far too often groups run into trouble because of their inability to mobilize the various components of power they have. Think of the European Jews during the Holocaust. Had channels of communication among them existed, there is little doubt that they would have fought back against the might of the Nazi state, perhaps not successfully, but certainly they would have put up more resistance than they did. But because they didn't know what was happening, they didn't fight back. In some cases they even unwittingly assisted the Nazis. There is the example of the chief rabbi of Budapest helping the Nazis round up all the Jews in the city because he believed that they would be safer in camps of some sort than they would be trying to live a normal life in a hostile anti-Semitic environment. They simply did not have the ability to mobilize the resources that existed within the group.

Whether two individuals within the same organization will in fact share more or less similar perceptions and identities may depend more upon what they do in the organization than the fact that they work for it. We know from all sorts of research that has been done, particularly in large organizations, that people in one division frequently cannot communicate with people in another division. There are good reasons for that. One is that different kinds of people become accountants, salespeople, engineers, human resources specialists, and so forth. They have different tastes, interests, languages; in sum, different cultures. They may work for the same organization, but the cultural differences among them may be greater than the cultural similarities of working for the same organization. That is a problem for every large group.

Years ago when NASA (the space agency) was getting started, its space scientists were essentially conceptualizers who said, "We can go to the moon." But conceptualizers, by themselves, couldn't get us there. That required engineers who could build the rockets and who could transform the conceptualizers' ideas into tangible results. Conceptualizers and engineers are from two distinct cultures. They do not think alike, and what's more, each is rather disdainful of the other. Communications between the two groups in NASA apparently were so difficult that it appeared for a while that no communication between them was possible. That was when NASA had the sense to bring in what amounted to the kind of bicultural people discussed in an earlier chapter—conceptualizing engineers. These people could speak to and understand both groups and knew how to communicate with each. Their primary job was essentially that of translator. They had to take a message or question from one group and translate it into language the other could understand before presenting it. (See figure 4.3. The same thing is being discussed here.)

From everything said thus far, it should be clear that intragroup communication—talking to one of us—should be among the easiest of all communications. And, if everything else is constant, it is. The problem is that no one is part of only one group. Shouldn't it be easiest for a Baptist to communicate with another Baptist? Well yes, but…. Is the other Baptist also white or black, urban or rural, north-

ern or southern, well-to-do or poor, devout or lapsed, educated or uneducated...? The more groups we share with
someone, the more *intragroup* the communication will be
and the easier it should be. The fewer groups we share, the
more difficult. In other words, this is exactly the same as was
said in discussing interpersonal communication earlier.

Intergroup Communication: How Do We Communicate with *Them*?

Let's start by recognizing that most intergroup communications are probably quite successful, and that is a direct
result of people's ability to communicate effectively with
people in other groups.

When Mr. A of the Apple Computer Corporation communicates with Ms. B of Packard Bell or with Mr. C of
Compaq Computer Corporation, they may come from different corporate cultures, but there are probably a hundred other identities that they share. For one thing, they
all would be computer literate. Most likely they are from
more or less the same educational, social, and economic
groups—meaning that they probably share a great many
common perceptions and codes among themselves. And
while there are differences between PC and Macintosh
cultures, they would still all share membership in the
broader culture of gigabytes and workstations. Vice presidents of one organization are most likely to speak to vice
presidents of other organizations, lawyers of one tend to
speak to lawyers of others, bookkeepers of one to bookkeepers of others, and so forth. Thus intergroup communication is facilitated because the people communicating
for their groups tend to share a high degree of similarity
of perception with the people of other groups with whom
they are likely to communicate. Further, even when people
in one group do communicate with people with a different function in another group, they probably share so many
other common group memberships the likelihood is that
they will have little difficulty communicating effectively.

This is not to say that problems of intergroup communication do not occur. Clearly they do, and one of the most common reasons they do is because the other people with whom we are communicating share so many group memberships with us that we tend to forget that there are some perceptions we do not share. The constant reminder that no two individuals can communicate 100 percent effectively—regardless of how many group perceptions they share—should help us communicate more effectively because we will try harder.

The intergroup communication model presented in figure 4.5 is a continuation of what was presented in figure 4.4. Each of the groups in communication will probably be made up of different people. (The fact that some groups have an overlapping of personnel sometimes can make communication between those groups easier, if those individuals are used constructively.) Each group will have its own culture. The more similar the culture of the two groups in question, the easier communication between them should be. The more different the culture between the groups, the more difficult communication should be. Everything that was said up to now about communicating interculturally applies just as much to communications between groups. They still have to send messages over channels, and they still have to have appropriate receivers, and they must know the appropriate codes to decode the messages. But essentially the communication process has already been described. What is different is the level of analysis.

If we don't know their group very well, that is the time it behooves us to find out more about them. Do we know who comprises their group? Do we know which codes members of their group know? Do we have individuals within our own group who understand their codes? After all, if it is we who want to communicate with them, it is we who will have to do something.

In discussing interpersonal communication I pointed out the importance of establishing trust by establishing common identities. So too in *intergroup* communication, it is possible to "build identity bridges" to the other group, as the more bridges we build, the more trust we are likely to engender. In the business world, building trust in relationships is crucial. It is more crucial in some countries than in others (Japan and Mexico, for instance, two major trading partners of the United States). In the case of Japan, one reason American business has had a difficult time breaking into the Japanese market is because Japanese business executives are not just looking for a profitable product. They are looking for a company they can trust the way they trust the Japanese partners and colleagues they've been working with for years. How do they know that the American company hurrying to make a deal with them will continue to deliver a product of the same quality and at the same price in the future, unless the American company spends the time to establish a good personal and professional relationship first. This is an oversimplification, to be sure. There are many other reasons why American firms have had difficulty breaking into the Japanese market, but one fact is that most of them traditionally have not taken the time to establish the relationships that are necessary to doing business in Japan. The successful American companies in Japan have invested the time and effort necessary to build those bridges of trust.

If the relationship is hostile, and we can't ask them directly the questions to which we need answers, and if we don't have any overlapping members, there is always the possibility of going to people from a third group (who are more familiar with them than we are) and asking those people what they can tell us about "them." Admittedly that is not as good a method as direct communication, but once again, some information may be better than none. Also, it is wise to be cautious and screen the answers received from people from the third group for biases toward "them" that the third-group people might consciously or subconsciously transmit.

As we have said repeatedly in this work, any relationship in which there is a lack of trust makes communication extremely difficult. However, as we have also said, one needn't give up.

For some reason, people generally find it easier to think about groups and nations exercising influence as opposed to individuals doing so. The question, "Does our group have sufficient power to achieve its goals?" is not an unusual one to hear. We constantly ask ourselves whether group resources are sufficient for achievement of its purposes. But while the question may not be alien or surprising, I am afraid that often we may ask it in its grossest form without considering which aspect of power is most appropriate for achieving which goal. That is, I suspect many groups believe that because they have sufficient resources of one sort, they do not stop to question whether that resource is the appropriate one to use to achieve a specific goal. "We have enough people on our side who support what we want to achieve, so we can't lose." Well, that may be true, but are they properly organized? Do they have sufficient skills to achieve that particular goal? Do they have the material equipment they need? Unfortunately, these and questions like them are not asked frequently enough.

"We know we are right; therefore, we can't lose" and "God is on our side" are two other statements (in exaggerated form, perhaps) that one frequently hears variants of. Now, moral and religious values are fine, and I don't mean to deprecate them, but in real life I am afraid that the good guys don't always win. We may consider ourselves good, right, or virtuous, but I am afraid that "they" consider themselves to be all of those things as well. Often groups fail to achieve their purpose simply because they haven't properly taken into account all of the components of power that would be necessary to achieve their goal in *a specific context*. Because we are "right" in no way assures us of success. Other groups are not going to do what we want them to do merely because "we" think that we are right. We have

Figure 4.5 Intergroup Communication Process

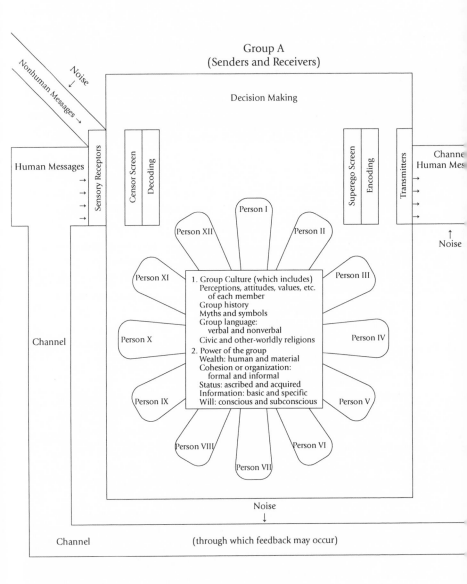

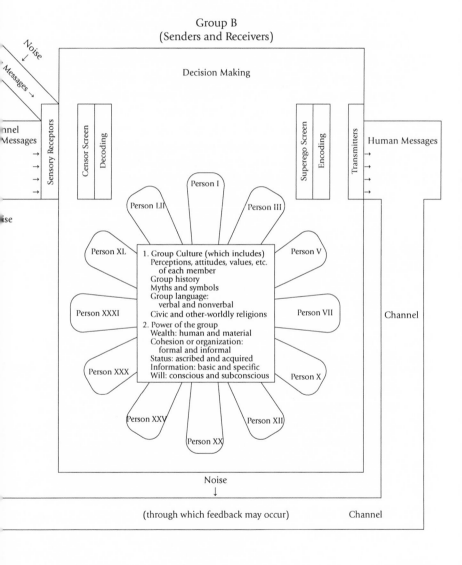

Group B
(Senders and Receivers)

Noise

Messages →

Decision Making

Channel
Messages
→
→
→
→

ise

Sensory Receptors

Censor Screen

Decoding

Superego Screen

Encoding

Transmitters

Human Messages
→
→
→
→

Person I

Person LII

Person III

Person XL

Person V

Person XXXI

Person VII

Person XXX

Person X

Person XXV

Person XII

Person XX

1. Group Culture (which includes)
   Perceptions, attitudes, values, etc.
      of each member
   Group history
   Myths and symbols
   Group language:
      verbal and nonverbal
   Civic and other-worldly religions
2. Power of the group
   Wealth: human and material
   Cohesion or organization:
      formal and informal
   Status: ascribed and acquired
   Information: basic and specific
   Will: conscious and subconscious

Channel

Noise
↓

(through which feedback may occur)

Channel

to convince them that we are. That means exercising influence over them. That means having sufficient amounts of the correct components (vis-à-vis them) to do so. That is precisely what power is all about.

Though it is often the difficulty of trying to open communication between groups who do not trust each other that gets the headlines in most newspapers—and consumes most of our attention and effort when we are involved in such a situation—let's not lose sight of the fact that most communication that occurs on a day-to-day basis actually does occur between people and groups who know and trust each other. Just think for a moment of the myriad of groups to which you belong. Then realize that someone from virtually every one of those groups—this very day— probably communicates with a host of other people from other groups. But the vast majority of those communications will take place between people who share some identities, and they will probably be between people who know and trust one another. If you yourself did not speak to a businessperson or a soldier or a blue-collar worker or a foreigner (or whatever) today, chances are great that someone from one of the groups of which you are a part did. Chances also are that the two who spoke were people who knew and trusted each other. Life really can be depicted as a kind of daisy chain. In the center is you—the reader. (See figure 4.6.) Each of the petals represents another of the groups to which you belong. It is this factor that makes most intergroup communications as successful as they are.

Figure 4.6

Intra- and International Communication: With Which Voice Do Nations Speak?

A nation[7] is a formal group like any other formal group. It has specific goals (usually to look after the safety and welfare of its population) and formal communication patterns between its leadership and the rest of the population.

---

[7] The political scientist makes a distinction between a nation and a state. The state is the formal legal entity that has a government, boundaries, and formal laws. A nation may have such things, but many nations do not. Often they share a territory with other nations, as the Tutsi and Hutu do in Rwanda, and as the Croats, Serbs, and Muslims do in Bosnia (or as maybe thirty others do around the world). Or they have no state at all, as the Jews until 1948 did not, or the Palestinians and others feel they still do not. Or they are divided into two states as were Germany and Vietnam before they were reunited, or as Korea still is. In this work I have been using the word *nation* when I really mean *state*. It is easier to refer to the United Nations by that name (since the more accurate "United States" was already taken), and to "international affairs" rather than "interstate affairs."

One thing that distinguishes a nation from all other groups is that it recognizes no legal authority above it. Therefore, it feels free to make any decisions it chooses concerning its own population within its boundaries. Those decisions can and often do include anything the government of a nation feels it has the power to enforce—including decisions about the life and death of its members. No other group legally has that authority, and few other groups take that prerogative, even illegally. The second characteristic of nations that distinguishes them from other groups is that they see themselves as being the "sole *legitimate* repository of force" within their own boundaries, and as having the "right" to use force against individuals, groups, and nations outside their boundaries whenever they *alone* decide that it is in their interest to do so and when they feel they have sufficient power to do so. No other group legally claims that right. (Gangs and crime organizations do, but they are considered illegal everywhere.)

Aside from those two characteristics, however, a nation can be viewed in exactly the same terms as any other formal organization. The nation is sometimes larger than most other groups, but not always. Approximately two dozen nations have populations smaller than the number of people who work for the General Motors Corporation.

A nation usually has many subgroups within it, many of whom identify on certain issues and in certain contexts more closely with groups living in other nations than they do with some of the groups that live in the same nation. (See figure 4.7.) What makes international communication so interesting to study is the fact that many communications across national boundaries are *less* intercultural than are many of the communications occurring among groups in the same nation. For example, a communication about a problem in physics between two physicists from different countries may often be far less intercultural than would be a communication on the same subject between the physi-

Figure 4.7 Multiple Group Identities: Relationships between Individuals, Groups, and States[8]

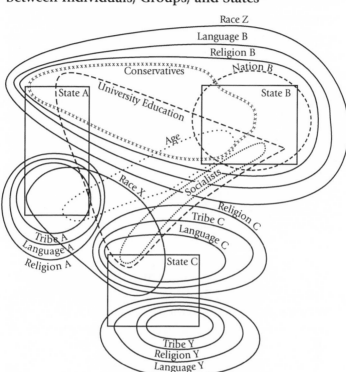

cist and a longshoreman from the same country. However, to the degree that both the longshoreman and the physicist identify with the symbols of their nation, any communication between nationals of the same country on a subject concerning the nation would be *intra*cultural, while any communication between them and someone from another country on a subject concerning national interest would almost automatically be *inter*cultural.

---

[8] This diagram appeared previously in the author's *Weak States in A World of Powers: The Dynamics of International Relationships* (New York: Free Press, 1972).

Intranational Communication:
People to People and Group to Group

Just as we have to determine the universe of the *members of a group* in order to ascertain accurately the collective group culture, so too do we have to determine the universe of all of the *groups in any nation* to ascertain that state's national culture. No nation has all and only the same groups as any other nation. Also, just as we have to find out who the dominant members of any group are so that we can determine the extent to which their perceptions have become the dominant perceptions of the group culture, so too do we have to find out which are the dominant groups in any nation to learn the degree to which their group cultures have become the predominant national culture. For example: In most of the former French and British colonies which achieved independence after World War II, French and English languages, customs, and values became the languages, customs, and values of the ruling elites. Even though the French and British have been gone for as many as fifty years, in some cases, those languages, customs, and values still predominate. In over half of those countries French and English are still either the *only* official language or one of the official languages. Often a nation is so large and contains so many different groups, with many conflicting values and attitudes, that the task of establishing which the most important groups are is not an easy one. Still, it is not an impossible one either.

There is no one set of attitudes and values to which all of the groups in any country subscribe. On the other hand, frequently there are within each country predominant attitudes and values on a whole range of issues. Many nations have a kind of "official view" on everything from what the proper functions of government ought to be, through how resources produced in the country ought to be divided among the various groups within the country, to who the enemies are both within and outside the national boundaries.

Decision-making functions go on in every nation. I say functions (plural) because I don't mean just governmental decisions, although that is certainly an important part. Most of the decisions that have great impact on a nation are made *not* by the government but by the people in positions to make private decisions daily that affect large numbers of people in very important ways. The decision of a large corporation to invest—or not to invest—in a particular country (or in a particular part of a particular country) can have a profound impact on that country. The decision of a union to demand, or not to demand, higher wages or better working conditions can have an enormous impact on inflation and working conditions in that nation.

Every country, regardless of size, has elites within it— and sometimes from outside—who are in a position to make the kinds of decisions, for purely private reasons, that can profoundly affect the lives and well-being of large numbers of people in that nation. In assessing the perceptions and identities of a nation, it is important to assess the perceptions and identities of the elite of the country who will be making most of those important decisions. In order to do that, we first have to identify them. After we have identified who the elites are, then we can assess their perceptions and identities.

Every nation, regardless of size, contains so many different groups, each with its own identity and values on so many different issues, that there is always going to be conflict in attitudes and values within the state. That is normal. The difficulty arises when one group (or a coalition of groups) within the nation is imposing its attitudes and values on the rest of the country—and some other groups within the country decide to do something about it. As long as most groups accept the other group's value system passively (and it is truly amazing just how long many groups passively accept other groups' definitions of national interest), there is no immediate problem. The problem arises either when they find, for whatever reason, that the divergence between their own values and the values of the dominant group or groups has become intolerable, or when they feel their own group power is sufficiently strong vis-à-vis the dominant group to challenge them, as in South Africa when the Afrikaners were forced out by a coalition of black tribes led by Nelson Mandela.

Every group's attitudes and values will reflect group self-interest. That becomes particularly apparent on the national level, where there are very big prizes at stake. The dominant group or groups almost always defines national interest in such a way that its own group interests are very well served. The question that every dominant group faces is how to get or keep enough control of the government so that there will be governmental protection of its needs and values. Usually it makes sure that some of the members of the primary elite of the dominant subsectors of the nation have a loud voice within the government of the country. Look at almost any country in the world and you will find that a large proportion of the primary governmental elite, including bureaucratic and military subsets, is made up of primary elites of other important subsets of the country. And that is as true in democratic states as it is in totalitarian states of both the left and the right.

I believe that it is in the long-term interest of the government of every country to look closely at the needs, values, and attitudes of the groups that comprise the nation and to consciously try to fulfill those needs before the deprived groups feel that the only way they can change how the pie is divided is to fight violently for what they see as their fair share.

The first thing for us to determine in any country we examine is which groups are in that country. Next we have to note which are the most powerful groups in the country. Then we need to find out their perceptions, attitudes, and values. We can do this by looking at the various components of power and asking which groups have how much of which component relative to the other groups in that country. Just as we found a symbiotic relationship between groups and the people of whom they are comprised, so too there is a symbiotic relationship between a country and the groups of which it is composed. Once we know which are the dominant groups in a country, chances are we will also know the dominant attitudes and values of the country as a whole.

Regardless of form of government every country has a governmental sector, which is relatively easy to identify. Within that sector, upon investigation it is not too difficult to identify those who are the primary, secondary, and tertiary elites. For example, within the United States it is fairly safe to argue that the president, his most influential advisers (who might or might not include specific cabinet members and has frequently included his wife), the heads of the most powerful standing committees of Congress, the majority leaders in both the House and Senate, and the members of the Supreme Court probably constitute the primary governmental elite in this country. The other members of Congress, the next highest level of federal judges, and powerful governors would probably constitute the secondary governmental elite, and so on. In a country like this it is sometimes difficult to determine exactly who fits where in the governmental elite, but one would be surprised at the degree of consensus one would find if, for example, one were to ask a panel of American government experts to do the analysis for us.

Almost every country also has an agricultural sector. Those who control the most land or cattle would be the primary agricultural elites, and those who control less, secondary and tertiary. The same would be true for all other sectors. That those same people might also be included in the governmental elite—and in other subsets as well—need not disturb us at all. Indeed the measure of any one individual's influence may be the number of different subsets in which he or she appears at the top.

In short, what I am suggesting is that if we go through this exercise for every identity group in every country, we would find, for example, that with but few exceptions each has a political sector (which may or may not be distinct from the governmental sector), a military sector, an agricultural sector, a commercial/industrial sector, a labor sector, a religious sector, an intellectual sector, a social aristocracy (official or unofficial), and so on. Some may be far more important in some countries than they are in others, but most of them are there in some form. The agricultural elite in Singapore or Hong Kong may be far less important than the agricultural elite in Australia, the United States, or Canada, but they are still there. There are also in every country some groups that are unique to that country. For example, if one wants to study Nigeria, one had better ask questions about Hausa, Ibo, and Yoruba elites as well as about all of the other tribal groups in the country. In the United States one probably ought to ask about elites among African Americans and the whole gamut of other ethnic Americans.

If one wants to be very specific, some sectors really should be divided still further by functions. For example, in certain situations (like at budget time) the military is far less likely to see itself as "the military"—and much more likely to see itself as "army," "air force," "navy," and "marines." Our ranking of identity groups changes in different contexts. The degree of specificity one chooses for examination in most would depend on the depth of analysis being undertaken.

In any event, each sector can be viewed as a pyramid. At the top is the primary elite of that sector, those who exercise the most influence *within that sector, at least.* Directly below it is the secondary elite, and below it, the tertiary elite. One could, of course, keep going, but let's stop there.

By drawing a pyramid of each of these subsectors of society and then tilting them so that all of the tops touch, one gets a diagram like figure 4.8.

Figure 4.8 <u>Intra</u>national Communication

Instead of drawing pyramids, however, I have chosen to draw them as pyramid-shaped petals to be consistent with what has been said before. But they are still pyramids. The ones at the top are upside down, with the small elite portion pointing to the center. To understand the individual, we had to ask: To which identity groups does the individual belong, and which are the most important to him or her? To understand the group, we had to ask: Which people are in the group, and who are the most powerful? Now, to understand the country, we have to ask: Which are the groups in the country, and which are the most powerful ones? Each of the petals represents a different identity group which can be found in any given country. People within each of these groups know who the elites of their group are. They are also able to communicate more easily with other people in their group because they do share a high degree of similarity of perception.

The tops of the pyramids are actually touching at the center. The innermost circle represents the primary elite of each group. The second circle represents the secondary elite, and the third represents the tertiary elite. The outermost portions of the petals represent the rank and file of that group. By drawing the groups this way one can see that the elites are physically closest to each other—and indeed in every country they do tend to live close in the better neighborhoods, they do tend to go to the same elite schools, and they do tend to belong to the same elite clubs. Hence communication among them is much easier than is communication among those rank-and-file members of the groups at the bottom, or outer ends, of the pyramid petals, who tend to communicate with each other very little. This is not to suggest that the attitudes and values of the elites in every country are homogeneous. They usually are not. Each elite normally views the world from the perspective of its own group and personal self-interest. Thus in every country one has to expect to find among elites some conflict in attitudes and values.

In every country the primary elite of every group will tend to have the most influence within its own group. The pope and cardinals will have most influence among Catholics; a general, among his officers in the same branch of the service; an intellectual, among fellow intellectuals. The farther up the pyramid one goes, the more crossing over there tends to be in terms of association and communication patterns. At the top of the commercial/industrial sector of society it is likely that the heads of corporations will not only see other heads of corporations, but will also see elite government people, generals, religious leaders, and so on.

At every level of analysis in which empirical research has been done, the findings have been the same: Influence seems to flow from the top down. What is more, people at the bottom tend to associate and communicate more with other people at the bottom—of their own subset—while people at the top tend to associate and communicate more with people at the top—not necessarily staying exclusively within their own subset. Thus if I wanted to send a message to someone in my own state but at the top of a group of which I was not a member, I would speak to one or two people above me—in my group. They in turn would probably speak to someone above them—in their group—who in turn would speak directly to the person I wanted to reach in the different group. The intended recipient would eventually receive the message from "one of us," however defined.

We need also to examine the collective experience of the groups which exist in the country, and look at their national history. How have the groups related to each other, and how have they related to other groups and countries in the world? I know of no more striking current example of the importance of this than to look at the country we used to call Yugoslavia. Though the Serbian and Croatian people and their languages are so similar that we called them by a single name for all the years that Yugoslavia existed, the fact is that Serbs, Croats, and Muslims have different languages, religions, histories, hatreds, myths, and symbols. In sum, they had different, frequently hostile national cultures. They were able to coexist within one state when the Austro-Hungarian Empire made them do so, or when the authoritarian Communist government at the center held them together. With the demise of communism in Yugoslavia, all it took was some politicians to throw lighted nationalist matches on the gasoline of those ethnic and religious animosities that had been there for centuries. The same was true of the Soviet Union.

International Communication: People to People, Group to Group, and Country to Country

Communication between nations falls into essentially two categories: (1) *official* communications, usually between the government of one country and the government of another, or some individual, group, or organization in another country, or an international organization, and (2) *unofficial* transactions that most frequently take place between and among private individuals, groups, or organizations and official government agencies. These are sometimes called "transnational interactions." When governments communicate with each other, on an official level, it is normally through official diplomatic channels involving representatives of their foreign offices (the Department of State in the United States) or through the international division of other governmental departments (for example, the Departments of Commerce, Agriculture, Defense, or Labor). While numerous when one considers that there are a multitude of different departments in over one hundred eighty countries around the world, these numbers pale by comparison when one considers the millions of unofficial messages sent across national borders by mail, fax, phone, e-mail, Internet, and World Wide Web, by millions of people acting either for their groups and organizations or privately. And I have not yet mentioned the mass media messages that go out to literally hundreds of millions of people simultaneously. Here I am talking about messages addressed to specific individuals. Many of these messages may be as trivial as selling a particular stock. But if thousands of stockholders begin to get frightened about the future of the economy and start selling their stocks, they can and do, frequently, have an enormous impact on the world economy.

Similarly, large private corporations in one of the more developed countries can make decisions for private profit motives to, for instance, substitute a synthetic product in place of the raw material currently being used in the production of one of their products and thereby nearly destroy the economies of the countries which produce that particular raw material. Or a private corporation might decide to move its manufacturing from countries with high labor costs—like the United States or Western Europe—to low-cost countries—like Malaysia, Honduras, or countries in Eastern Europe—and put thousands of workers in the high-cost countries out of work while stimulating economic expansion in the lower-cost countries.

It is not just private trade or investment that has an impact on people in different countries; so does working or going to school or touring or doing any of the things that people from one country do in other countries every day of the year. The important points to summarize are:

1. There are many more transnational interactions between peoples, groups, and organizations across national borders than there are official governmental interactions.
2. These transnational ties may be far more important in affecting the lives of the people in both countries on a day-to-day basis than most official government-to-government communications.
3. All international communications, whether official or unofficial, tend to move in almost exactly the same, predictable ways. That is, just as within most hierarchies, most international communications occur among countries at the top of the international hierarchy, fewer between countries at the top and those in the middle, even fewer between those at the top and those at the bottom, and almost none between those at the bottom of the different hierarchies.

Most interactions, both official and unofficial, occur among people and organizations from the most powerful states. The second greatest number of communications occur among people and organizations from the most powerful states and regional powers within the big states' own sphere. While even fewer occur among those at the top and those at the very bottom, the fewest occur among countries at the bottom of different spheres. Thus one would find very few transactions among, say, Bolivia, Bulgaria, Benin, and Brunei.

Let us look for a moment at the implications of this for international communication. Yes, there are *official* communications among all the major countries of the world. In actual fact, however, it is the big powers that communicate (officially) with most of the rest of the world. The weak countries simply cannot afford to have embassies and consulates in any but those few countries that are most important to them, usually in the capitals of each of the major powers, in the capitals of a few middle powers (usually the ones that are in their geographic region or the middle powers of their sphere), and some in the capitals of their neighbors. The big powers, on the other hand, not only have embassies in most capitals of the world, but also have consulates in all the major cities in the countries with which they have diplomatic relations. Just think of the enormous advantage this gives businesspeople from the more powerful countries, to have representatives of their countries reporting business opportunities everywhere else in the world back to their home country.

In some ways the international communication process is much more complicated than any of the others I have presented thus far. (See figure 4.9.) Nations don't communicate, people do, sometimes in the name of the state and sometimes representing one of the groups in a state. But it doesn't really matter who is doing the communicating, the process is more or less the same. In a moment I will discuss group-to-group communication, but let me start with government-to-government communication. Official messages going to government, regardless of how they started out, wind up in official receptors, which are not only embassies and consular offices, but also the intelligence officers dispatched to different countries (if their countries can afford them) to try to gather as much information that might help the country as possible. During the Cold War one used to think of spies trying to find out military secrets about the other country. And to a certain extent that was true. But just as important then, and now, are industrial secrets that Country A might want to acquire from Country B. In the age of sophisticated computer technology, the new software package may be the most important weapon in a nation's economic arsenal. Of course it is the corporations in Country A that stand to gain most by acquiring those secrets, but because of the symbiotic relationship between groups and countries, what's good for American companies A, B, and C is also good for the United States. Hence, American diplomats around the world are always looking for any advantage that an American corporation might find doing business in other countries. Just think of the diplomatic negotiations between the United States and Japan in the past two decades. The major disputes have been over how many American cars the Japanese are going to buy. With China the controversy is over protection of intellectual property and American corporate copyrights, and with France it is how many American television shows and motion pictures they will allow in.

International messages do go through censor screens, and they have to be decoded, in the sense that merely to avoid information overload some minor official, in some office somewhere, decides which information to pass on to others for decisions, and also the meaning of certain messages. If the official is not sophisticated enough to recognize that some piece of information about some highly technological subject could be of major importance to a specific company in the country, or to a particular government agency, that country could miss an advantage it might otherwise have had. There is so much information flowing into countries from every conceivable source that it is almost impossible to monitor it, and the vast bulk of those messages are unofficial.

From there we get to the part in the process that most distinguishes communication between countries. The national culture of each country is different. No two countries have only and all of the same groups within them;

Figure 4.9 <u>International Communication Process</u>

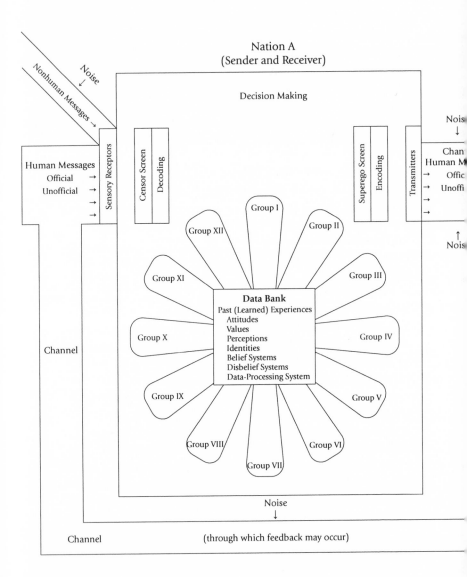

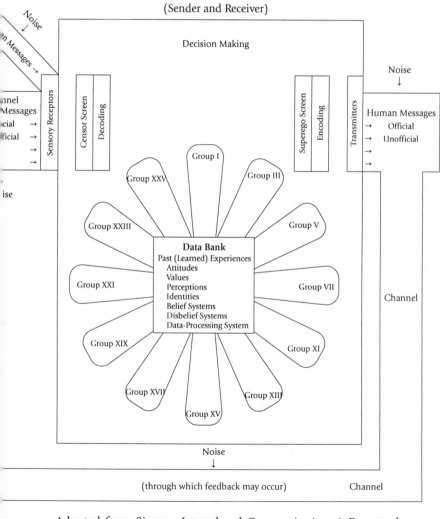

Nation B
(Sender and Receiver)

Adapted from Singer, *Intercultural Communication: A Perceptual Approach,* 1st ed. (Englewood Cliffs, NJ: Prentice-Hall, 1987), 70.

hence, the perceptions, attitudes, and values of the groups that comprise the state will be different in different countries. What's more, the power of different groups will also be different. Every country may have a military, but in some countries the military is the most important group in the country; in others it is less powerful. In some countries the religious leaders wield enormous amounts of power (think of Iran); in others, the industrial leaders. And while the power of the groups that make up the country varies, so too does the determination regarding which group values will dominate. And that will have a direct impact on decision making in the country.

Of course, the collective experience and history of each country will be different and will have a profound effect on how it behaves as a country. Russia's deep distrust of the Chinese stems in no small measure from three hundred years of being occupied by the Mongol Empire. While France and Germany may be cooperating in the European Union now, centuries of war leave many historic scars.

Finally there is the power of the country itself, relative to the countries with which it must interact. In part the question is whether the country has the power, in the aggregate, to do what it wants and achieve the goals it has set for itself. But there is also the question of whether it has enough of the correct components of power to achieve its goals. Material wealth is important, to be sure, but I believe that the United States—which had many more of the objective components of power than Vietnam in the 1960s and 1970s, lost the war there because it didn't have the will to win (which, remember, I consider one of the components of power), just as the Russians lost in Afghanistan in the 1980s.

What does a "Superego Screen" mean on the national level? As with groups, I am not suggesting a libidinal basis for countries, but I do think that most countries, through their official actions, are very sensitive about the image they project in the world and thus are careful not to say what they really would like to say, but rather say what it is appropriate to say. Finally, while governments can use governmental transmitters to send out international messages, they are just as likely to use the international press, where they know they will get wide distribution.

Nonofficial International Communication

When the international communication being considered is from a nonofficial person or group, there is some change in the international communication process, but not much. Any message is likely to go through all of the same steps. What changes are the channels used. Instead of government channels picking up messages, it may be private channels, and instead of governmental decision making, it may be private group decision making.

If there are thousands of government-to-government communications daily, there are millions of nongovernmental international communications daily. Aside from the myriad of business transactions that occur across international boundaries, add to that communications of the several thousand nonprofit organizations that exist worldwide, like the International Red Cross, Catholic Charities (and the hundreds of other religious organizations that operate internationally), Greenpeace (and the scores of environmental groups with international chapters), along with organizations as diverse as Boy Scouts and Girl Scouts, animal rights organizations, and philatelist societies. The list is almost as endless as human imagination. They are all out there and they are communicating daily. Some are doing it more easily because they share similarities of perception centered on what it is they do or are interested in, and some are struggling with the problems caused by the "spin" the unique national cultures give to the functional work the international organization is supposed to be doing.

Whether they are doing it as well as they might or not, they are communicating. To the degree that they are doing it well, they are reinforcing their similarities of perception and therefore should communicate with more ease in the future. To the degree that they are doing it poorly, they are making tomorrow's communication that much more difficult. Indeed, there may be no communication tomorrow, because of intercultural misunderstandings that occurred today.

With the vast increase in unofficial international communications that are spreading around the globe at an exponential rate, one can only hope that as the various groups practice communicating with each other, they will get better at it. They are, after all, working on calibrating their similarity of perceptions, and the more they succeed in doing that, the easier international intercultural communication should become.

Despite everything that has been said in these pages about how difficult it is to communicate effectively across cultural barriers in countries other than their own, huge numbers of people do it every day. While most of them may have experienced at least some difficulty communicating at least some of the time, a large majority has been able to communicate relatively successfully. It is not that all of those people who do so are intuitively better communicators than those who do not (although there may be some merit in the argument that those who are willing to take the risk just might be). I think that the reason they are relatively successful is that the people with whom they must communicate most intensely day-to-day probably have developed intercultural communication skills and thus know better and better how to learn about what they need to know to communicate more effectively with their counterparts. The more people continue to work, go to school, and live in countries other than their own, the more successful intercultural communicators there are likely to be in the future.

The Communication Revolution

The National Broadcasting Corporation, NBC, claimed that three and one-half billion people watched the opening ceremonies of the 1996 Olympics in Atlanta, Georgia. If true, that would mean that almost three out of every four people on earth watched the same program at the same time. Even if it is not true, and only two and a half billion people watched, the numbers are still staggering.

What does this communication revolution which has occurred since the end of World War II mean? For one thing it means that there is an international socialization and sharing of perceptions possible now that was previously unthinkable. Not only do people know what Coke, Reebok, McDonald's, Levi's, and other brand names refer to, they want them. But it is not just consumer products that people all over the world can now hear about and come to want, it is also popular culture. American jazz is played around the world. In the 1960s the Beatles would claim, with some degree of accuracy, that more people knew who they were than knew who Jesus Christ was. Probably more people worldwide recognize the faces of Michael Jackson and Madonna than would recognize the face of any American except, maybe, the president of the United States. And while no rock group is as famous now as the Beatles were, within months of the release of a new CD by a major rock group, whether in Britain, the United States, or France, there is a demand for it in Tokyo, Warsaw, Rio, and Bombay.

Use of the Internet has skyrocketed. People from Dushanbe, Tajikistan, are in chat rooms and can see and speak with people from Des Moines, Dakar, and Damascus. The subjects can, and do, range from Medieval European Literature to politics to cooking to sex. Just think about this for a moment. In the first chapter I talked about identity groups forming where people with a similarity of perception could find someone with similar perceptions with whom they could form an identity group. But until recently that was usually limited to people in one's immediate vicinity. That is all changing for those who have access to electricity, television, and computers.

While the gap between those who do and those who don't have access to those things is, at least for the moment, getting wider, some of my friends in the computer industry believe that too will eventually change. It is claimed that there will soon be computers that will enable people to speak into them in any language and convey the message verbally to the listener in the listener's language. If and when that happens, being literate will no longer be a factor in international communication. Certainly these new machines would make obsolete the need for literacy and a common world language, but we may still be quite some time away from that. While there are still many villages in the world that don't have electricity, the transistor radio broke that barrier. Perhaps a transistorized computer will break this barrier. (Indeed, some would say that the laptop has done precisely that.)

What all of this means, of course, is that:

1. there is a more rapid and widespread possibility of sharing similarity of perceptions among more diverse people than anyone thought possible less than a generation ago
2. there is the possibility of the creation and reinforcement of a plethora of identity groups worldwide, unthinkable until now
3. there is a rapidly increasing number of channels of communication available to people and that offers the opportunity for people to communicate who previously could not

Communication, as I have emphasized, is not a panacea, but as the numbers who communicate increase, so does the possibility of meaningful dialogue taking place. We aren't going to build one culture any time soon, but if current trends continue, more people than ever before will be building and reinforcing identity groups across national boundaries. Although not everyone will be part of this brave new communications world, unbelievable numbers will. Just think of an address book with the e-mail numbers of half the population of the world. Not only that, but as more and more of them engage in communication, they will be calibrating perceptions and developing increasing spirals of similarities of perception. Ultimately a significant portion of them might come to understand and respect your values and attitudes while you come to understand and respect theirs. Not at all a bad start in building the global village of the future.

Propositional Summary for Chapter 4

Communicating at different levels: Organizations, groups, and nations don't communicate, people do—in the name of the unit they represent. The difference is the level of analysis being discussed. The *process*, whether on the individual, group, or international level, is the same.

The role of power in communication: Power is the *ability* to exercise influence over others and the *ability* to prevent influence from being exercised over oneself. Regardless of which level of analysis is being considered, it is relative and contextual.

Intrapersonal communication: Getting in touch with what it is we really want, either in life or in a communication relationship, is not only the first thing we need to do to communicate effectively, it is also the most important.

Interpersonal communication: In order to do it effectively we have to make the effort to get to know another's perceptions, attitudes, and values, then put our message into language that the other can understand and accept.

Cultural diversity: Intercultural communication is not just about communicating with people in other countries. It is about communicating *effectively* with people who are different from ourselves, and they are all around us, at work, in school, virtually everywhere we look—even in our own families.

Distortion in communication: The more steps a communication has to go through to reach its intended destination, the more likely there is to be distortion. The more steps, the more distortion is likely to occur. Therefore, the general rule is to avoid as many steps as possible.

Networks: Networks of people we know and trust are among the most important channels of communication through which messages flow. Any message is much more likely to be accepted if the receiver knows and trusts the sender. Hence it sometimes pays to violate the previous rule and add extra people to the message network, if that will accomplish the goal of making the message more acceptable to the receiver.

Groups: Each group is different because few if any groups contain all and only the same members, and each member brings to the group his or her own values and belief system. There is a symbiotic relationship between the group and its members. Each affects the other.

Environment and history also have impacts on groups: There is no certainty that all groups will continue to exist. Either they adjust to their environment, or they could perish. Similarly, the history of the group frequently determines both individual and group behavior within the group and toward other groups.

Intragroup communication: Communication within the group is determined in large measure by the group culture, including which individuals have the most power in the group. It is frequently they who set the group norms, attitudes, and values.

Intergroup communication: It is not groups that communicate, but rather people who communicate in the name of the group. The more similar the people in each group, the easier communication should be; the more different, the more difficult.

Intranational communication: No nation contains all and only the same groups as any other nation. To determine international culture it is important to know not only the groups in the country, but also which groups have the most power. The elites of each of the groups in the country are the ones who usually determine group norms and behaviors.

International communication: International communications are generally of two types: official (government to government) or transnational (private people to people, or group to group, or even private people or groups to governments). There are many more transnational communications every day than there are official ones. There is also a kind of international pecking order, with the most powerful governments and organizations communicating more with other powerful governments and organizations than with those less so.

The communication revolution: The incredible increase of communication channels that have opened since World War II has made it possible for more people to communicate, over more channels, than at any other time in history. Hopefully this explosion in communication will lead to the strengthening of identity groups and the spiraling of similarities of communication among a vast array of different people around the world who could never have communicated before.

Bibliography

5

Books

Abelson, R. P., E. Aronson, W. J. McGuire, T. M. Newcomb, M. J. Rosenberg, and P. H. Tannenbaum. *Theories of Cognitive Consistency: A Source Book.* Chicago: Rand McNally, 1968.

Akin, Johnnye, Alvin Goldberg, Gail Myers, and Joseph Stewart, eds. *Language Behavior: A Book of Readings in Communication.* The Hague: Morton, 1970.

Allport, F. H. *Theories of Perception and the Concept of Structure.* New York: John Wiley & Sons, 1955.

Allport, Gordon W., and L. Postman. *The Psychology of Rumor.* New York: Holt, Rinehart & Winston, 1947.

Almond, Gabriel A. *The American People and Foreign Policy.* New York: Praeger, 1960.

Althen, Gary. *The Handbook of Foreign Student Advising*, rev. ed. Yarmouth, ME: Intercultural Press, 1995.

Argyle, Michael. *Bodily Communication*. New York: International Universities Press, 1975.

Asante, Molefi Kete, and William B. Gudykunst, eds. *Handbook of International and Intercultural Communication*. Newbury Park, CA: Sage, 1989.

Asante, Molefi Kete, Eileen Newmark, and Cecil A. Blake, eds. *Handbook of Intercultural Communication*. Beverly Hills: Sage, 1979.

Bache, Ellen. *Culture Clash*, 2d ed. Wilmington, NC: Banks Channel Books, 1994.

Bandler, Richard, and John Grinder. *Frogs into Princes: Neuro-Linguistic Programming*. Moab, UT: Real People Press, 1979.

Bem, Daryl J. *Beliefs, Attitudes, and Human Affairs*. Belmont, CA: Brooks/Cole, 1970.

Benedict, Ruth. *Patterns of Culture*. 1934. Reprint. New York: New American Library, 1959.

Berelson, Bernard, and Gary A. Steiner. *Human Behavior: An Inventory of Scientific Findings*. New York: Harcourt, Brace & World, 1964.

Berlo, David K. *The Process of Communication*. New York: Holt, Rinehart & Winston, 1960.

Berry, John W. *Human Ecology and Cognitive Style: Comparative Studies in Cultural and Psychological Adaptation*. Beverly Hills: Sage, 1974.

Berry, John W., and P. R. Dasen, eds. *Culture and Cognition: Readings in Cross Cultural Psychology*. London: Methuen, 1974.

Berry, John W., and W. J. Lonner, eds. *Applied Cross-Cultural Psychology*. Amsterdam: Swets and Zeitlinger, 1975.

Biddle, Bruce J. *Role Therapy: Expectations, Identities and Behaviors*. New York: Academic Press, 1979.

Birdwhistell, Ray L. *Kinesics and Context: Essays on Body Motion Communication*. Philadelphia: University of Pennsylvania Press, 1970.

Bjorn-Andersen, Niels, ed. *Information Society: For Richer, For Poorer*. New York: North-Holland, 1982.

Boulding, Kenneth E. *The Image*, 6th ed. Ann Arbor: University of Michigan Press, 1968.

Blubaugh, Jon A., and Dorthy L. Pennington. *Crossing Difference: Inter-Racial Communication*. Columbus, OH: Charles E. Merrill, 1976.

Brislin, Richard W. *Understanding Culture's Influence on Behavior*. Fort Worth, TX: Harcourt Brace, 1993.

——. *Cross-Cultural Encounters: Face-to-Face Interaction*. New York: Pergamon, 1981.

——. *Culture Learning: Concepts, Applications and Research*. Honolulu: East-West Center and University Press of Hawaii, 1977.

——, ed. *Topics in Culture Learning*, vol. 4. Honolulu: East-West Center, 1976.

Brislin, Richard W., and Paul Pedersen. *Cross-Cultural Orientation Programs*. New York: Gardner Press, 1976.

Broadbent, D. E. *Perception and Communication*. London: Pergamon Press, 1958.

Cantril, Hadley. *The Pattern of Human Concerns*. New Brunswick, NJ: Rutgers University Press, 1966.

Carbaugh, Donal, ed. *Cultural Communication and Intercultural Contact*. Hillsdale, NJ: Lawrence Erlbaum, 1990.

Casmir, Fred L., ed. *International and Intercultural Communication Annual*, vol. 3. Falls Church, VA: Speech Communication Association, 1976.

——, ed. *International and Intercultural Communication Annual*, vol. 2. Falls Church, VA: Speech Communication Association, 1975.

——, ed. *International and Intercultural Communication Annual*, vol. 1. Falls Church, VA: Speech Communication Association, 1974.

Casse, Pierre. *Training for the Multicultural Manager*. Washington, DC: Society for Intercultural Education, Training and Research, 1982.

————. *Training for the Cross-Cultural Mind,* 2d ed. Washington, DC: Society for Intercultural Education, Training and Research, 1981.

Cherry, Colin. *On Human Communication: A Review, a Survey and a Criticism.* Cambridge: MIT Press; and New York: John Wiley & Sons, 1957. Reprint. New York: Science Editions, 1961.

Clevenger, Theodore Jr., and Jack Matthews. *The Speech Communication Process.* Glenview, IL: Scott Foresman, 1971.

Combs, James E., and Michael W. Mansfield, eds. *Drama in Life: The Uses of Communication in Society.* New York: Hastings House, 1976.

Condon, John C. *With Respect to the Japanese: A Guide for Americans.* Yarmouth, ME: Intercultural Press, 1984.

Condon, John C., and Fathi S. Yousef. *An Introduction to Intercultural Communication.* Indianapolis: Bobbs-Merrill, 1975.

Cornish, Edward, ed. *Communications Tomorrow: The Coming of the Information Society.* Bethesda, MD: World Future Society, 1982.

Dance, Frank E. X., ed. *Human Communication Theory.* New York: Holt, Rinehart & Winston, 1967.

Daniel, Norman. *The Cultural Barrier: Problems in the Exchange of Ideas.* Edinburgh: University Press, 1975.

Davey, William G. *Intercultural Theory and Practice: A Case Method Approach.* Washington, DC: Society for Intercultural Education, Training and Research, 1981.

Deese, James E. *The Structure of Associations in Language and Thought.* Baltimore: Johns Hopkins Press, 1966.

De Rivera, Joseph H. *The Psychological Dimension of Foreign Policy.* Columbus, OH: Charles E. Merrill, 1968.

Deutsch, Karl W. *The Nerves of Government.* New York: Free Press, 1963.

————. *Nationalism and Social Communication: An Inquiry into the Foundations of Nationality.* Cambridge: Technology Press of MIT; and New York: John Wiley & Sons, 1953.

Dilts, Robert, John Grinder, Richard Bandler, Leslie C. Bandler, and Judith De Lozier. *Neuro-Linguistic Programming: The Study of the Structure of Subjective Experience,* vol. 1. Cupertino, CA: Meta Publications, 1980.

Dodd, Carley H. *Perspectives on Cross-Cultural Communication.* Dubuque, IA: Kendall/Hunt, 1977.

Ekman, Paul. *The Face of Man: Expressions of Universal Emotions in a New Guinea Village.* New York: Garland STPM Press, 1980.

―――. *Universals and Cultural Differences in Facial Expressions of Emotion.* Lincoln: University of Nebraska Press, 1971.

Ellis, Willis D. *A Source Book of Gestalt Psychology.* New York: Humanities Press, 1967.

Erikson, Erik H. *Identity and the Life Cycle.* New York: W. W. Norton, 1979.

Fast, Julius. *Body Language.* New York: Pocketbooks, 1971.

Festinger, Leon. *A Theory of Cognitive Dissonance.* Stanford, CA: Stanford University Press, 1957.

Fischer, Heinz-Dietrich. *International and Intercultural Communication.* New York: Hastings House, 1976.

Fischer, Heinz-Dietrich, and J. C. Merrill, eds. *International Communication: Media, Channels, and Functions.* New York: Hastings House, 1970.

Fisher, Glen. *American Communication in a Global Society.* Norwood, NJ: Ablex Publishing, 1979.

―――. *International Negotiation: A Cross-Cultural Perspective.* Chicago: Intercultural Press, 1980.

Fitzgerald, Thomas K., ed. *Social and Cultural Identity: Problems of Persistence and Change.* Athens: University of Georgia Press, 1974.

Giffin, Kim, and Bobby R. Patton. *Fundamentals of Interpersonal Communication.* New York: Harper & Row, 1971.

Glenn, Edmund S., and Christine Glenn. *Man and Mankind and Communication between Cultures.* Norwood, NJ: Ablex Publishing, 1981.

Gordon, Thomas. *P.E.T.: Parent Effectiveness Training.* New York: New American Library, 1970.

Grove, Cornelius Lee. *Communications across Cultures: A Report on Cross-Cultural Research.* Washington, DC: National Educational Association of the U.S., 1976.

Gudykunst, William B., ed. *Intercultural Communication Theory: Current Perspectives* (which is also *International and Intercultural Communication Annual*, vol. 7). Beverly Hills, CA: Sage, 1983.

Gudykunst, William B., and Young Y. Kim, eds. *Methods for Intercultural Communication Research* (which is also *International and Intercultural Communication Annual*, vol. 8). Beverly Hills,CA: Sage, 1984.

Hagen, Everett E. *On a Theory of Social Change: How Economic Growth Begins.* Homewood, IL: Dorsey Press, 1962.

Haigh, Robert W., George Gerbner, and Richard B. Byrne. *Communication in the Twenty-First Century.* New York: John Wiley & Sons, 1981.

Hall, Edward T. *The Dance of Life: The Other Dimension of Time.* New York: Anchor/Doubleday, 1983.

———. *Beyond Culture.* New York: Anchor/Doubleday, 1976.

———. *The Silent Language.* New York: Anchor/Doubleday, 1973.

———. *The Hidden Dimension.* Garden City, NY: Doubleday, 1966.

Harms, Leroy Stanley. *Intercultural Communication.* New York: Harper & Row, 1973.

Harper, Robert G., Arthur N. Wiens, and Joseph D. Matarazzo. *Nonverbal Communication: The State of the Art.* New York: John Wiley & Sons, 1978.

Harrington, Michael. *The Other America: Poverty in the United States.* New York: Macmillan, 1962.

Harris, Philip R., and Robert T. Moran. *Managing Cultural Differences*, 4th ed. Houston: Gulf, 1996.

──────. *Managing Cultural Synergy*. Houston: Gulf, 1982.

Hofstede, Geert. *Cultures and Organizations: Software of the Mind*. London: McGraw-Hill, 1991.

──────. *Culture's Consequences: International Differences in Work-Related Values*. abridged ed., 7th printing. Newbury Park, CA: Sage, 1991.

Hoijer, Harry, ed. *Language in Culture*. Chicago: University of Chicago Press, 1954.

Homaus, G. C. *The Human Group*. New York: Harcourt, Brace, 1950.

Hoopes, David S., ed. *Readings in Intercultural Communication*, vol. 5, *Intercultural Programming*. Pittsburgh: Intercultural Communications Network, 1976.

Hoopes, David S., and Paul Ventura, eds. *Intercultural Sourcebook: Cross-Cultural Training Methodologies*. Chicago: Intercultural Press, 1979.

Horowitz, Donald L. *Ethnic Groups in Conflict*. Berkeley: University of California Press, 1985.

Huntington, Samuel P. *The Clash of Civilizations and the Remaking of World Order*. New York: Simon & Schuster, 1997.

Inkeles, Alex. *Public Opinion in Soviet Russia: A Study in Mass Persuasion*. Cambridge: Harvard University Press, 1950.

Isaacs, Harold. *Idols of the Tribe: Group Identity and Political Change*. New York: Harper & Row, 1977.

──────. *Scratches on Our Minds: American Images of China and India*. New York: J. Day, 1958.

Jain, Nemi C., ed. *International and Intercultural Communication Annual*, vol. 6. Falls Church, VA: Speech Communication Association, 1982.

──────, ed. *International and Intercultural Communication Annual*, vol. 5. Falls Church, VA: Speech Communication Association, 1979.

──────, ed. *International and Intercultural Communication Annual*, vol. 4. Falls Church, VA: Speech Communication Association, 1977.

Jervis, Robert. *Perception and Misperception in International Politics.* Princeton, NJ: Princeton University Press, 1976.

Jussawalla, Meheroo. *Bridging Global Barriers: Two New International Orders, NIEO, NWIO.* Honolulu: East-West Communication Institute, 1981.

Keller, Joseph. *Intercommunity Understanding: The Verbal Dimension.* Washington, DC: University Press of America, 1977.

Kelly, George. *A Theory of Personality: The Psychology of Personal Constructs.* New York: W. W. Norton, 1963.

Kelman, Herbert C., ed. *International Behavior: A Social-Psychological Analysis.* New York: Holt, Rinehart & Winston, 1965.

Keohane, Robert O., and Joseph S. Nye. *Transnational Relations and World Politics.* Cambridge: Harvard University Press, 1972.

Key, Wilson Bryan. *Subliminal Seduction: A Media's Manipulation of a Not So Innocent America.* New York: Thomas Y. Crowell, 1968.

Kilpatrick, Franklin P., ed. *Explorations in Transactional Psychology.* New York: New York University Press, 1961.

Klineberg, Otto. *The Human Dimension in International Relations.* New York: Holt, Rinehart & Winston, 1964.

Knapp, Mark L. *Nonverbal Communication in Human Interaction,* 2d ed. New York: Holt, Rinehart & Winston, 1978.

Kohls, L. Robert, and John M. Knight. *Developing Intercultural Awareness: A Cross-Cultural Training Handbook,* 2d ed. Yarmouth, ME: Intercultural Press, 1994.

Landis, Dan, and Richard W. Brislin, eds. *Handbook of Intercultural Training,* vol. 2. *Issues in Training Methodology.* New York: Pergamon, 1983.

Lasswell, Harold D. *Power and Personality.* New York: W. W. Norton, 1948.

———. *Politics: Who Gets What, When, How.* New York: McGraw-Hill, 1936.

Lasswell, Harold D., and Abraham Kaplan. *Power and Society: A Framework for Political Inquiry*. New Haven, CT: Yale University Press, 1950.

Lawrence, Charles R., ed. *Man, Culture and Society*. New York: Brooklyn College Press, 1962.

Lerner, Daniel. *The Passing of Traditional Society: Modernizing the Middle East*. Glencoe, IL: Free Press, 1958.

Levitt, Harold. *Managerial Psychology*, 2d ed. Chicago: University of Chicago Press, 1964.

Levitt, Harold, and Louis R. Pondy, eds. *Readings in Managerial Psychology*, 2d ed. Chicago: University of Chicago Press, 1963.

Lewis, Oscar. *Five Families: Mexican Case Studies in the Culture of Poverty*. New York: New American Library, 1959.

Lippitt, Gordon L., and David S. Hoopes. *Helping across Cultures*. Washington, DC: International Consultants Foundation, 1978.

Littlejohn, Stephen W. *Theories of Human Communication*. Columbus, OH: Charles E. Merrill, 1978.

Lloyd, Barbara B. *Perception and Cognition: A Cross-Cultural Perspective*. Baltimore: Penguin Books, 1972.

Luft, Joseph. *Group Processes: An Introduction to Group Dynamics*, 2d ed. Palo Alto, CA: National Press, 1970.

———. *Of Human Interaction*. Palo Alto, CA: National Press, 1969.

Makler, Harry, Albert Martinelli, and Neil Smelser, eds. *Many Voices, One World: Communication and Society Today and Tomorrow: Towards a New More Just and More Efficient World Information and Communication Order*. Report by the International Commission for the Study of Communication Problems. New York: Uniput, 1980.

Malloy, John T. *Dress for Success*. New York: P. H. Weyden, 1975.

Maslow, Abraham H. *Motivation and Personality,* 2d ed. New York: Harper & Row, 1970.

McCall, George J., and J. L. Simmons. *Identities and Interactions: An Examination of Human Associations in Everyday Life*, rev. ed. New York: Free Press, 1978.

McClelland, David C. *The Achieving Society*. Princeton, NJ: Van Nostrand, 1961.

Mehrabian, Albert. *Silent Messages: Implicit Communication of Emotions and Attitudes*, 2d ed. Belmont, CA: Wadsworth, 1981.

Merriam, Charles E. *Political Power*. New York: Collier Books, 1964.

Miller, James G. *Living Systems*. New York: McGraw-Hill, 1978.

Misra, Bhabagrahi, and James Preston, eds. *Community, Self, and Identity*. The Hague: Morton, 1978.

Morain, Genelle. *Kinesics and Cross-Cultural Understanding*. Arlington, VA: Center for Applied Linguistics, 1978.

Morris, Desmond, Peter Collett, Peter Marsh, and Marie O'Shaughnessy. *Gestures*. New York: Stein & Day, 1979.

Mortenson, David. *Basic Readings in Communication Theory*. New York: Harper & Row, 1973.

Nisbitt, Richard, and Lee Ross. *Human Inference: Strategies and Shortcomings of Social Judgment*. Englewood Cliffs, NJ: Prentice-Hall, 1980.

Northrup, F. S. L., and H. H. Livingston. *Cross-Cultural Understanding: Epistemology in Anthropology*. New York: Harper & Row, 1964.

Osgood, Charles E., William H. May, and Murray S. Miron. *Cross-Cultural Universals of Affective Meaning*. Urbana: University of Illinois Press, 1975.

Paige, R. Michael, ed. *Education for the Intercultural Experience*, 2d ed. Yarmouth, ME: Intercultural Press, 1993.

Parsons, Talcott. *The Social System*. Glencoe, IL: Free Press, 1951.

Parsons, Talcott, R. F. Bales, and Edward A. Shils. *Toward a General Theory of Action*. Glencoe, IL: Free Press, 1953.

————, eds. *Working Papers in the Theory of Action.* Cambridge: Harvard University Press, 1951.

Pedersen, Paul, ed. *Readings in Intercultural Communication,* vol. 4. *Cross-Cultural Counseling.* Pittsburgh: Intercultural Communications Network, 1974.

Pool, Ithiel De Sola, Wilber Schramm, Fredrick W. Frey, Nathan Maccoby, and Edwin B. Parker, eds. *Handbook of Communication.* Chicago: Rand McNally, 1973.

Prosser, Michael H., ed. *Intercommunication among Nations and Peoples.* New York: Harper & Row, 1973.

Pusch, Margaret D., ed. *Multicultural Education: A Cross-Cultural Training Approach.* Chicago: Intercultural Press, 1981.

Pye, Lucien W., ed. *Communication and Political Development.* Princeton, NJ: Princeton University Press, 1963.

Redfield, Robert. *Peasant Society and Culture: An Anthropological Approach to Civilization.* Chicago: University of Chicago Press, 1956.

Renwick, George W. *Evaluation Handbook for Cross-Cultural Training and Multicultural Education.* La Grange Park, IL: Intercultural Press, 1979.

————. *State of the Art Study: A Longitudinal Analysis and Assessment of Intercultural Education, Training and Research, 1932-1984.* Unpublished Ph.D. dissertation, Pittsburgh: University of Pittsburgh, Graduate School of Public and International Affairs, 1991.

Rich, Andrea L. *Interracial Communication.* New York: Harper & Row, 1974.

Riesman, David, with Nathan Glazer and Revei Denny. *The Lonely Crowd: A Study of the Changing American Character.* New Haven, CT: Yale University Press, 1961.

Robertson, Roland, and Burkhart Holzner, eds. *Identity and Authority: Explorations in the Theory of Society.* New York: St. Martin's Press, 1980.

Robinson, Glen O., ed. *Communication for Tomorrow: Policy Perspectives for the 1980s.* New York: Praeger, 1978.

Rogers, Everett M. *Diffusion of Innovations*, 3d ed. New York: Free Press, 1983.

Rogers, Everett M., and Rekha Agarwala-Rogers. *Communication in Organizations.* New York: Free Press, 1976.

Rogers, Everett M., and F. Floyd Shoemaker. *Communication of Innovations: A Cross-Cultural Approach.* New York: Free Press, 1971.

Rokeach, Milton. *The Nature of Human Values.* New York: Free Press, 1973.

————. *The Open and Closed Mind: Investigations into the Nature of Belief Systems and Personality Systems.* New York: Basic Books, 1960.

Rosen, Robert H. *Leading People: Transforming Business from the Inside Out.* New York: Viking, 1996.

————. *The Healthy Company: Eight Strategies to Develop People, Productivity, and Profits.* Los Angeles: Jeremy P. Tarcher, 1991.

Rosenblith, W. A., ed. *Sensory Communication.* New York: John Wiley & Sons, 1961.

Ruhly, Sharon. *Orientations to Intercultural Communication.* Chicago: Science Research Associates, 1976.

Samovar, Larry A. *Understanding Intercultural Communication.* Belmont, CA: Wadsworth, 1981.

Samovar, Larry A., and Richard E. Porter. *Communication between Cultures.* Belmont, CA: Wadsworth, 1991.

————, eds. *Intercultural Communication: A Reader.* 8th ed. Belmont, CA: Wadsworth, 1997.

Schiller, Herbert I. *Communication and Cultural Domination.* New York: International Arts and Sciences Press, 1976.

Seelye, H. Ned. *Teaching Culture: Strategies for Intercultural Communication.* Lincolnwood, IL: NTC, 1993.

Seelye, H. Ned, and V. Lynn Tyler. *Intercultural Communicator Resources.* Provo, UT: Brigham Young University, 1977.

Segall, Marshall H., D. T. Campbell, and M. J. Herskovits. *The Influence of Culture on Visual Perception.* Indianapolis: Bobbs-Merrill, 1966.

Shannon, C. E., and Warren Weaver. *The Mathematical Theory of Communication.* Urbana: University of Illinois Press, 1949.

Siegman, Aron W., and Stanley Feldstein. *Nonverbal Behavior and Communication.* New York: Halsted Press, 1978.

Singer, Marshall R. *The Emerging Elite: A Study of Political Leadership in Ceylon.* Cambridge: MIT, 1964.

————. *Weak States in a World of Powers: The Dynamics of International Relationships.* New York: Free Press, 1972.

Sitaram, K. S., and Roy R. Cogdell. *Foundation of Intercultural Communication.* Columbus, OH: Merrill, 1976.

Smith, Alfred G. *Communication and Culture.* New York: Holt, Rinehart & Winston, 1966.

Smith, Anthony. *The Geopolitics of Information: How Western Culture Dominates the World.* New York: Oxford University Press, 1980.

Smith, Elise C., and Louise Fiber Luce, eds. *Toward Internationalism: Readings in Cross-Cultural Communication.* Rowley, MA: Newbury House, 1979.

Smitherman, Geneva. *Talkin and Testifyin: The Language of Black America.* Boston: Houghton Mifflin, 1977.

Sprott, W. J. H. *Human Groups.* Harmondsworth, England: Penguin Books, 1958.

Stewart, Edward C., and Milton J. Bennett. *American Cultural Patterns: A Cross-Cultural Perspective,* rev. ed. Yarmouth, ME: Intercultural Press, 1991.

Stewart, John, and Gary D'Angelo. *Together: Communicating Interpersonally.* Reading, MA: Addison-Wesley, 1976.

Szalay, Lorand B., and James E. Deese. *Subjective Meaning and Culture: An Assessment through Word Associations.* New York: Halsted Press, 1978.

Taguiri, Ron, and L. Petrollo. *Personal Perception and Interpersonal Behavior*. Stanford, CA: Stanford University Press, 1958.

Taylor, Howard F. *Balance in Small Groups*. New York: Van Nostrand Reinhold, 1970.

Thibaut, John W., and Harold H. Kelley. *The Social Psychology of Groups*. New York: John Wiley & Sons, 1959.

Triandis, Harry C. *Individualism and Collectivisim*. Boulder, CO: Westview Press, 1995.

———. *The Analysis of Subjective Culture*. New York: John Wiley & Sons, 1972.

Uttal, W. R. *The Psychology of Sensory Coding*. New York: Harper & Row, 1973.

Verderber, Rudolph F., and Kathleen Verderber. *Inter-Act: Using Interpersonal Communication Skills*. Belmont, CA: Wadsworth, 1995.

Vetter, Charles T. Jr. *Citizen Ambassadors*. Provo, UT: David M. Kennedy International Center, 1983, rev. ed. *Citizen Diplomacy*, 1995.

Weaver, Gary, R. ed. *Culture, Communication and Conflict: Readings in Intercultural Relations*, 2d ed. Needham Heights, MA: Simon & Schuster, 1998.

Weitz, Shirley, ed. *Non-Verbal Communication: Readings with Commentary*. Oxford: Oxford University Press, 1974.

White, E. B. *The Second Tree from the Corner*. New York: Harper and Brothers, 1935.

Whorf, Benjamin Lee. *Language, Thought and Reality: Selected Writings of Benjamin Lee Whorf*, edited by J. B. Carroll. Cambridge: MIT Press, 1956.

Wiener, Norbert. *Human Use of Human Beings*. New York: Houghton Mifflin, 1964.

———. *Cybernetics*. Cambridge: Technology Press of MIT; and New York: John Wiley & Sons, 1948.

Wilentz, Joan S. *The Senses of Man*. New York: Thomas Y. Crowell, 1968.

Wolfgang, Aaron, ed. *Nonverbal Behavior: Applications and Culture Implications*. New York: Academic Press, 1979.

Chapters in Books

Adler, Peter S. "Beyond Cultural Identity: Reflections on Cultural and Multicultural Man." In *Intercultural Communication: A Reader*, 4th ed., edited by Larry A. Samovar and Richard E. Porter. Belmont, CA: Wadsworth, 1985.

Andersen, Janis F. "Educational Assumptions Highlighted from a Cross-Cultural Comparison." In *Intercultural Communication: A Reader*, 4th ed., edited by Larry A. Samovar and Richard E. Porter. Belmont, CA: Wadsworth, 1985.

Arkoff, Abe, Falak Thaver, and Leonard Elkind. "Mental Health and Counseling Ideas of Asian and American Students." In *Readings in Intercultural Communication*, vol. 4, *Cross-Cultural Counseling*, edited by Paul Pedersen. Pittsburgh: Intercultural Communications Network, 1974.

Barna, La Ray M. "Stumbling Blocks in Intercultural Communication." In *Intercultural Communication: A Reader*, 4th ed., edited by Larry A. Samovar and Richard E. Porter. Belmont, CA: Wadsworth, 1985.

Barnlund, Dean C. "Communication in a Global Village." In *Intercultural Communication: A Reader*, 4th ed., edited by Larry A. Samovar and Richard E. Porter. Belmont, CA: Wadsworth, 1985.

———. "The Cross-Cultural Arena: An Ethical Void." In *Intercultural Communication: A Reader*, 4th ed., edited by Larry A. Samovar and Richard E. Porter. Belmont, CA: Wadsworth, 1985.

————. "A Transactional Model of Communication." In *Language Behavior: A Book of Readings in Communication*, edited by Johnnye Akin, Alvin Goldberg, Gail Myers, and Joseph Stewart. The Hague: Morton, 1970.

Barnlund, Dean C., and Naoki Nomura. "Decentering Convergence, and Cross-Cultural Understanding." in *Intercultural Communication: A Reader*, 4th ed., edited by Larry A. Samovar and Richard E. Porter. Belmont, CA: Wadsworth, 1985.

Bennett, Milton J. "Toward Ethnorelativism: A Developmental Model of Intercultural Sensitivity." In *Education for the Intercultural Experience*, edited by R. Michael Paige. Yarmouth, ME: Intercultural Press, 1993.

Bloombaum, Milton, Joe Yamamoto, and Quinton James. "Cultural Stereotyping among Psychotherapists." In *Readings in Intercultural Communication*, vol. 4, *Cross-Cultural Counseling*, edited by Paul Pedersen. Pittsburgh: Intercultural Communications Network, 1974.

Boxer, Marilyn J. "Are Women Human Beings? Androcentricity as a Barrier to Intercultural Communication." In *Intercultural Communication: A Reader*, 4th ed., edited by Larry A. Samovar and Richard E. Porter. Belmont, CA: Wadsworth, 1985.

Brein, Michael, and Kenneth H. David. "Intercultural Communication and the Adjustment of the Sojourner." In *Readings in Intercultural Communication*, vol. 4, *Cross-Cultural Counseling*, edited by Paul Pedersen. Pittsburgh: Intercultural Communications Network, 1974.

Brislin, Richard W. "Prejudice in Intercultural Communication." In *Intercultural Communication: A Reader*, 4th ed., edited by Larry A. Samovar and Richard E. Porter. Belmont, CA: Wadsworth, 1985.

Bruneau, Tom. "The Time Dimension in Intercultual Communication." In *Intercultural Communication: A Reader*, 4th ed., edited by Larry A. Samovar and Richard E. Porter. Belmont, CA: Wadsworth, 1985.

Carmichael, Carl W. "Cultural Patterns of the Elderly." In *Intercultural Communication: A Reader*, 4th ed., edited by Larry A. Samovar and Richard E. Porter. Belmont, CA: Wadsworth, 1985.

Clarke, Clifford H. "Personal Counseling across Cultural Boundaries." In *Readings in Intercultural Communication*, vol. 4, *Cross-Cultural Counseling*, edited by Paul Pedersen. Pittsburgh: Intercultural Communications Network, 1974.

Cooley, Ralph E. "Codes and Contexts: An Argument for Their Description." In *Intercultural Communication Theory: Current Perspectives*, 3d printing, edited by William B. Gudykunst. Newbury Park, CA: Sage, 1989.

Daniel, Jack. "The Poor: Aliens in an Affluent Society: Cross-Cultural Communication." In *Intercultural Communication: A Reader*, 4th ed., edited by Larry A. Samovar and Richard E. Porter. Belmont, CA: Wadsworth, 1985.

Deetz, Stanley. "Metaphor Analysis." In *Methods for Intercultural Communication Research*, edited by William B. Gudykunst and Young Y. Kim. Beverly Hills, CA: Sage, 1984.

Eakins, Barbara Westbrook, and R. Gene Eakins. "Sex Differences in Nonverbal Communication." In *Intercultural Communication: A Reader*, 4th ed., edited by Larry A. Samovar and Richard E. Porter. Belmont, CA: Wadsworth, 1985.

Edgerton, Robert B., and Marvin Karno. "Mexican-American Bilingualism and the Perception of Mental Illness." In *Readings in Intercultual Communication*, vol. 4, *Cross-Cultural Counseling*, edited by Paul Pedersen. Pittsburgh: Intercultural Communications Network, 1974.

Ehrenhaus, Peter. "Culture and the Attribution Process: Barriers to Effective Communication." In *Intercultural Communication Theory Current Perspectives*, 3d printing, edited by William B. Gudykunst. Newbury Park, CA: Sage, 1989.

Fearing, Franklin. "An Examination of the Conceptions of Benjamin Whorf in the Light of Theories on Perception and Cognition." In *Language in Culture*, edited by Harry Hoijer. Chicago: University of Chicago Press, 1954.

Folb, Edith A. "Vernacular Vocabulary: A View of Interracial Perceptions and Experiences." In *Intercultural Communication: A Reader*, 4th ed., edited by Larry A. Samovar and Richard E. Porter. Belmont, CA: Wadsworth, 1985.

———. "Who's Got the Room at the Top? Issues of Dominance and Nondominance in Intracultural Communication." In *Intercultural Communication: A Reader*, 4th ed., edited by Larry A. Samovar and Richard E. Porter. Belmont, CA: Wadsworth, 1985.

Go, Mae Jean. "Quantitative Content Analysis." In *Methods for Intercultural Communication Research*, edited by William B. Gudykunst and Young Y. Kim. Beverly Hills, CA: Sage, 1984.

Grey, Alan L. "The Counselling Process and Its Cultural Setting." In *Readings in Intercultural Communication*, vol. 4, *Cross-Cultural Counseling*, edited by Paul Pedersen. Pittsburgh: Intercultural Communications Network, 1974.

Gudykunst, William B., et al. "Language and Intergroup Communication." In *Handbook of International and Intercultural Communication*, edited by Molefi Kete Asante and William B. Gudykunst. Newbury Park, CA: Sage, 1989.

Hall, Edward T. Interviewed by Kenneth Friedman. "Learning the Arabs' Silent Language." In *Culture, Communication and Conflict: Readings in Intercultural Relations*, 2d ed., edited by Gary R. Weaver. Needham Heights, MA: Simon & Schuster, 1998.

———. "Context and Meaning." In *Intercultural Communication: A Reader*, 4th ed., edited by Larry A. Samovar and Richard E. Porter. Belmont, CA: Wadsworth, 1985.

Hecht, Michael L., Peter A. Andersen, and Sidney A. Ribeau. "The Cultural Dimensions of Nonverbal Communication." In *Handbook of International and Intercultural Communication*, edited by Molefi Kete Asante and William B. Gudykunst. Newbury Park, CA: Sage, 1989.

Hoijer, Harry. "The Sapir-Whorf Hypothesis." In *Intercultural Communication: A Reader*, 7th ed., edited by Larry A. Samovar and Richard E. Porter. Belmont, CA: Wadsworth, 1994.

Jakobson, Roman. "Nonverbal Signs for 'Yes' and 'No'." In *Intercultural Communication: A Reader*, 2d ed., edited by Larry A. Samovar and Richard E. Porter. Belmont, CA: Wadsworth, 1976.

Jensen, J. Vernon. "Perspective on Nonverbal Intercultural Communication." In *Intercultural Communication: A Reader*, 4th ed., edited by Larry A. Samovar and Richard E. Porter. Belmont, CA: Wadsworth, 1985.

Johnson, Kenneth R. "Black Kinesics: Some Non-Verbal Communication Patterns in Black Culture." In *Intercultural Communication: A Reader*, 4th ed., edited by Larry A. Samovar and Richard E. Porter. Belmont, CA: Wadsworth, 1985.

Kim, Young Y. "Communication and Acculturation." In *Intercultural Communication: A Reader*, 4th ed., edited by Larry A. Samovar and Richard E. Porter. Belmont, CA: Wadsworth, 1985.

————. "Intercultural Personhood: An Integration of Eastern and Western Perspectives." In *Intercultural Communication: A Reader*, 4th ed., edited by Larry A. Samovar and Richard E. Porter. Belmont, CA: Wadsworth, 1985.

————. "Searching for Creative Integration." In *Methods for Intercultural Communication Research*, edited by William B. Gudykunst and Young Y. Kim. Beverly Hills, CA: Sage, 1984.

King, Stephen W. "A Taxonomy for the Classification of Language Studies in Intercultural Communication." In *Intercultural Communication: A Reader*, 4th ed., edited by Larry A. Samovar and Richard E. Porter. Belmont, CA: Wadsworth, 1985.

Kochman, Thomas. "Cultural Pluralism: Black and White Styles" and "Force Fields in Black and White Communication." In *Cultural Communication and Intercultural Contact*, edited by Donal Carbaugh. Hillsdale, NJ: Lawrence Erlbaum, 1990.

Korzenny, Felipe, and Betty Ann Griffis Korzenny. "Quantitative Approaches: An Overview." In *Methods for Intercultural Communication Research*, edited by William B. Gudykunst and Young Y. Kim. Beverly Hills, CA: Sage, 1984.

La Barre, Weston. "Paralinguistics, Kinesics and Cultural Anthropology." In *Intercultural Communication: A Reader*, 4th ed., edited by Larry A. Samovar and Richard E. Porter. Belmont, CA: Wadsworth, 1985.

Lewis, Sasha Gregory. "Sunday's Women: Lesbian Life Today." In *Intercultural Communication: A Reader*, 4th ed., edited by Larry A. Samovar and Richard E. Porter. Belmont, CA: Wadsworth, 1985.

Maslow, Abraham H. "A Theory of Human Motivation." In *Readings in Managerial Psychology*, 2d ed., edited by Harold Levitt and Louis R. Pondy. Chicago: University of Chicago Press, 1963.

Mehrabian, Albert. "Communication without Words." In *Culture, Communication and Conflict: Readings in Intercultural Relations*, 2d ed., edited by Gary R. Weaver. Needham Heights, MA: Simon & Schuster, 1998.

Miller, Milton, Eng-Kung Yeh, A. A. Alexander, Marjorie Klein, Kwo-Kwa Tseng, Fikre Workneh, and Hung-Ming Chu. "The Cross-Cultural Student: Lessons in Human Nature." In *Readings in Intercultural Communication*, vol. 4, *Cross-Cultural Counseling*, edited by Paul Pedersen. Pittsburgh: Intercultural Communications Network, 1974.

Morten, George, and Derald Wing Sue. "Minority Group Counseling: An Overview." In *Intercultural Communication: A Reader*, 4th ed., edited by Larry A. Samovar and Richard E. Porter. Belmont, CA: Wadsworth, 1985.

Palmer, Mark T., and George A. Barnett. "Using a Spatial Model to Verify Language Translation." In *Methods for Intercultural Communication Research*, edited by William B. Gudykunst and Young Y. Kim. Beverly Hills, CA: Sage, 1984.

Pedersen, Anne B., and Paul B. Pedersen. "The Cultural Grid: A Personal Cultural Orientation." In *Intercultural Communication: A Reader*, 4th ed., edited by Larry A. Samovar and Richard E. Porter. Belmont, CA: Wadsworth, 1985.

Pedersen, Paul. "The Transfer of Intercultural Training Skills." In *Intercultural Communication: A Reader*, 4th ed., edited by Larry A. Samovar and Richard E. Porter. Belmont, CA: Wadsworth, 1985.

Pennington, Dorthy L. "Intercultural Communication." In *Intercultural Communication: A Reader*, 4th ed., edited by Larry A. Samovar and Richard E. Porter. Belmont, CA: Wadsworth, 1985.

Pool, Ithiel De Sola. "Communication Systems." In *Handbook of Communication*, edited by Ithiel De Sola Pool, et al. Chicago: Rand McNally, 1973.

Porter, Richard E., and Larry A. Samovar. "Approaching Intercultural Communication." In *Intercultural Communication: A Reader*, 4th ed., edited by Larry A. Samovar and Richard E. Porter. Belmont, CA: Wadsworth, 1985.

————. "Communicating Interculturally." In *Intercultural Communication: A Reader*, 2d ed., edited by Larry A. Samovar and Richard E. Porter. Belmont, CA: Wadsworth, 1976.

Price-Williams, D. "Cross-Cultural Studies." In *New Horizons in Psychology*, edited by Brian M. Foss. New York: Penguin Books, 1966. Reprinted in *Intercultural Communication: A Reader*, 2d ed., edited by Larry A. Samovar and Richard E. Porter. Belmont, CA: Wadsworth, 1976.

Ramsey, Sheila J. "Nonverbal Behavior: An Intercultural Perspective." In *Handbook of Intercultural Communication*, edited by Molefi Kete Asante, Eileen Newmark, and Cecil A. Blake. Beverly Hills: Sage, 1979.

————. "To Hear One and Understand Ten: Nonverbal Behavior in Japan." In *Intercultural Communication: A Reader*, 4th ed., edited by Larry A. Samovar and Richard E. Porter. Belmont, CA: Wadsworth, 1985.

Rosen, Robert H. "Diversity." In *Leading People: Transforming Business from the Inside Out*. New York: Viking, 1996.

————. "Our Strengths Lie in Celebrating Differences." In *The Healthy Company: Eight Strategies to Develop People, Productivity, and Profits*. Los Angeles: Jeremy P. Tarcher, 1991.

Ruben, Brent D. "Human Communication and Cross-Cultural Effectiveness." In *Intercultural Communication: A Reader*, 4th ed., edited by Larry A. Samovar and Richard E. Porter. Belmont, CA: Wadsworth, 1985.

Samovar, Larry A., and Richard E. Porter. "Co-Cultures: Living in Two Cultures." In *Intercultural Communication: A Reader*, 8th ed., edited by Larry A. Samovar and Richard E. Porter. Belmont, CA: Wadsworth, 1997.

———. "Cultural Diversity in Perception: Alternative Views of Reality." In *Communication between Cultures*, Belmont, CA: Wadsworth, 1991.

Sarbaugh, Lawrence E. "An Overview of Selected Approaches." In *Methods for Intercultural Communication Research*, edited by William B. Gudykunst and Young Y. Kim. Beverly Hills, CA: Sage, 1984.

Sarett, Carla J. "Observational Methods." In *Methods for Intercultural Communication Research*, edited by William B. Gudykunst and Young Y. Kim. Beverly Hills, CA: Sage, 1984.

Sechrest, Lee, Todd L. Fay, and S. M. Zaidi. "Problems of Translation in Cross-Cultural Communication." In *Intercultural Communication: A Reader*, 4th ed., edited by Larry A. Samovar and Richard E. Porter. Belmont, CA: Wadsworth, 1985.

Shuter, Robert. "Naturalistic Field Research." In *Methods for Intercultural Communication Research*, edited by William B. Gudykunst and Young Y. Kim. Beverly Hills, CA: Sage, 1984.

Sprang, Alonzo. "Counseling the Indian." In *Readings in Intercultural Communication*, vol. 4, *Cross-Cultural Counseling*, edited by Paul Pedersen. Pittsburgh: Intercultural Communications Network, 1974.

Stanback, Marsha Houston, and W. Barnett Pearce. "Talking to 'the Man': Some Communication Strategies Used by Members of 'Subordinate' Social Groups." In *Intercultural Communication: A Reader*, 4th ed., edited by Larry A. Samovar and Richard E. Porter. Belmont, CA: Wadsworth, 1985.

Starosta, William J. "On Intercultural Rhetoric." In *Methods for Intercultural Communication Research*, edited by William B. Gudykunst and Young Y. Kim. Beverly Hills, CA: Sage, 1984.

Sue, Derald Wing, and Stanley Sue. "Counseling Chinese-Americans." In *Readings in Intercultural Communication*, vol. 4, *Cross-Cultural Counseling*, edited by Paul Pedersen. Pittsburgh: Intercultural Communications Network, 1974.

Tafoya, Dennis W. "Research and Cultural Phenomena." In *Methods for Intercultural Communication Research*, edited by William B. Gudykunst and Young Y. Kim. Beverly Hills, CA: Sage, 1984.

Ting-Toomey, Stella. "Qualitative Research: An Overview." In *Methods for Intercultural Communication Research*, edited by William B. Gudykunst and Young Y. Kim. Beverly Hills, CA: Sage, 1984.

Van Mannen, J., and Edwin Schein. "Toward a Theory of Organization Socialization." Quoted in Norman G. Dinges and William S. Maynard, "Intercultural Aspects of Organizational Effectiveness." In *Handbook of Intercultural Training*, vol. 2, *Issues in Training Methodology*, edited by Dan Landis and Richard W. Brislin. New York: Pergamon, 1983.

Weaver, Gary R. "Section II: Managing Diversity." In *Culture, Communication and Conflict: Readings in Intercultural Relations*, 2d ed., edited by Gary R. Weaver. Needham Heights, MA: Simon & Schuster, 1998.

Weber, Shirley N. "The Need to Be: The Socio-Cultural Significance of Black Language." In *Intercultural Communication: A Reader*, 4th ed., edited by Larry A. Samovar and Richard E. Porter. Belmont, CA: Wadsworth, 1985.

Woelfel, Joseph, and Nicholas R. Napoli. "Measuring Human Emotion: Proposed Standards." In *Methods for Intercultural Communication Research*, edited by William B. Gudykunst and Young Y. Kim. Beverly Hills, CA: Sage, 1984.

Wolfson, Kim, and Martin F. Norden. "Measuring Responses to Filmed Interpersonal Conflict: A Rules Approach." In *Methods for Intercultural Communication Research*, edited by William B. Gudykunst and Young Y. Kim. Beverly Hills, CA: Sage, 1984.

Wrenn, C. Gilbert. "The Culturally Encapsulated Counselor." In *Readings in Intercultural Communication*, vol. 4, *Cross-Cultural Counseling*, edited by Paul Pedersen. Pittsburgh: Intercultural Communications Network, 1974.

Wright, Joseph E. "The Implications of Cognitive Science." In *Methods for Intercultural Communication Research*, edited by William B. Gudykunst and Young Y. Kim. Beverly Hills, CA: Sage, 1984.

Yum, June Ock. "Network Analysis." In *Methods for Intercultural Communication Research*, edited by William B. Gudykunst and Young Y. Kim. Beverly Hills, CA: Sage, 1984.

Journal Articles

Abe, Hiroko, and Richard L. Wiseman. "A Cross-Cultural Confirmation of the Dimensions of Intercultural Effectiveness." *International Journal of Intercultural Relations* 7, no. 1 (1983).

Asuncion-Lande, Nobeleza C. "Implications of Intercultural Communication for Bilingual and Bicultural Education." In *International and Intercultural Communication Annual*, vol. 2, edited by Fred L. Casmir. Falls Church, VA: Speech Communication Association, 1975.

Badami, Mary Kenny. "Interpersonal Perceptions in a Simulation Game of Intercultural Contact." In *International and Intercultural Communication Annual*, vol. 1, edited by Fred L. Casmir. Falls Church, VA: Speech Communication Association, 1974.

Baldassini, Jose G., and Vincent F. Flaherty. "Acculturation Process of Colombian Immigrants into the American Culture in Bergen County, New Jersey." *International Journal of Intercultural Relations* 5, no. 2 (1981).

Bennett, Janet. "Transition Shock: Putting Culture Shock in Perspective." In *International and Intercultural Communication Annual*, vol. 4, edited by Nemi C. Jain, Falls Church, VA: Speech Communication Association, 1977.

Benson, Philip G. "Measuring Cross-Cultural Adjustment: The Problem of Criteria." *International Journal of Intercultural Relations* 2, no. 1 (1978).

Berry, Elizabeth, Joan B. Kessler, John T. Fodor, and Masakatsu Wato. "Intercultural Communication for Health Personnel." *International Journal of Intercultural Relations* 7, no. 4 (1983).

Borden, George A., and Jean M. Tanner. "The Cross-Cultural Transfer of Educational Technology: A Myth." *International Journal of Intercultural Relations* 7, no. 1 (1983).

Brashen, Henry M. "Research Methodology in Another Culture: Some Precautions." In *International and Intercultural Communication Annual*, vol. 2, edited by Fred L. Casmir. Falls Church, VA: Speech Communication Association, 1975.

Briggs, Nancy E., and Glenn R. Harwood. "Training Personnel in Multinational Businesses: An Inoculation Approach." *International Journal of Intercultural Relations* 6, no. 4 (1982).

Broome, Benjamin J. "Facilitating Attitudes and Message Characteristics in the Expression of Differences in Intercultural Encounters." *International Journal of Intercultural Relations* 5, no. 3 (1981).

Burgoon, Michael, James P. Dillard, and Noel E. Doran. "Cultural and Situational Influences on the Process of Persuasive Strategy Selection." *International Journal of Intercultural Relations* 6, no. 1 (1982).

Burk, Jerry L. "Intercultural Communication Vistas: Description, Concept, and Theory." In *International and Intercultural Communication Annual*, vol. 2, edited by Fred L. Casmir. Falls Church, VA: Speech Communication Association, 1975.

———. "The Effects of Ethnocentrism upon Intercultural Communication." In *International and Intercultural Communication Annual*, vol. 3, edited by Fred L. Casmir. Falls Church, VA: Speech Communication Association, 1976.

Clark, M. L., and Willie Pearson, Jr. "Racial Stereotypes Revisited." *International Journal of Intercultural Relations* 6, no. 4 (1982).

Clark, Robert R. "African Healing and Western Psychotherapy: Meetings between Professionals." *International Journal of Intercultural Relations* 6, no. 1 (1982).

Cline, Rebecca J., and Carol A. Puhl, "Gender, Culture, and Geography: A Comparison of Seating Arrangements in the United States and Taiwan." *International Journal of Intercultural Relations* 8, no. 2 (1984).

Condon, Eliane C. "Cross-Cultural Inferences Affecting Teacher-Pupil Communication in American Schools." In *International and Intercultural Communication Annual*, vol. 3, edited by Fred L. Casmir. Falls Church, VA: Speech Communication Association, 1976.

Cushman, Donald, and Gordon C. Whiting. "An Approach to Communication Theory: Towards Consensus on Rules." *Journal of Communication* 22 (September 1972).

Da Silva, Edgar J. "Microbial Technology: Some Social and Intercultural Implications in Development." *International Journal of Intercultural Relations* 8, no. 4 (1984).

Delgado, Melvin. "Cultural Consultation: Implications for Hispanic Mental Health Services in the United States." *International Journal of Intercultural Relations* 6, no. 3 (1982).

Diamond, C. T. Patrick. "Understanding Others: Kellyian Theory, Methodology and Applications." *International Journal of Intercultural Relations* 6, no. 4 (1982).

Douglas, Donald G. "The Study of Communication Messages and the Conflict over Global Eco-Patience." In *International and Intercultural Communication Annual*, vol. 2, edited by Fred L. Casmir. Falls Church, VA: Speech Communication Association, 1975.

Dyal, James A., and Ruth Y. Dyal. "Acculturation Stress and Coping: Some Implications for Research and Education." *International Journal of Intercultural Relations* 5, no. 4 (1981).

Edwards, Walter F. "Some Linguistic and Behavioral Links in the African Diaspora: Cultural Implications." *International Journal of Intercultural Relations* 5, no. 2 (1981).

Esfandiari, M., and J. Hamadanizadeh. "An Investigation of the Iranian's Attitudes towards Goals of Education." *International Journal of Intercultural Relations* 5, no. 2 (1981).

Everett, James E., Bruce W. Stening, and Peter A. Longton. "Stereotypes of the Japanese Manager in Singapore." *International Journal of Intercultural Relations* 5, no. 3 (1981).

Farmer, Helen S., Nayereh Tohidi, and Elisabeth R. Weiss. "Study of the Factors Influencing Sex Differences in the Career Motivation of Iranian High School Students." *International Journal of Intercultural Relations* 6, no. 1 (1982).

Flemings, Corinne K. "National and International Conferences Relating to International and Intercultural Communication." In *International and Intercultural Communication Annual*, vol. 3, edited by Fred L. Casmir. Falls Church, VA: Speech Communication Association, 1976.

Florian, Victor. "Cross-Cultural Differences in Attitudes towards Disabled Persons: A Study of Jewish and Arab Youth in Israel." *International Journal of Intercultural Relations* 6, no. 3 (1982).

Frideres, James, and S. Goldenberg. "Ethnic Identity: Myth and Reality in Western Canada." *International Journal of Intercultural Relations* 5, no. 2 (1981).

Fyans, Leslie J. Jr., Barbara Kremer, Farideh Salili, and Martin L. Maehr. "The Effects of Evaluation Conditions on 'Continuing Motivation': Study of the Cultural Personological and Situational Antecedents of a Motivational Pattern." *International Journal of Intercultural Relations* 5, no. 1 (1981).

Graham, Morris A. "Acculturative Stress among Polynesian, Asian and American Students on the Brigham Young University-Hawaii Campus." *International Journal of Intercultural Relations* 7, no. 1 (1983).

Gudykunst, William B. "Toward a Typology of Stranger-Host Relationships." *International Journal of Intercultural Relations* 7, no. 4 (1983).

———. "Intercultural Contact and Attitude Change: A Review of Literature and Suggestions for Future Research." In *International and Intercultural Communication Annual*, vol. 4, edited by Nemi C. Jain. Falls Church, VA: Speech Communication Association, 1977.

Guthrie, George M., Tomas L. Fernandez, and Nenita O. Estrera. "Small-Scale Studies and Field Experiments in Family Planning in the Philippines." *International Journal of Intercultural Relations* 8, no. 4 (1984).

Hawes, Frank, and Daniel J. Kealey. "An Empirical Study of Canadian Technical Assistance: Adaptation and Effectiveness on Overseas Assignment." *International Journal of Intercultural Relations* 5, no. 3 (1981).

Hecht, Michael L., and Sidney Ribeau. "Ethnic Communication: A Comparative Analysis of Satisfying Communication." *International Journal of Intercultural Relations* 8, no. 2 (1984).

Hepworth, Janice C. "Some Empirical Considerations for Cross-Cultural Attitude Measurements and Persuasive Communications." In *International and Intercultural Communication Annual*, vol. 1, edited by Fred L. Casmir. Falls Church, VA: Speech Communication Association, 1974.

Herberg, Dorothy C. "Discovering Ethnic Root Behavior Patterns: Towards an Applied Canadian Ethnic Studies." *International Journal of Intercultural Relations* 5, no. 2 (1981).

Hui, Chi-Chiu Harry. "Locus of Control: A Review of Cross-Cultural Research." *International Journal of Intercultural Relations* 6, no. 3 (1982).

Inglis, Margaret, and William B. Gudykunst. "Institutional Completeness and Communication Acculturation: A Comparison of Korean Immigrants in Chicago and Hartford." *International Journal of Intercultural Relations* 6, no. 3 (1982).

Ivey, Allen E., and Suzanne Jessop McGowan. "Sociolinguistics: The Implications of a Sociological Approach in Examining the Counseling Relationship." *International Journal of Intercultural Relations* 5, no. 1 (1981).

Jeffres, Leo W., and K. Kyoon Hur. "Communication Channels within Ethnic Groups." *International Journal of Intercultural Relations* 5, no. 1 (1981).

Jun, Suk-Ho. "Communication Patterns among Young Korean Immigrants." *International Journal of Intercultural Relations* 8, no. 4 (1984).

Kaplan, Robert B. "Cultural Thought Patterns in Inter-Cultural Education." *Language Learning* 16, nos. 1 and 2 (1966).

Kim, Young Y. "Inter-Ethnic and Intra-Ethnic Communication: A Study of Korean Immigrants in Chicago." In *International and Intercultural Communication Annual,* vol. 4, edited by Nemi C. Jain. Falls Church, VA: Speech Communication Association, 1977.

Koenig, Edna L. "Language and Ethnicity in Intergroup Communication." In *International and Intercultural Communication Annual,* vol. 2, edited by Fred L. Casmir. Falls Church, VA: Speech Communication Association, 1975.

Korzenny, Felipe, and Kimberly A. Neuendorf. "The Perceived Reality of Television and Aggressive Predispositions among Children in Mexico." *International Journal of Intercultural Relations* 7, no. 1 (1983).

La France, Marianne, and Clara Mayo. "Cultural Aspects of Nonverbal Communication: A Review Essay." *International Journal of Intercultural Relations* 2, no. 1 (1978).

Lampe, Philip E. "Ethnicity and Crime: Perceptual Differences among Blacks, Mexican Americans, and Anglos." *International Journal of Intercultural Relations* 8, no. 4 (1984).

———. "Interethnic Dating: Reasons For and Against." *International Journal of Intercultural Relations* 5, no. 2 (1981).

Lessing, Elise E., Chester C. Clarke, and Lisa Gray-Shellberg. "Black Power Ideology: Rhetoric and Reality in a Student Sample." *International Journal of Intercultural Relations* 5, no. 1 (1981).

Maehr, Martin L., and Anton Lysy. "Motivating Students of Diverse Sociocultural Backgrounds to Achieve." *International Journal of Intercultural Relations* 2, no. 1 (1978).

Martin, Judith N. "The Intercultural Reentry: Conceptualization and Directions for Future Research." *International Journal of Intercultural Relations* 8, no. 2 (1984).

Matsumoto, David, and Hiromu Kishimoto. "Developmental Characteristics in Judgements of Emotion from Nonverbal Vocal Cues." *International Journal of Intercultural Relations* 7, no. 4 (1983).

Meehan, Anita, and Glynis Bean. "Tracking the Civil Rights and Women's Movements in the United States." *International Journal of Intercultural Relations* 5, no. 2 (1981).

Mendenhall, Mark, Gary Oddou, and David V. Stimpson. "Enhancing Trainee Satisfaction with Cross-Cultural Training Programs via Prior Warning." *International Journal of Intercultural Relations* 6, no. 4 (1982).

Neel, Robert G., Oliver C. S. Tzeng, and Can Baysal. "Comparative Studies of Authoritarian-Personality Characteristics across Culture, Language and Methods." *International Journal of Intercultural Relations* 7, no. 4 (1983).

Newmark, Eileen, and Molefi Kete Asante. "Perception of Self and Others: An Approach to Intercultural Communication." In *International and Intercultural Communication Annual*, vol. 2, edited by Fred L. Casmir. Falls Church, VA: Speech Communication Association, 1975.

Nilan, Michael S. "Development Communication Expectations in Occupational Contexts: A Comparison of U.S. and Foreign Graduate Students." *International Journal of Intercultural Relations* 5, no. 2 (1981).

Nomura, Naoki, and Dean C. Barnlund. "Patterns of Interpersonal Criticism in Japan and the United States." *International Journal of Intercultural Relations* 7, no. 1 (1983).

Nwankwo, Robert L. "Minoritarianism and Ethnic Groups Communication." In *International and Intercultural Communication Annual*, vol. 2, edited by Fred L. Casmir. Falls Church, VA: Speech Communication Association, 1975.

Nwankwo, Robert L., and Humphrey A. Regis. "The Perception of Transcendent Interest: Communication and Identification in an Emergent Community." *International Journal of Intercultural Relations* 7, no. 4 (1983).

Pedersen, Paul. "International Conferences: Significant Measures of Success." *International Journal of Intercultural Relations* 5, no. 1 (1981).

Pettersen, Duane D. "Language and Information Processing: An Approach to Intercultural Communication." In *International and Intercultural Communication Annual*, vol. 3, edited by Fred L. Casmir. Falls Church, VA: Speech Communication Association, 1976.

Pool, Ithiel De Sola, and Manfred Kochen. "Contacts and Influence." *Social Networks* 1 (1978/79).

Pruitt, France J. "The Adaptation of African Students to American Society." *International Journal of Intercultural Relations* 2, no. 1 (1978).

Renwick, George W. "Intercultural Communication: State-of-the-Art Study." In *International and Intercultural Communication Annual*, vol. 5, edited by Nemi C. Jain. Falls Church, VA: Speech Communication Association, 1979.

Rich, Yisrael, Yehuda Amir, and Rachel Ben-Ari. "Social and Emotional Problems Associated with Integration in the Israeli Junior High School Motivational Pattern." *International Journal of Intercultural Relations* 5, no. 3 (1981).

Ripple, Richard E., Gail A. Jaquish, H. Wing Lee, and John Spinks. "Intergenerational Differences in Descriptions of Life-Span Stages among Hong Kong Chinese." *International Journal of Intercultural Relations* 7, no. 4 (1983).

Ruhly, Sharon. "The Major Triad Revisited: A Potential Guide for Intercultural Research." In *International and Intercultural Communication Annual*, vol. 3, edited by Fred L. Casmir. Falls Church, VA: Speech Communication Association, 1976.

Ruszkowski, Andrew. "Role of the Holy See Observer to the United Nations as Intercultural Communication." In *International and Intercultural Communication Annual*, vol. 3, edited by Fred L. Casmir. Falls Church, VA: Speech Communication Association, 1976.

St. Martin, Gail M. "Intercultual Differential Decoding of Nonverbal Affective Communication." In *International and Intercultural Communication Annual*, vol. 3, edited by Fred L. Casmir. Falls Church, VA: Speech Communication Association, 1976.

Salili, Farideh, Martin L. Maehr, and Leslie J. Fyans Jr. "Evaluating Morality and Achievement: A Study of the Interaction of Social Cultural and Developmental Trends." In *International Journal of Intercultural Relations* 5, no. 2 (1981).

Sarbaugh, Lawrence E. "A Systematic Framework for Analyzing Intercultural Communication." In *International and Intercultural Communication Annual*, vol. 5, edited by Nemi C. Jain. Falls Church, VA: Speech Communication Association, 1979.

Sarmad, Zohreh. "Pattern of Some Measured Mental Abilities among Persian Bilingual and Monolingual Children." In *International Journal of Intercultural Relations* 5, no. 4 (1981).

Schein, Edgar H. "Coming to a New Awareness of Organizational Culture." *Sloan Management Review* 26 (Winter 1984).

Schneider, Michael J., and William Jordan. "Perception of the Communicative Performance of Americans and Chinese in Intercultural Dyads." *International Journal of Intercultural Relations* 5, no. 2 (1981).

Shamir, Boas. "Some Differences in Work Attitudes between Arab and Jewish Hotel Workers." *International Journal of Intercultural Relations* 5, no. 1 (1981).

Shuter, Robert, and Judith Fitzgerald Miller. "An Exploratory Study of Pain Expression Styles among Blacks and Whites." *International Journal of Intercultural Relations* 6, no. 3 (1982).

Singer, Marshall R. "Culture: A Perceptual Approach." *Vidya,* no. 3 (Spring 1969).

Smith, Alfred G. "Taxonomies for Planning Intercultural Communication." In *International and Intercultural Communication Annual*, vol. 5, edited by Nemi C. Jain. Falls Church, VA: Speech Communication Association, 1979.

Smutkupt, Suriya, and LaRay M. Barna. "Impact of Non-verbal Communication in an Intercultural Setting: Thailand." In *International and Intercultural Communication Annual*, vol. 3, edited by Fred L. Casmir. Falls Church, VA: Speech Communication Association, 1976.

Stein, Howard F. "Adversary Symbiosis and Complementary Group Dissociation: An Analysis of the U.S./U.S.S.R. Conflict." *International Journal of Intercultural Relations* 6, no. 1 (1982).

Stewart, Edward C. "The Survival Stage of Intercultural Communication." In *International and Intercultural Communication Annual*, vol. 4, edited by Nemi C. Jain. Falls Church, VA: Speech Communication Association, 1977.

Szalay, Lorand B. "Intercultural Communication—A Process Model." *International Journal of Intercultural Relations* 5, no. 2 (1981).

Ting-Toomey, Stella. "Ethnic Identity and Close Friendship in Chinese-American College Students." *International Journal of Intercultural Relations* 5, no. 4 (1981).

Tyler, Vernon Lynn. "Dimensions, Perspectives and Resources of Intercultural Communication." In *International and Intercultural Communication Annual*, vol. 1, edited by Fred L. Casmir. Falls Church, VA: Speech Communication Association, 1974.

Useem, John, and Ruth Hill Useem. "American-Educated Indians and Americans in India: A Comparison of the Two Modernizing Roles." *Journal of Social Issues* 24, no. 4 (1968).

Viglionese, Paschal C. "Text and Metatext in Hersey's *A Single Pebble* from the Perspective of Intercultural Communication." *International Journal of Intercultural Relations* 6, no. 1 (1982).

Weimann, Gabriel. "Images of Life in America: The Impact of American T.V. in Israel." *International Journal of Intercultural Relations* 8, no. 2 (1984).

White, Ralph K. "Misperception and the Vietnam War." *Journal of Social Issues* 22, no. 3 (July 1966).

Wong-Rieger, Durhane. "Testing a Model of Emotional and Coping Responses to Problems in Adaptation: Foreign Students at a Canadian University." *International Journal of Intercultural Relations* 8, no. 2 (1984).

Yamamoto, Kaoru, O. L. Davis Jr., and Gail McEachron-Hirsch. "International Perceptions across the Sea: Patterns in Japanese Young Adults." *International Journal of Intercultural Relations* 7, no. 1 (1983).

Yinon, Yoel, and Yehuda Ron. "Ethnic Similarity and Economic Status of the Potential Helper as Determinants of Helping Behavior." *International Journal of Intercultural Relations* 6, no. 3 (1982).

Yousef, Fathi S., and Nancy E. Briggs. "The Multinational Business Organization: A Schema for the Training of Overseas Personnel in Communication." In *International and Intercultural Communication Annual*, vol. 2, edited by Fred L. Casmir. Falls Church, VA: Speech Communication Association, 1975.

Index

A

Affirmative action, 183

African American identity, 61-62, 61n, 75-76, 77, 129-31, 134-35, 184

Allport, Gordon W., 129-31

American identity, 71, 72, 73, 75-76, 79, 82, 88-89 133. *See also* Immigrant identity

Anthropology. *See* Cultural anthropology, early research in

Arafat, Yasar, 119

Aristotle, 14, 108

Art culture, 126

Assimilation, in U.S. workplace, 185

Athenian identity, 69-70

Attitudes
    definition of, 27, 52
    ranking of, 93-94

Attitudinal framework, 28-29

Attribution theory, 176-77
Authoritarian-oriented cultures, 43
Authoritarian-oriented individuals, 43
Authority, attitudes toward, 42-43

B

Bandaranaike, Sirimavo, 196
Barbarians, 70
Barnlund, Dean C., 151, 152-54
Behavior. *See also* Context
    effects of identity on, 82-83
    influence of perceptions on, 10-11
    group-learned, 3
    nonverbal, 119
    norms of, 2
    of managers and workers, 38-39
    power-oriented, 164
Belief system, 13, 137
    definition of, 39, 53
Beliefs
    core, 40-41
    derivative, 41
    impact on intercultural communication, 41
    secondary, 40-41
Belonging, 7
Benedict, Ruth, 6
Berelson, Bernard, 118
Beyond Culture, 135-36
Bias, 176
Biological inheritance, 4, 15-16, 19
Biological needs, 3, 6-7
Biological process, impact of on identity, 95
Black/white identity, 62, 129-31, 134
Blindness caused by conflicting identities, 91
Body language, 4n
Books, reality of, 44-45, 48
Brain-lobe dominance, 121

British identity, 71, 90-91, 216
Buddhist identity, 28
Building bridges, 181-82, 192, 208

C

Caterpillars, fried, 9-10, 124
Catholic identity, 20-21, 61, 70, 80, 193. *See also* Latin
    Catholic identity
Censor screens, 11, 28, 126-31, 160, 203-04
        construction of, 127-28
Channels of communication, 147-49, 161, 187, 204, 234
Childhood,nonverbal communication in, 116. *See also*
    Formative years
Chinese identity, 23, 70
Circle of causality, 13, 84
Civil rights, 183
Clan, as identity group, 66
Class identity, 72
Coercion, 166, 169
Cognition, 87-88
Cognitive dissonance, 87-88
Cold War, 75, 81, 148, 226
Collective experience, 223, 230
Collective history, 230
Collective memory, 85-86
Collectivity, 56n
Communication. See also Channels of communication;
    Face-to-face communication; Intergroup communica-
    tion; International communication; Interpersonal
    communication; Intragroup communication;
    Intrapersonal communication
    as means to categorizing groups, 59, 197-98
    barriers to, 24, 37, 43, 63, 113, 131, 138, 151, 208-09
    breakdown in, 98-99
    breaking barriers of, 234
    definition of, 68
    difficulties inherent in, 107-09

distortions in, 185-87, 190, 235-36
ease of in family groups, 66
impact of overlapping identity groups on, 65
impact of sensory styles on, 122
increasing effectiveness of, 8
influence of elites on, 222
needs-based, 36
official, 223-24
physical barriers to, 16, 19
purpose of, 107-08, 158
reality-based, 50-51
role of feedback in, 68, 156-57
role of symbols in, 24
role of values in, 37-38
spiraling of, 63, 99. *See also* Spiral of similarity of
    perception, Spiral of trust
steps to, 191
unofficial, 224
Communication process, 103, 109, 158, 179
Barnlund's model of, 151, 152-54
complexity of, 157
Singer's model of, 110-11
steps in, 106, 185-87
within groups, 200-02
Communication revolution, 232-35, 237
Communism, 80-81, 223
Conflict, 89, 107. *See also* Ethnic conflict; Religious con-
    flict
intranational, 217-18
resolution, 49, 75-76
situations, misperceptions in, 49, 74-77
Consciousness, 13
Contamination, cultural, 7
Context, 72-73, 82-83, 89, 132, 209
Conti, Richard, 45-46
Core beliefs, 42, 124, 175
Corporate America, 184

Corporate culture, 206, 208
Cottam, Richard, 79
Cross-cultural communication, barriers to, 8
Cultural adaptation, 193-94
Cultural anthropology, early research in, 6-7
Cultural barriers, communicating effectively across, 34
Cultural boundaries, 96-97
Cultural change, 101
Cultural conditioning, 3-5, 12
Cultural differences
    effect of, 9
    evolution of, 63-64
Cultural diversity, 182-85, 235
    workplace benefits of, 183-84
Cultural groups. *See* Identity groups
Cultural identity, 4, 68-69, 81n
Cultural inheritance, 4
Cultural language, 76-77, 142
Cultural neutrality, 19
Cultural norms, violation of, 1-2
Cultural patterns, 7
Cultural perceptions. *See* Perceptions.
Cultural similarities, 8
    importance of in communication, 33-34
Culturally identical, 84
Culturally neutral, 156
Culturally unique, 13, 30, 33-34, 84, 178
Culture. *See also*, Group culture; Individual culture; Popu-
    lar culture
    changing definition of, 7
    definition of, 5-6, 11, 52
    impact of on behavior, 98
Culture of poverty, 58
Cultures. *See* Identity groups
Culture's Consequences, 38

D

Daisy chain, 212-13
Data bank, 11, 85, 132, 136-38, 142, 160
        effect on communication, 138
Decision making, 159-60, 203, 217
Decoding, 131-36, 160, 180, 203
        mechanisms, 11, 28
Democracy, 80-81
Democratic identity, 128
Dialects, 7, 179
Differences, acclimation to, 72
Diffusion, 8
Diplomatic relations, 226, 227
Disbelief systems, 13, 137
        definition of, 39, 53
Distance, 119-20
Distortion. See Communication, distortions in
Diversity. *See* Cultural diversity
Dominance, 71, 216, 218
Double-value orientation, 92

E

Ego, 139
Egyptian identity, 24-25
Elite(s), 203, 216, 217, 219-20
        and government control, 218-19
        communication among, 222
        definition of, 199
        diagram of, 221
        primary, 199
        secondary, 199
        tertiary, 199
Encoding, 141, 160, 204
Environment. *See also* Foreign environment; Neutral turf
        adaptation to, 193-94
        impact of on communication, 92-94, 101
Ethnic conflict, 81-82, 167-68, 223

Ethnic group, 180
Ethnic identity, 61
        environment and, 73-74
Ethnic inferiority complex, 71
Ethnic nationalism, 81
Ethnic neighborhoods, 73-74
Ethnic purity, 81-82
Eye contact, 134-35
Eye of the Beholder, The, 45-46
Eyes, as sensory receptors, 14
Eyes, reading of, 118-19

F

Face-to-face communication, 112, 148, 149, 151, 185-87, 190
Family identity, 66, 95-96. *See also* Nuclear family
        as network, 187
        breakdown of, 66-67
Father identity, 36
Feedback, 65, 68, 133
        role of in communication, 151-57, 162
Festinger, Leon A., 87-88
Filipino identity, 70
Fingerprints, 14-15
Foreign environment
        adaptation to, 76
        as challenge to identity, 93-94
Foreign service, 77
Formative years, 4-5, 6, 13, 20, 59-60, 95-96, 106
French identity, 216
Freud, Sigmund, 138-39, 146. *See also* Freudian slip
Freudian slip, 119, 146
Friendship and shared identities, 67

G

Gandhi, Indira, 196
Gandhi, Rajiv, 168

Genetics, role of in identity, 4
German identity, 70
German-Jewish identity, 61-62
Global village, 235
Goal achievement through communication, 106-07
Going native, 77, 93-94
Government
    functions of, 216, 218
    power of, 214
Government-to-government communication, 226
Green, Sam, 50-51, 98, 167
Group(s). *See also* Group-learned experiences, Identity
    groups, Informal groups
    assumption of good, 69, 71
    attitudes of, 27-29
    characteristics of, 197
    codes of, 132, 136
    cohesion of, 21
    culture of, 52, 85, 100, 199-200, 216
    decision making within, 199
    explanation of, 194-99
    functions of, 198
    goals of, 198
    history of, 202
    identity of, 3, 29, 34, 78, 179-81
    impact of environmental factors on, 192-94, 236
    impact of historical factors on, 192-94, 236
    membership in, 86
    memory of, 200
    myths of, 202
    multiple identities of, 215
    needs of, 37
    norms of, 139
    power of, 202
    protection of, 82
    ranking of values within, 37
    response to stimuli, 129

role of judgments in, 28-29
rules and regulations of, 199
subtleties of, 67
trust, 69, 207
values of, 30, 37-39, 202
Group-learned experiences, 4
Guatemalan identity, 50-51

H

Hall, Edward T., 119, 135-36
Hallucinations, 46
Hess, E. H., 118
Hierarchy of needs, 34-35
Hindi, 105
Hindu identity, 105, 128
Hofstede, Geert, 11, 38-39, 42
Hoijer, Harry, 8
Holocaust, 204
Homosexual identity, 74, 118
Hoopes, David S., 68
Human identity, 75-76
Hussein, Saddam, 75
Hypnosis, 133

I

Id, 137, 138-39
Identity, 13. *See also* Individual identity
    conflicting, 88, 90-91
    finding common experiences in, 179-81
    primary, 78-80, 82, 88, 195
    ranking of, 78, 84, 86, 89, 100, 220
    recognition of, 99
    secondary, 78-79, 88
    sharing of, 99
    subconscious assumptions of, 67, 172-73
    tertiary, 78-79, 90

Identity group(s), 5, 6, 8, 56n, 59, 99, 197
    culture of, 6
    formation of, 59-62, 233-34
    learning in, 60
    loyalty to, 66, 79-80
    overlapping of, 30, 64-68, 188-89, 207
    power structure of, 220
    ranking of, 84
    value systems of, 32-33
Image projection, 230
Immigrant identity, 67, 73
Indian identity, 194
Individual attitudes, 12-13
Individual cultures, 84, 100
Individual identity, 5, 11, 12-13, 85
Individualism vs. collectivism, 38
Inferiority complex. See Ethnic inferiority complex
Influence, 187, 209, 222-23
    definition of, 164-65
    determinants of, 219
    effect of context upon, 166
Informal groups, 197-98
Information, as component of power, 171
Ingram, Harrington, 174-75
Inheritance. See Biological inheritance; Formative years
Insanity, 47
Institutions, 198
Intercultural communication skills, 14, 96-99, 106-07, 171, 178, 232
Intergroup communication, 206-12, 236
    problems in, 63, 207
Intergroup communication model, 207, 210-11
Intermediary, 208
International affairs, 75, 213
Internal communication, 172-73
International communication, 214-15, 223-33, 237
International communication process model, 228-29

Internet, 233-34
Interpersonal communication, 163, 178-82, 207-08, 235
Interpersonal communication process, Singer model of, 110-11
Intragroup communication, 57-59, 199-206, 236
Intragroup communication model, 201
Intranational communication, 216-23, 236-37
Intranational communication model, 221
Intrapersonal communication, 153, 171-78, 235. *See also* Internal communication
Involuntary message, 161
Involuntary response, 145
Irish identity, 193
Isolated cultures, 7

J

Japanese identity, 133, 208
Jewish identity, 25, 31-32, 70, 79. *See also* German-Jewish identity
Johari Window, 174, 179, 181
    explanation of, 175-76

K

Kaplan, Robert B., 41-42
Key, Wilson Bryan, 117, 123-24
Kinesthetic sensory mechanism, 124
Kissinger, Henry, 83
Klineberg, Otto, 130

L

Language. *See also* Whorf/Sapir hypothesis
    as symbols, 23-24
    definition of, 4, 4n
    determined by dominant group, 216
    effect of technology on, 234
    role of in shaping patterns of thought, 7, 41-42
    translation of, 205

Language learning, 4, 60, 132-33
Latin Catholic identity, 22-23, 61
Leadership, 165, 202
Levitt, Harold, 154
Libidinal urges, 139
Life expectancy, 193-94
Linguistic groups, 41-42
Linguistic relativity. *See* Whorf/Sapir hypothesis
Long-term vs. short-term time horizons, 38
Luft, Joseph, 174-75

M

Mandela, Nelson, 218
Marketing, effect of miscommunication on, 183-84
Marriage, influence of culture upon, 193-94
Masculinity vs. femininity, 38
Maslow, Abraham H., 34-35
Media, 157, 224, 231
Meier, Golda, 196
Merriam, Charles E., 169
Message(s), 158-59
    camouflaging of, 116-17
    conflicting, 144
    conscious, 117, 143-44, 161
    definition of, 113-14
    distortion of, 130-31, 185-87
    frequency of, 224
    hierarchy in communication of, 223
    human, 115-17, 159
    internal, 172
    involuntary, 120, 145-46, 161
    nonhuman, 114-15, 159
    nonverbal, 115-17, 120, 133-34, 143-44
    ordering of, 127
    subconscious, 103-04, 117, 119, 120, 146-47, 161
    subliminal, 117-19, 122, 146-47, 159. *See also*
        Neurolinguistic programming
    verbal, 115-17, 143

Middle Eastern identity, 25
Minority groups, 72-74
Minority identity, 73
Misperceptions, 107
    definition of, 49, 52
Miscommunication, 105
Mixed race, 62n
Muller-Lyer illusion, 18
Multinational corporations, 38
Music culture, 126

N
NASA (National Aeronautics and Space Administration), 205
Nation(s)
    characteristics of, 214
    definition of, 8n, 86, 213
    influence of, 165-66
National culture, 100-01, 216, 227-28
National history, 223
National interest, 218
Nationalism, 75, 80-81
Nationalist conflicts, 81
Nature, dependency on, 58
Needs, 29-30
    compared to values, 35
    conflicting, 35-39
    substitutions for, 36-37
Networks, 187-92, 236
Neurolinguistic programming (NLP), 118, 120, 121-23, 126, 133, 147
Neuro-muscular sets, 152
Neutral turf, 94
Nigerian identity, 135
Nobel Peace Prize, 168
Noise, 115, 149-51, 161-62
Nonprofit organizations, 231

Nonverbal
    behavior, 134, 152
    codes, 136
    languages, 104-06
    signals, 104n, 104-05, 177
Nuclear family, 183
Nurse identity, 26

O

Objective reality, 43
Odor as a message, 115
Official communication, 226
Organization, as component of power, 170-71
Origins of (hu)mankind, 70
Overpopulation, 193

P

Pacifist identity, 90-91
Parent identity, 96
Parents, role of in identity, 4-5
Peasant culture, 57-58
Penny Foundation of Guatemala, 50
Perception(s). *See also* Similarity of perception; Visual perception
    altered by behavior, 13
    as reality, 44
    assumption of accuracy, 26-27
    definition of, 10-11, 52
    determinants of, 53
    effect of on physical response, 10
    environmental determinants of, 16-19
    factors that affect, 11-12
    learned determinants of, 11, 19-27
    of others, 46, 62, 176
    of self, 46, 62, 175
    passed from generation to generation, 5
    physical determinants of, 14-16

sharing of, 63
uniqueness of, 17
Perceptual group, 56, 56n, 99
Personal space, 119-20
Personality
    role of in perception, 15
Physical identity, 4, 15-16
Physical inheritance. *See* Biological inheritance
Physical reactions, 10
Political behavior, 171
Political power, 167-68
Popular culture, 233
Porter, Richard, 104n
Postman, L., 129-31
Poverty. *See* Culture of poverty; Peasant culture; Urban poor
    identity
Power, 209, 212, 230. *See also* Political power
    components of, 170-71, 204, 218-19, 230
    definition of, 164-65
    instruments of, 166, 170
    role of in communication, 164, 235
Power distance, 38
Powerlessness, created by foreign environment, 93
Primitive peoples, 6-7
Private cues, 152-53
Professional identity, 89
Psychosomatic illness, 90-91
Public cues, 152-53
Public image, 204

R

Racial identity, 72
Racial neighborhoods, 73-74
Ranking. *See also* Identity, ranking of
    of groups, 78
    of values, attitudes, and needs, 37, 93

Reality
>   alternate perceptions of, 45-46
>   devices for constructing, 47-48
>   fact-driven observations of, 47
>   incorrect perceptions of, 48
>   perceptions of, 43, 47, 53
Receivers, 112-13
Relativity, principle of, 3
Religious conflicts, 81-82
Religious identity, 28, 39. *See also* Buddhist identity; Catholic identity; Jewish identity; Latin Catholic identity; Sikhs
Republican identity, 128
Responses, involuntary, 145-46
Rokeach, Milton, 42-43

S
Samovar, Larry A., 104n
Sapir, Edward, 7
Screening devices, 115
Selective attention, 129
Self, conscious awareness of, 172
Self-actualization, 34-35
Self-awareness, 175
Self-interest, 69
Senders, 112-13
Senses. *See* Sensory receptors
Sensory data, 19
Sensory language, 122
Sensory-preference style of communicating, 120-22, 123
Sensory receptors, 11, 14, 44, 112-13, 120-21, 123, 124-26, 132, 143, 159, 202-03
>   compensation for loss of, 125
>   physical variations in, 15
Sensory strategies, 121-22
Sensory transmitters, 112-13
Sikhs, 28

Similarity of perception(s), 4, 19-20, 22, 56-57, 60-61, 65,
        78, 206, 231-32, 234
    assumption of, 26-27
    communication of, 59
    degree of, 20-21, 62-63, 67
    recognition of, 59
Six degrees of separation, model of, 189
Socialization process, 5, 59, 98, 128, 139-40, 200
Societal groups, 6
Software of the mind, 11. *See* Hofstede, Geert
Spiral of similarity of perception, 235
Spiral of trust, 192
Sri Lankan identity, 44, 91-92, 96-97, 104-05
Status, as component of power, 171
Steiner, Gary A., 118
Stereotyping, 130
Stimuli, 10-11. *See also* Messages
Subconscious perception of needs or values, 13, 36
Subghettoization, 74
Subliminal messages. *See* Messages, subliminal
Subset, formulation of, 48
Superego, 137, 139, 140
Superego screen, 138-41, 160, 203-04, 230-31
Surroundings. *See* Environment
Swastika, 25-26
Symbols, 21-27, 132, 215
        assigning meaning to, 23-24
Synchronized body motion, 135-36

T

Tamil-Sinhalese conflict, 167-68
Teacher identity, 21
Teenage rebellion, 5
Temperament, role of in perception, 15
Thatcher, Margaret, 196
Time, 119-120
Transmitter, 142-47, 160-61

Transmutation of sensory data, 130
Transnational interactions, 224, 225
Transnational ties, 225
Twins, 19-20

U

Uncertainty avoidance, 38
United States government, power structure of, 219
Unofficial communication, 227
Urban poor identity, 58
Urban societies, 66-67
"Us" versus "Them," 13-14, 59-60, 68-74, 75, 76-77, 85-
    86, 93, 97, 150-51, 166, 174-75, 184, 209, 212

V

Value(s)
    compared to needs, 35
    conflicting, 30, 35-39, 88-89, 101
    definition of, 29-30, 52
    ranking of, 30-34, 89, 93-94
    synthesis of, 92
Value system, definition of, 52
Verbal codes, 136
Visual perception, 17-19

W

Wealth, as component of power, 170
White/black identity, 62, 129-31
White flight, 74
Whorf, Benjamin Lee, 3, 7
Whorf/Sapir hypothesis, 7
Will, as component of power, 171
World War I, 80, 90-91
World War II, 216

Worldview
     expansion of, 95-96
     identity groups as determinants of, 79
     limited, 57-58
Women, role of in politics, 196

Z
Zipper, open, 1-2, 150